Praise for *A Framework for Understanding Poverty*

This is some of the most important work of our time. In Georgia, 23% of students live below the poverty line. The majority of those students are from marginalized groups, but 60% of teachers in Georgia are white and middle class. When you consider these facts, it becomes very evident why educators need to understand the impact of poverty on students.

> –Rachel Spates, Executive Director, West Georgia
> Regional Educational Service Agency, Grantville, GA

With the number of students in poverty on the rise, this should be required reading in colleges of education for all prospective teachers and administrators. In addition, members of local boards of education need to read *A Framework for Understanding Poverty* to improve board policies and better guide the educational process.

> –Christopher D. Sullens, Ed.D., Superintendent, Kewanee
> Community Unit School District #229, Kewanee, IL

Framework is crucial reading not just for teachers and education professionals, but for parents, clergy, business owners—anyone with a desire to make poverty escapable. It encourages communities to take a holistic approach that sees people as assets to develop rather than liabilities to manage. Payne's work challenges conventional thinking, provides practical strategies, and gets the conversation started.

> –Laurie Lee, Chairman of the Board,
> The Reform Alliance, Little Rock, AR

This book belongs in every congregation's tool kit for training volunteers who interact with children and families in poverty. Its concise format, framed by research and supporting stories, addresses issues facing our communities today and offers effective implementation strategies for teachers and community leaders.

> –Tamara Tillman Smathers, Minister of Education and
> Administration, First Baptist Church of Rome, GA

Framework examines poverty by taking into account the current social complexities of race, class, and health disparities. Luckily, the effects of the environment of poverty on cognitive development can be mediated. This book is an invaluable tool for your organization.

> –Evan Whitehead, M.Ed., Director of Special Services,
> Lindop School District #92, Broadview, IL

SIXTH EDITION

a framework for
UNDERSTANDING
POVERTY

A Cognitive Approach

FOR EDUCATORS, POLICYMAKERS, EMPLOYERS, AND SERVICE PROVIDERS

Ruby K. Payne, Ph.D.
    A Framework for Understanding Poverty: A Cognitive
    Approach. 6th Revised Edition.
    297 pp.
    Bibliography pp. 249–274

    ISBN 13: 978-1-948244-18-3

        For information, address
        aha! Process, Inc.
        P.O. Box 727
        Highlands, TX 77562-0727
        ahaprocess.com

Book design by Paula Nicolella
Cover design by Amy Alick Perich

Printed in the United States of America

"Human Learning Process" graphic from *Building Expertise: Cognitive Methods
for Training and Performance* (pp. 50–51), by R. C. Clark, 2008, San Francisco, CA:
Pfeiffer. Copyright 2008 by John Wiley & Sons. Reprinted with permission.

"Why SES Shapes Brain Development" graphic from "State of the Art Review:
Poverty and the Developing Brain" by S. Johnson, J. L. Riis, & K. G. Noble as
published in *Pediatrics.* Reprinted with permission.

Ruby K. Payne, Ph.D.

SIXTH EDITION

a framework for UNDERSTANDING POVERTY

A Cognitive Approach

FOR EDUCATORS, POLICYMAKERS, EMPLOYERS, AND SERVICE PROVIDERS

Other Selected Titles by Ruby K. Payne, Ph.D.

Emotional Poverty in All Demographics: Reducing Anger, Anxiety, and Violence in the Classroom
(Payne)

Research-Based Strategies: Narrowing the Achievement Gap for Under-Resourced Students, Revised Edition
(Payne & Tucker)

Removing the Mask: How to Identify and Develop Giftedness in Students from Poverty, Third Edition
(Payne, Slocumb, & Williams)

Bridges Out of Poverty: Strategies for Professionals and Communities
(Payne, DeVol, & Dreussi-Smith)

Bridges to Health and Healthcare: New Solutions for Improving Access and Services
(Payne, Dreussi-Smith, Shaw, & Young)

From Understanding Poverty to Developing Human Capacity: Ruby Payne's Articles on Transforming Individuals, Families, Schools, Churches, and Communities
(Payne)

School Improvement: 9 Systemic Processes to Raise Achievement
(Payne & Magee)

Under-Resourced Learners: 8 Strategies to Boost Student Achievement
(Payne)

Hidden Rules of Class at Work
(Payne & Krabill)

Crossing the Tracks for Love: What to Do When You and Your Partner Grew Up in Different Worlds
(Payne)

What Every Church Member Should Know About Poverty
(Payne & Ehlig)

Dedication

I thank all of the educators, practitioners, social workers, et al. who have told me their stories—and especially those who have used this work to reach out to children in poverty. This book is for you. Every time someone tells me a story of how the information helped, I am grateful. There is so much undeveloped talent in individuals in poverty simply because the understandings and the tools for transitioning out of poverty (if one chooses to make the transition) have not been available. To each of you who provides hope, it is an immeasurable gift.

Table of Contents

Introduction

It has been more than two decades since the original "red book," *A Framework for Understanding Poverty,* was published in 1995. I have added three new chapters to reflect current concerns: one on the intersectionality of class and other factors, one on poverty and the development of the brain, and one on who the parents of children in poverty are.

In the intervening years, many practitioners have expanded on the ideas I introduced in 1995 and, in many cases, also have done their own original research. The work of countless scholars, researchers, and practitioners, along with the continuing work of my company, aha! Process, has contributed to greater understanding of children's experience of poverty and the critical role schools can play in helping children and teens exit poverty—when those schools have the tools they need to understand and respond with care. In addition to education, I have been gratified by the way the work has expanded into other areas and arenas by those who understand and adapt the *Framework* concepts to their particular settings. These include businesses, healthcare providers, social service agencies, religious entities, higher education, and Bridges Out of Poverty communities.

I believe that this book is even more necessary now than it was in 1995. Due to economic conditions, childhood poverty is on the rise. We have more information than ever on the economic costs of poverty—not only to individuals, but to all of us. Since 2002, the U.S. federal government's insistence on publishing student achievement data has shown just how great the achievement disparities are between economically disadvantaged children and their more advantaged peers.

One of the persistent debates in social-stratification research and theory pertains to the causation of both poverty and wealth.[1] In fact, four prevalent theories are extant: individual choice, exploitation/colonialism, economic and social systems, and resources of a community. I would suggest a fifth explanation: the cognition and knowledge base of the individual and that individual's relationships.

All disciplines move through three research stages: classification, correlation, and causation. For example, when people first saw the stars, they named them and called it astrology. Then Galileo came along and said the stars moved in relationship to each other and called that astronomy. And then Newton appeared and said there is a reason they do that and called it gravity. In social theory, however, there is no clear agreement about what causes social class.

Most legislation in the United States in the last 70 years has been based on social determinism. In the 1800s, Western civilization tended to believe in genetic determinism. Who you were and what could happen to you were based largely on your genetic inheritance. Then the women's movement and the civil rights movement came along and said it didn't matter what you were born with. If you weren't allowed to vote, own property, or be educated, then your genes were essentially a moot point. This is called social determinism. It's "the system" that holds you back. Beginning in the 1940s, we began to look at artificial intelligence, brain and MRI scans, and eventually computer programming. We became very interested in how individuals process and manipulate information and knowledge. It would seem it is time for a cognitive model of social class. In other words, what thinking and knowledge are necessary to function in different social-class environments? How can individual initiative—based on resources— overcome, even transcend, the very real impact of social determinism?

Social determinism is based on correlation models that use numbers as their main point of proof. In cognitive models of brain processing, the brain tends to process in patterns. As a person has greater expertise in a situation or discipline, that person processes very rapidly in patterns.[2] So a cognitive model would rely more heavily on patterns of thinking as evidenced in patterns of behaviors. Many researchers are uncomfortable looking at patterns and would prefer the "safety" and proof of numbers. Yet experts in any discipline would agree that there are patterns of response among human beings.

Social determinism cannot answer the following questions:

- Why do only 42% of children born to parents in the lowest-earning quintile stay in the lowest-earning quintile?[3]

- Why do only 36% of the children born to households in the highest-earning quintile stay there?

- Why do 7% of individuals make it from the lowest-earning 20% of households to the highest-earning 20% of households?

- Why are 75% of the Forbes list of the 400 wealthiest people in America new money?

- Why is there such a "great divide" in income by educational attainment?

Based upon Bandura's work on social cognition, I will argue that there is a relationship between the demands of the environment, the resources one has, and the knowledge base one has.

This relationship among and between who and what you know (relationships and knowledge), what the environment demands for survival, and your resources impacts how you negotiate your environment and create mindsets.

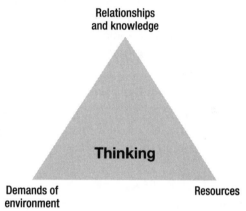

This work is not without its critics. In the early 2000s, a group of social justice professors became quite vocal in their criticism of my work because it did not approach poverty as a social justice issue but rather as a social cognitive issue—an application of Bandura's theories. My approach to poverty is eminently practical: Having worked for many years in schools and school districts, I know firsthand that teachers need down-to-earth, relevant strategies in addition to theory. Their mission—and it is a critically important one—is to reach the children in their classrooms. They are on the front lines of social change, one student at a time.

The purpose of the book is to help those teachers, principals, district leaders, counselors, school nurses, and the many other educators who work with the poor to positively impact the opportunities of their students/clients by:

1. Naming the experience of generational poverty
2. Identifying the tools and resources necessary to become educated
3. Providing intervention strategies
4. Increasing the intergenerational transfer of knowledge

5. Understanding the thinking in generational poverty

6. Helping to understand the situated-learning reality of generational poverty so that individuals can successfully make the transition to the decontextualized world of school and work[4]

Research Base of This Book

This work is based on a naturalistic, longitudinal inquiry based on a convenience sample. I was closely involved with a neighborhood of people from generational poverty for 32 years. The neighborhood included 50–70 people (counts fluctuated over time based on situation, death, and mobility), mostly white. During this time I—coming from a middle-class upbringing—encountered the vast range of ways that the neighborhood's understandings, actions, and responses differed from my own. I undertook an interdisciplinary analysis of the research to explain these differences. Additionally, I lived in Haiti for three and a half months to study poverty and engage in service while in college. Then I lived among the wealthy for six years while my former husband was working with the Chicago Board of Trade, which taught me much about wealth.

During and after these experiences, I took on the methodology of the anthropologist: I "went native" and then relied on research to explain these experiences. Subsequently, I have spoken with thousands of people in China, India, Australia, Canada, Trinidad and Tobago, Slovakia, Hungary, Great Britain, New Zealand, and the United States. The 2005 edition of the *Framework* book is being used in Jamaica and Korea. While every experience has unique elements, the commonalities and patterns within the experience of poverty— and the conflicts between children of poverty and middle-class schools—are much greater. For more on this topic, see "What Information Does *A Framework for Understanding Poverty* Have That Cannot Be Obtained Easily from Other Sources? Why Do Critics Love to Hate It and Practitioners Love to Use It?" in the Appendix.

Myths About Poverty and Wealth

1. *Myth:* Poverty belongs to minorities. *Fact:* Sixty-seven percent of all individuals in poverty in the United States are white.[5]

2. *Myth:* Poverty is caused almost totally by the system and exploitation. *Fact:* In addition to systemic and exploitation causes, poverty is also caused by individual choices, addiction, illness, war, lack of education, lack of employment, mindsets, disabilities, and thinking.

3. *Myth:* People in poverty are lazy. *Fact:* Actually, people in poverty are often problem solvers with limited resources who may or may not have the knowledge bases, tools, bridging social capital, and transportation to be employed.

4. *Myth:* Wealthy people do not pay taxes. *Fact:* Two thirds of U.S. federal taxes are paid by the highest-earning 20% of households.[6]

5. *Myth:* Your IQ is lower if you are poor. *Fact:* IQ is largely a measure of acquired knowledge. If your environment does not provide that knowledge or vocabulary, you cannot show evidence of it on a test.

6. *Myth:* Poverty is about money. *Fact:* Poverty is about a combination of resources.

7. *Myth:* In wealth, assets are more important than income. *Fact:* Assets are important, but income is what allows one to live every day. If none of the assets is producing income (or if they produce insufficient income) to live, then you are in significant trouble.

8. *Myth:* Poverty is mostly an urban problem. *Fact:* Poverty is equally found in rural areas, and to a surprising degree, in suburban areas as well.

Some Key Points to Remember

1. Poverty and wealth are relative to the environment in which you live. In Manhattan, $1,000 is insignificant. In Haiti, $1,000 will allow you to live for a long time.

2. Poverty occurs in all races and all countries.

3. Economic class is a continuous line, not a clear-cut distinction.

4. Resources in generational and situational poverty are different, just as in new money and old money.

5. This work is a cognitive study based on patterns, not on stereotypes. All patterns have exceptions. If this work is used to stereotype—i.e., to indicate that everyone in a given group is a certain way—then the work is misunderstood.

6. Privilege is as much about the intergenerational transfer of knowledge as it is about money and social access.

7. Individuals bring with them the hidden rules of the class in which they were raised.

8. Most schools and businesses operate from middle-class norms and use the hidden rules of middle class.

9. For our students/clients to be successful, we must understand their hidden rules and teach them the rules that will make them successful at school and work. "Code switching" is a term often used to describe this. We tell students that there are rules for basketball and rules for football. To use the football rules in a basketball game is to lose the game. We tell students that there are rules for school and rules for out of school, and they are not the same. You use the rules in the situation that will help you win in that situation.

10. We can neither excuse people nor scold them for not knowing; as educators, we must teach the students and provide support, insistence, and high expectations.

11. To move from poverty to middle class or middle class to wealth, an individual must give up relationships for achievement (at least for some period of time). The issue is time; there is not enough time to have both.

12. Four things that move you out of poverty are employment, education, relationships of bridging social capital (relationships with people who are different from you), and/or a future story.

13. Four reasons one leaves poverty are: It's too painful to stay, a vision or a goal, a special talent or skill, and/or a key relationship.

It is my hope that as you read this book, you will understand your students in a deeper way and therefore increase your own happiness and satisfaction with teaching, as well as have better outcomes for your students.

Chapter 1

Resources, 'Reality,' and Interventions: How They Impact 'Situated Learning'

To better understand students and adults from poverty, a working definition of poverty is "the extent to which an individual does without resources."

Regardless of which country or race or gender, certain things happen when resources are in short supply. The fewer the resources, the more a person lives on the left-hand side of the chart. The greater the resources, the more a person lives on the right-hand side of the chart. Resources are always on a continuum and are not static. They fluctuate and may change over a lifetime.

Resource Continuum

Under-Resourced		Resourced
Instability/crisis	. . . .	Stability
Isolation	. . . .	Community
Dysfunction	. . . .	Functionality
Concrete reality	. . . .	Abstract, representational reality
Casual, oral language	. . . .	Formal, written language
Thought polarization	. . . .	Option seeking
Survival	. . . .	Abundance
Poverty	. . . .	Wealth
No work/ intermittent work	. . . .	Work/careers/ larger cause
Less educated	. . . .	More educated

Using resources as an analytical tool is a strength-based model and acknowledges the many strengths that students, including students from poverty, bring to school. The purpose of knowing the resources of a student is to know which interventions will work and which ones will not. Interventions will work only when the needed resources for that intervention are available. In other words, you have to work from strengths. These resources are the following:

Financial: Having the money to purchase goods and services.[7]

Emotional: Being able to choose and control emotional responses, particularly to negative situations, without engaging in self-destructive behavior. This is an internal resource and shows itself through stamina, perseverance, and choices.[8]

Mental/cognitive: Having the mental abilities and acquired skills (reading, writing, computing) to deal effectively with daily life.[9]

Spiritual: Believing in divine purpose and guidance.[10]

Physical: Having physical health and mobility.[11]

Support systems: Having friends, family, and backup resources available to access in times of need. These are external resources.[12]

Relationships/role models: Having frequent access to individual(s) who are appropriate, who are nurturing, and who do not engage in self-destructive behavior.[13]

Knowledge of hidden rules: Knowing the unspoken cues and habits of different groups.[14]

Language/formal register: Having the vocabulary, language ability, and negotiation skills necessary to succeed in school and/or work settings.

Typically, poverty is thought of in terms of *financial resources* only. However, the reality is that financial resources, while very important, do not explain the differences in the success with which some individuals leave poverty nor the reasons that many stay in poverty.[15] The ability to leave poverty is more dependent on other resources than it is on financial resources. Each of these resources plays a vital role in the success of an individual.[16]

Emotional resources provide the stamina to withstand difficult and uncomfortable emotional situations and feelings. Emotional resources allow you to *not* engage in destructive behaviors—to others or yourself. Emotional resources may well be the most important of all resources because, when present, they allow the individual not to return to old patterns. In order to move from poverty to middle class or middle class to wealth, individuals must suspend their "emotional memory bank" because the situations and hidden rules are so unlike what they have experienced previously.[17] Therefore, a certain level of persistence and an ability to stay with the situation until it can be learned (and therefore feel comfortable) are necessary. This persistence (i.e., staying with the situation) is evidence that emotional resources are present. Emotional resources come, at least in part, from role models.[18]

Mental/cognitive resources are simply being able to process information and use it in daily living. If an individual can read, write, and compute, that individual has a decided advantage. That person can access information from many different free sources, as well as be or become self-sufficient.

Spiritual resources are the beliefs that help can be obtained from a higher power, that there is a purpose for living, and that worth and love are gifts from God. This is a powerful resource because individuals do not see themselves as hopeless and useless, but rather as capable and having worth and value. Furthermore, spiritual resources provide a person with a "future story," which gives that person hope for the future.

Physical resources are having a body that works, that is capable and mobile. The individual can be self-sufficient.

Support systems are having friends, family, and backup resources to access in times of need. These are external resources. To whom does one go when help is needed? Those individuals who are available and will help are resources. When the child is sick and you have to be at work, who takes care of the child? Where do you go when money is tight and the baby needs medicine? Support systems are not just about meeting financial or emotional needs. They are about knowledge bases as well. How do you get into college? Who sits and listens when you get rejected? Who helps you negotiate the mountains of paper? Who assists you with your algebra homework when you don't know how to do it? These people all constitute support systems.

Relationships/role models are resources. All individuals have role models. The question is the extent to which the role model is nurturing or appropriate. Can the role model parent? Work successfully? Provide a gender role for the individual? It is largely from role models that the person learns how to live life on an emotional level.[19]

No significant learning occurs without a significant relationship.

–Dr. James Comer[20]

Knowledge of hidden rules is crucial to whatever social group or class in which you wish to live.[21] Hidden rules, sometimes called mores, exist in poverty, in middle class, and in wealth, as well as in ethnic groups and other units of people. Hidden rules are about the salient, unspoken understandings that cue the members of the group that a given individual does or does not fit.[22] For example, three of the hidden rules in poverty are the following: The noise level is high (the TV is almost always on, and everyone may talk at once), the most important information is nonverbal, and one of the main values of an individual to the group is an ability to entertain. There are also hidden rules about food, dress, decorum, etc. Generally, in order to successfully move from one class to the next, it is important to have a spouse or mentor from the class to which you wish to move to model and teach you the hidden rules.

Language/formal register is an acquired skill and constitutes the vocabulary and sentence structure necessary for navigating school and work.

Case Studies

The following case studies have been supplied by educators across the United States. After each case study, identify the resources available to the student and those available to the adult. NOTE: Names have been changed, but the stories are true.

Case Study #1: Alexa (from a mid-size town in southern Mississippi)

Background

Alexa is a 12-year-old white girl who recently moved with her mother to live with her maternal grandmother in a new city. Alexa's father committed suicide after Hurricane Katrina destroyed their home and drained their finances. The family's homeowner's insurance did not pay to repair or replace the home because the damage was caused by flooding, which the policy didn't cover. The emotional stress of the hurricane combined with the financial losses proved too much for Alexa's father. Because he committed suicide, all life insurance policies became null and void. What little savings the family had were used to cover expenses from the hurricane and the subsequent move to a new city.

You are Alexa's mother, Sharon, a 32-year-old housewife who has been suddenly thrust back into the workforce because of your husband's death. It has been less than a month since your husband committed suicide, and you have had no time to grieve. The hurricane destroyed everything you had, and you and your daughter were left with nothing but a few sets of clothes, some family memorabilia, and important documents. You have no choice but to move in with your mother, who is disabled and on a fixed income, while your disabled sister and two children also live with her. You must find employment to support yourself and child and to try to build a nest egg to start on your own. You have been a housewife since marrying your husband when you were 18. Your last job was a minimum-wage position in high school, and you have no formal training.

You find a minimum-wage position as a clerk in a convenience store during the day and as a receptionist overnight for a towing company. You have applied for food stamps and have begun secretarial training classes at the community job center. You work 16 hours a day, however, and have little time to improve your employment prospects, never mind spending time with your daughter. You spend virtually all your time working or sleeping in order to make ends meet—and to avoid an emotional breakdown from your recent trauma.

Current Situation

Alexa is in the gifted program at her new school. Because she is new at the school, has been through a very traumatic experience, and is shy by nature, the school counselor has stressed the importance of Alexa's involvement in the gifted program. The counselor invites Alexa to take part in a weekly after-school volunteer program for gifted students at the local library. She says it would be a great opportunity to get to know her fellow students, plus students are required to participate in order to stay in the gifted program. Alexa would be required to have transportation home from the library after school.

You have secretarial classes three nights a week from 4 to 6 p.m. If you don't take the classes, you likely will be stuck in minimum-wage jobs and not be able to support yourself and Alexa. On the other hand, your daughter is the most important part of your life and she has the chance to do something great with her academic ability. You know she needs to become part of a community and work through the issues of the past few months. But there is no way you can pick her up *and* take the classes at the job center. There is no public transportation, and no one in the family has transportation to pick her up. You want Alexa to have every opportunity to succeed and achieve great things, but in order to survive, you must work while improving your skills.

Using a scale of 0 to 4 (with 4 being high), how would you assess the resource base of Alexa and her mother? Put a question mark if you are uncertain, if the information is not available, or if a response cannot be inferred.

Resource Assessment

Resource	Alexa (student)	Sharon (mother)
Financial		
Emotional		
Mental/cognitive		
Spiritual (future story)		
Physical		
Support systems		
Relationships/role models		
Knowledge of hidden rules at school and work		
Language/formal register		

[To compare your analysis of Alexa with the author's, please see Appendix A.]

Case Study #2: Duane (from a mid-size town in Mississippi)

Background

Duane is a 12-year-old African-American male who lives with his father and two younger siblings in public housing. His mother left when Duane was 6, leaving his father with three children under the age of 7. Duane goes directly home after school each day to watch his younger siblings while his father is at work. There is often nothing but baloney and Kool-Aid for dinner. Duane is responsible for feeding his siblings, bathing them, helping with homework, and getting them to bed. This leaves Duane little time for his own homework. School is a struggle for Duane, but he is a gifted athlete. He has already drawn the interest of the high school football coach who believes he has a bright future as a player.

You are Duane's father, Roney, a 29-year-old male. Duane was born while you were a junior in high school and his mother, Cydney, was 16. You and Cydney were married shortly after Duane was born. You dropped out of school to work to support Duane and his mother. You had a good job changing oil at a local service station and were able to support your wife and child so Cydney could stay home. Duane's brother, Walker, was born four years later, but Cydney had a difficult pregnancy, and soon after Walker was born the station you worked at closed.

Cydney became despondent and often went out with friends, leaving you with the children. You were able to take odd jobs fixing cars but didn't make enough to support your family. You and the children were forced to move in with your mother, who was in her mid-50s and an alcoholic. She was on disability with a fixed income and struggled herself to make ends meet.

With your mother there to watch the children at night while Cydney went out, you were able to secure a minimum-wage position as a delivery driver. Between the odd jobs fixing cars during the day and the delivery job at night, you were beginning to catch up financially. After your third child was born, Cydney left you without warning and moved to a distant state. Within a month, your mother lost her battle with alcoholism and died.

Current Situation

You leave for work before your children get home from school. You are dependent on Duane to help with your other children at night so you can work. However, Duane is becoming more frustrated with school and is causing problems. His teacher calls to set up a parent/teacher conference, which means you will be late for work. You want Duane to graduate because you know the importance of an education, so you make it a priority to get involved.

At the meeting, the high school coach is present and expresses his interest in Duane's ability. He says playing football would help Duane build self-esteem and work harder to succeed in school. The teacher agrees and thinks Duane should practice with the high school team after school two days a week. He also offers to stay after school to tutor Duane and help him with his reading comprehension.

You want Duane to have the opportunity to play football because you feel it will help him build self-confidence, which in turn will help him in school. You also appreciate the teacher offering help academically and you understand Duane needs extra help. But you need Duane at home to watch his siblings so you can work. There is no one else to watch your two youngest children.

Using a scale of 0 to 4 (with 4 being high), how would you assess the resource base of Duane and his father? Put a question mark if you are uncertain, if the information is not available, or if a response cannot be inferred.

Resource Assessment

Resource	Duane (student)	Roney (father)
Financial		
Emotional		
Mental/cognitive		
Spiritual (future story)		
Physical		
Support systems		
Relationships/role models		
Knowledge of hidden rules at school and work		
Language/formal register		

[To compare your analysis of Duane with the author's, please see Appendix A.]

Case Study #3: Michael (from a mid-size town in Texas)

Background

Michael, a young white male, recently came to live with his father who is an independent truck driver. Michael was living with his mother and brother who is a senior in high school. Michael came to live with the father because his mother stabbed his brother one night when she came home intoxicated. The mother's behavior had escalated within the past six months, but she had not been violent; however, she was verbally abusive. Michael's brother had helped him get the necessities while the mother was absent, but now his brother has moved in with a friend in order to finish high school.

Michael, a freshman, has to change school districts. Michael doesn't like change and doesn't make friends easily. He has been in special education since he was 9 years old with a learning disabled classification. When he was 12, he started a fire and was hospitalized for emotional problems; after the incident, Michael's primary condition was changed to emotionally disturbed. Also, Michael was sexually abused by a neighbor when he was 8 years old. In his old school, Michael had several teachers who had taught him for several years and looked out for him and encouraged him in schoolwork. They also made sure he and his brother had Christmas.

Michael's dad loves his sons but is on the road much of the time. He knows things aren't good for his boys, but he feels helpless because of his job. The previous year, Michael's dad met a young woman who has a 2-month-old baby. They live in a two-bedroom mobile home in a rural area. He knows Michael can be challenging but wants to make sure his son is safe and in school. He isn't sure how his girlfriend and Michael will get along, but he moves Michael into the mobile home. Money is tight for the family, what with the truck note, the price of fuel, and the new baby.

Michael is afraid of his mother because of the behavior she has exhibited over the past year. He doesn't want to see her, and he doesn't want her to know where he's living. He wears glasses, but he left them at his old home and doesn't want to go back to get them. His dad doesn't have the money to buy new glasses for him.

Michael and his father go to the new school, which is a very large high school, at the beginning of the second semester thinking he will begin school the next day. They are told by the attendance clerk that Michael cannot enroll because the dad doesn't have legal custody. Michael's father must leave to go on a long truck haul to Mississippi. Michael stays alone until his father returns.

Dad contacts the lawyer who handled the divorce and tells him of the situation. The lawyer requires $5,000 as a retainer fee to file for temporary custody. Michael's dad borrows the money from his mother who loathes the ex-wife and is glad Michael is away from her. Michael misses his friends from his old school and doesn't know what to do. He calls one of his friends from the old school who comes and picks up Michael for the weekend. When his dad returns from the trip, Michael is missing. Within a few hours, however, Michael calls his dad.

Dad returns to school to enroll Michael with the temporary custody order. Dad tells school officials that Michael is in special education. The registrar tells Michael he will be in regular classes until the special ed documentation is received from the former school.

He finally gets enrolled in high school. Michael lives with his father and stepmother and really likes his stepmother. He goes to church with his stepmother's parents. His stepmother's mom is a school administrator and works with him to get the help he needs at school. He has friends but doesn't do well with crowds. He plays football and is on the water polo team at the high school. Michael is small for his age, so he doesn't get to participate until the teams are winning. He is hoping to go into the military.

Michael's paternal grandmother lives in Georgia and isn't able to help him financially because her husband is in bankruptcy. His maternal grandparents give him pocket money, bought him his first suit so he could go to a banquet with a girl, ordered a cake with his name on it for his birthday, and had his school picture taken and ordered.

Using a scale of 0 to 4 (with 4 being high), how would you assess the resource base of Michael and his father? Put a question mark if you are uncertain, if the information is not available, or if a response cannot be inferred.

Resource Assessment

Resource	Michael	Father
Financial		
Emotional		
Mental/cognitive		
Spiritual (future story)		
Physical		
Support systems		

Resource	Michael	Father
Relationships/role models		
Knowledge of hidden rules at school and work		
Language/formal register		

[To compare your analysis of Michael with the author's, please see Appendix A.]

Case Study #4: Wadell and Destinie (from a reservation in New Mexico)

Background

Wadell is a 17-year-old Native American male. His father was killed two years ago in an auto accident. His mother is serving the first year of a three-year prison sentence for felony possession of methamphetamine. Wadell and his 11-year-old sister, Destinie, live with their grandmother in a one-bedroom trailer in a small community on the reservation. The trailer is old, does not have running water or electricity, and the family is often without fuel to run the generator and without food to eat. Grandmother cares for the children, but due to age is not always able to provide support. Wadell never learned to drive, and public transportation isn't available, so he and Destinie walk just about everywhere.

When he isn't at school, Wadell spends most of his time caring for Destinie and his grandmother. Sometimes their "cousin brother," who lives 300 miles away, comes to visit, but he doesn't stay very long. Wadell and Destinie both qualify for and receive tribal services (e.g., clothing and medical services). Wadell values tradition, attends tribal gatherings, and wants to learn more about his family and culture. He especially loves the drums and songs.

You, a teacher, first met Wadell when he was a student in your ninth-grade class. He confides in you and another teacher at the high school. After the death of his father, Wadell swore he would never drink or do drugs. For the past three years Wadell has scored at the advanced level in mathematics on the state math assessment.

Current Situation

Wadell and Destinie have nearly perfect attendance. Since Wadell transferred to the alternative high school, his grades have improved, and his current GPA is 3.0. His technology skills are exceptional; he loves all types of music, works as an assistant in the school's technology lab, and creates soundtracks and digital art. Wadell tends to be very quiet and doesn't talk much, but he has shared his dream of taking Destinie and his mother to Disney World, owning a music company, and having his own record label.

Students admire Wadell's talent and strength, but he doesn't have a best friend, nor does he associate with one specific group of students. You and Wadell have a relationship of mutual respect and meet at school regularly to discuss his progress and options. After reviewing this year's final grades and his transcript, you realize that Wadell can graduate at midyear next school year.

Using a scale of 0 to 4 (with 4 being high), how would you assess the resource base of either Wadell or Destinie and their grandmother? Put a question mark if you are uncertain, if the information is not available, or if a response cannot be inferred.

Resource Assessment

Resource	Wadell or Destinie	Grandmother
Financial		
Emotional		
Mental/cognitive		
Spiritual (future story)		
Physical		
Support systems		
Relationships/role models		
Knowledge of hidden rules at school and work		
Language/formal register		

[To compare your analysis of Wadell and Destinie with the author's, please see Appendix A.]

Case Study #5: Julius (from rural West Virginia)

Background

You are teaching summer school. Mr. Brandon brings his granddaughter, Halley, to school the first day of summer school and attends the session. He receives a stipend of $50 a day for bringing a child and attending the session, which is teaching nonreaders how to use a signing strategy to decode sounds. At midmorning, Mr. Brandon removes his hand from the pocket of his bib overalls, waves his arm, and asks, "If I bring another grandchild, will I get $100 a day?" The principal in charge investigates, then tells him yes, he can earn double for bringing another grandchild whose name is on the approved list.

The next day Julius, a white male, whom his grandfather calls "Jughead," appears. His eyes express constant apprehension, and he is reluctant to communicate. Julius can decode some two- and three-letter words, but he lacks the skills to read more challenging texts. Throughout the ensuing three-week period, Julius actively yet quietly participates in learning the skills you are teaching him, pointing to words with dirty fingers.

While cousins Julius and Halley participate in classroom activities, Mr. Brandon sits in the back of the room and tells stories to the other parents and grandparents sitting around him. One of the most remarkable is about one of his wives leaving him and marrying his father. Because they all lived in the same house, she simply changed bedrooms. He also tells how Julius knows exactly how to set a car on fire to collect insurance money. When the conversation moves to topics such as cockfighting and justification for killing one's wife, the principal interrupts the conversation and refocuses Mr. Brandon's and his audience's attention on the reading instruction.

Each day when the class is over, the Brandon children walk up the side of the hill behind the school and pick berries. Once, Julius signs "hi" to you from the side of the hill.

Over the course of the three weeks, Julius's confidence grows. By the end of the program he can read a large number of words, including *shark, motion,* and *saucer.* Mr. Brandon expresses concern over the possibility that if Julius learns to read, the family might stop drawing money. The principal assures him that because of Julius's age of 13, the money would continue even if Julius learns to read well. Often Julius says, "I'm not going to that high school. They'll mess you up." When you ask Julius who told him that, he answers, "Everybody."

You and your students plan a celebration for the last day of the summer program and invite family members to attend. The principal makes a bet with you that none of the Brandon family members will be there. With very little confidence you bet they will. The time arrives for the celebration and student readings— no Brandons. You have just begun the reading celebration when you hear a tremendous noise in the stairwell. Moments later Julius bursts into the room, smiling broadly. He is followed by his cousin, Halley, then Mr. Brandon, then wives #2 and #3. They are followed by seven other family members of various ages and relationships. All show pride in Julius's and Halley's academic progress, and all stay for refreshments, taking the leftovers home with them.

A few weeks later you find a donor willing to give a scholarship to encourage the Brandon family to allow Julius to continue taking classes on into high school. The Brandons turn the money down.

Using a scale of 0 to 4 (with 4 being high), how would you assess the resource base of Julius and his grandfather? Put a question mark if you are uncertain, if the information is not available, or if a response cannot be inferred.

Resource Assessment

Resource	Julius ('Jughead')	Grandfather
Financial		
Emotional		
Mental/cognitive		
Spiritual (future story)		
Physical		
Support systems		
Relationships/role models		
Knowledge of hidden rules at school and work		
Language/formal register		

[To compare your analysis of Julius with the author's, please see Appendix A.]

Case Study #6: Gabriela (from a small town in New Mexico)

Background

Gabriela is a 16-year-old Hispanic female. Her mother and father are both in jail on drug-related charges. Gabriela lives in her parents' house with her grandmother and four younger brothers and sisters. Gabriela is responsible for her family—managing the day-to-day challenges they face. Gabriela's grandmother is 83 and lived in Mexico until she moved in with the family a year ago. Grandmother speaks limited English and sometimes requires as much attention as the younger children. Gabriela's brothers are 8 and 10; her sisters are 5 and 12.

Gabriela is part of the third generation of a local family that migrated to the area from Mexico; she is very proud of her heritage. Three of her uncles started a large groundskeeping business that has been very profitable and provides jobs for several family members.

Gabriela is a pretty girl, with many friends. She just started driving the family car, has her own cell phone, and dresses well. At school Gabriela works hard in some classes, but in others teachers report she is disrespectful and won't work at all. This year she received several disciplinary referrals for being disrespectful and responding inappropriately when she was angry.

Current Situation

You teach a career class at the high school. This semester Gabriela has been one of your highest achieving students. Based on career and college exploration, Gabriela has determined she likes media and photography. She asks if you will help her look for a scholarship or financial assistance so she can take a class at the local community college. The class begins in two weeks.

One day as you're working at your desk, Gabriela shows up and asks for your advice on how to respond to a message from her brother's teacher about his behavior. Gabriela says she also has concerns about changes in his behavior but wonders what to do since his teacher has been rude and talked down to her in previous meetings.

Using a scale of 0 to 4 (with 4 being high), how would you assess the resource base of Gabriela and her grandmother? Put a question mark if you are uncertain, if the information is not available, or if a response cannot be inferred.

Resource Assessment

Resource	Gabriela	Grandmother
Financial		
Emotional		
Mental/cognitive		
Spiritual (future story)		
Physical		
Support systems		
Relationships/role models		
Knowledge of hidden rules at school and work		
Language/formal register		

[To compare your analysis of Gabriela with the author's, please see Appendix A.]

Case Study #7: Raymond (from an inner city in Texas)

Background

Raymond is a Hispanic male, and his father is a skilled laborer. Since before Raymond could walk, his father referred to him as his little football hero. Raymond's father was considered to be passionate and aggressive. Up until eighth grade, Raymond often witnessed his father make degrading remarks to his mother. Raymond was encouraged to play and perfect his football techniques, and his grades followed a predictable pattern during most of his academic career. He would fail throughout most of the grading period. As the time for report cards approached, his father would make a call or an appointment with the teacher(s) and request that Raymond be allowed to make up some of his grades or be given an opportunity for extra credit. While not always successful, it worked often enough for Raymond to get promoted year after year.

One month after Raymond's 13th birthday, his mother told him of her intentions to divorce his father. That day his mother noticed Raymond speaking to her in the same harsh manner her husband had for many years. Raymond blamed his mother for all the family troubles. Between eighth and 11th grade, Raymond lived between two households. His parents got along better as a result of the divorce, and relations were amicable for the most part.

When Raymond qualified for the football team, his father expressed great pride to anyone who would listen. He attended every football game; Raymond's mother came to most of them and sat with her friends. Despite Raymond's success on the football field, his relations with authority figures (particularly females) grew increasingly defiant. His father's interventions on Raymond's behalf became less and less successful during Raymond's high school years, and he soon started blaming Raymond's teachers for his son's academic struggles.

Current Situation

Raymond has made a name for himself on the football field. He has obvious talent that has been noticed by some college scouts. When his academic records are looked at, he is told there are concerns but that he can be provided tutors if certain conditions are met. As a result of this and some earnest conversations with school staff members who have expressed concern about Raymond, he begins to examine his decision-making process. He comes to realize that he has never taken school seriously and starts thinking about how academics will play an important role in college—and in his vocational pursuits.

Following some painful self-examination, Raymond announces that he is quitting football in order to concentrate more on his grades. Most staff members are stunned by his decision. Raymond begins to take ownership of his temper and becomes more studious, however difficult it is for him to do. Some of his teachers begin to notice that increasingly they are talking to his mother, while his father has become less accessible. It is midyear before his teachers learn that Raymond's father cut his son off in every way after learning of his decision to quit football. Raymond now faces the reality that he is too far behind in his classes to catch up and graduate with his friends—and can no longer depend on his father for support. In late November, Raymond drops out of school.

Using a scale of 0 to 4 (with 4 being high), how would you assess the resource base of Raymond and his mother or father? Put a question mark if you are uncertain, if the information is not available, or if a response cannot be inferred.

Resource Assessment

Resource	Raymond	Mother or father
Financial		
Emotional		
Mental/cognitive		

Resource	Raymond	Mother or father
Spiritual (future story)		
Physical		
Support systems		
Relationships/role models		
Knowledge of hidden rules at school and work		
Language/formal register		

[To compare your analysis of Raymond with the author's, please see Appendix A.]

Case Study #8: Ciera (from rural New Mexico)

Background

Ciera is a 13-year-old Native American girl who is in eighth grade. She lives with her father and two younger brothers in a motel room they rent by the week. Her father used to find work driving a truck, but he has been without work for several months.

Ciera's mother and two older sisters live in a town 15 miles away. Both of her sisters quit school and are currently involved with members of a local gang. When her oldest sister was 15, she had a baby. Ciera loved her little niece, but when she was 6 months old the baby died under suspicious circumstances. Ciera's mother is currently under house arrest for possession of methamphetamines.

When Ciera was in sixth grade she decided she didn't want to end up like her mother or sisters and began to apply herself at school. Since that time she has consistently been on the honor roll. Both Ciera's mother and sisters ridicule Ciera and call her "school girl" for making good grades. Ciera has developed a trusting relationship with a counselor at her school. The counselor has continuously encouraged and reinforced the good choices Ciera has made.

Most summers Ciera's father can find work as a wildland firefighter. During this time she and her brothers go and stay with her father's elderly grandparents who live in a traditional hogan in a remote community on the reservation.

Current Situation

Ciera's dad has been arrested for DUI (driving under the influence) and is going to serve jail time. The motel is paid up through Sunday, but after that Ciera and her brothers will have to leave the motel.

Using a scale of 0 to 4 (with 4 being high), how would you assess the resource base of Ciera and her father? Put a question mark if you are uncertain, if the information is not available, or if a response cannot be inferred.

Resource	Ciera	Father
Financial		
Emotional		
Mental/cognitive		
Spiritual (future story)		
Physical		
Support systems		
Relationships/role models		
Knowledge of hidden rules at school and work		
Language/formal register		

[To compare your analysis of Ciera with the author's, please see Appendix A.]

Discussion of Case Studies

Significantly, each case study illustrates variety in the amount and kinds of resources available, as well as variations on the theme of poverty.

For example, the jail incident in the Ciera case study is one aspect of poverty. For many individuals who live in poverty, jail is a part of their lives on a fairly regular basis—for several reasons. First of all, if an individual is in generational poverty, organized society is viewed with distrust, even distaste. The line between what is legal and illegal is thin and often crossed. A lack of resources means that individuals will need to spend periods of time in jail for crossing those lines because they do not have the resources to avoid it. The reality is that middle class and upper class also cross the lines, but not with the frequency of those in poverty. In addition, when the upper and middle classes do cross the line, they usually have the resources to avoid jail. The poor simply see jail as a part of life and not necessarily always bad. Local jails provide food and shelter and, as a general rule, are not as violent or dangerous as state incarceration.

Throughout these case studies, though seldom directly mentioned, is the issue of money and how it is used and viewed. One of the hidden rules of poverty is that extra money is shared. Middle class puts a great deal of emphasis on being self-sufficient. In poverty, the clear understanding is that one will never get ahead, so when extra money is available, it is either shared or immediately spent, often on some type of entertainment because entertainment takes away the pain. There are always emergencies and needs; one might as well enjoy the moment. If you don't share your money, the next time you're in need, you'll most likely be left out in the cold. It's the hidden rule of the support system.

In poverty, people are possessions, and people rely on each other in order to survive. After all, that is all you have—people.

The Raymond case study is included because another aspect of generational poverty is that discipline is usually about penance and forgiveness, not about change. The father criticizes and blames the mother but asks for special treatment for his son to make up his failing grades. While not stated in the case study, it's likely that at home he criticizes his son as well, but at school he defends his son. Furthermore, when his son drops out of football, he refuses to see Raymond again. The relationship is totally cut off; it is the final punishment, and in this case there is no forgiveness.

Punishment in poverty is almost always in the negative. In their study, Hart and Risley found that a child in a welfare home received two negative comments to one positive while a child in a professional household received six positives to one negative.[23] In educated households, adults spend a great deal of time coaching the child on appropriate behavior. In poverty, the focus is on stopping the behavior but not necessarily on change.

One of the mistakes educators make is to misunderstand the role of punishment in generational poverty. As stated, punishment is not really about change, it's about penance and forgiveness. Individuals in poverty usually have a strong belief in fate and destiny. Therefore, to expect changed behavior after a parent/teacher conference is, in most cases, a false hope. This doesn't mean that you shouldn't have parent/teacher conferences. It does mean that the expectations around the conference tend to be middle class. Middle-class teachers expect that there will be changed behavior. You might want to follow up the conference with a letter that has three parts:

- What the school will do

- What the student will do

- What the parent will do

It is in this manner that expectations have been clarified. When you meet again, there is at least a starting place for the conversation, i.e., let's visit how the follow-up has been since the last time we met … It will be through the relationships and ongoing support that change has the best chance of occurring.

The Julius ("Jughead") story is included to make points about the isolation that occurs in generational poverty, especially in rural areas, and the "incestuous" patterns in thinking and relationships that can occur as a result of this isolation. Julius has been told by "everybody" that to go to high school will "mess you up." The grandfather openly admits that his wife left him and went to be with his father simply by changing bedrooms. In addition, the grandfather refuses the money to help Julius go on to high school because it will mess him up. Patterns of thinking are hard to change.

The Ciera case study, mentioned above, is included for another reason as well: to point out the role of drugs and gangs in poverty. Gangs are a type of support system and often a source of revenue due to the drug trade. They provide virtually all of the resources needed for survival.

Fighting and physical violence also are a part of poverty. People living in poverty need to be able to defend themselves physically, or they need someone to be their protector. Middle class uses space to deal with conflict and disagreement, i.e., they go to a different room and cool off; they purchase enough land so they aren't encroached upon; they live in neighborhoods where people put up fences and keep their distance. But in poverty, physical separation is not always an option. Ciera has separated herself from her mother and sisters by living with her father. But with his DUI and pending jail time, that may not be an option either. Therefore, when you cannot separate from the person or situation, the only way to defend oneself is physically. Also, individuals in poverty are seldom going to call the police, for two reasons: First, the police may be looking for them; second, the police will probably be slow to respond. So why bother calling?

Many of these case studies involve students being raised by grandparents because of the growing number of children not living with their parents—and the effect this has on the emotional resources of the children. Emotional resources come from observing how role models deal with adverse situations and social interactions. Wadell will come out of the situation knowing that he doesn't want to be like his father—but also that he doesn't want to be like his grandmother. So it will be difficult for him to identify an appropriate male role model unless he finds one at school or in the tribe. To have emotional resources that are healthy, one needs to have an identity. One uses role models to build that identity. Because of the limited financial resources, Wadell's access to appropriate role models will be limited to appropriate tribal males and the few males in the school setting.

The Duane case study highlights the number of children who are in situational poverty because of divorce. Duane's mother is an example of what happens when an individual's difficulties erode emotional resources. Duane's grandmother's alcoholism is another example of low emotional resources. (The reverse is also true, i.e., her emotional weakness leads to her dependence on alcohol.) Of all the resources, emotional resources seem to be paramount in maintaining a lifestyle with some semblance of order. When emotional resources are lacking or absent, the slide into poverty is almost guaranteed.

A few of these case studies involve drugs, addiction, or biochemical issues. Considerable debate has happened around which came first—the chicken or the egg. Was it the poverty that caused the addiction or the addiction that caused the poverty? Regardless of the cause, addiction breaks relationships, decimates emotional resources, destroys support systems, and eliminates role models— regardless of your class. Middle class and wealth in particular have a greater reserve of resources with which to mitigate the damage. But in any social class, addiction is destructive to resources. And addiction in poverty, because there are fewer resources, is particularly damaging to children.

In conclusion, the resources that individuals have vary significantly from situation to situation. Poverty is more about other resources than it is about money. The good news is that the other resources are those that educators can influence greatly.

Resources and Interventions

For each case study, go to Appendix A and look at how the resources were identified and the possible interventions for each.

How Do You Discover a Student's Resources?

Many educators ask, *How can I find out about my students' resources? I have 150 students. I cannot know them all.* First of all, you don't need to know them all. Many students come with support systems and relationships outside of school, so they don't need interventions.

Often it occurs through a conversation. A teacher I know at the secondary level starts school each year by showing pictures of herself and her family to her students, then she talks about why she is qualified to teach them and her hopes for them in the upcoming school year. She then invites students to write back to her and tell her about themselves. Questions include:

- What do you like about school?

- What do you hate?

- What kinds of things does a teacher do that help you learn?

- Are there things in your life that make getting homework done a problem? A job? Younger siblings to care for? Someone with a disability whom you care for?

Bonding and Bridging Social Capital

Bonding social capital is people you know who are like you. Bridging social capital is people you know who are different from you. Bridging social capital allows you to get to know new ways of thinking and is also crucial in moving between classes.[24]

What Is the Difference Between a Dysfunctional Household and Poverty? Between Dysfunction and Resources?

Dysfunction almost always occurs when resources are limited for the children— or when the adults themselves have limited resources. When individuals cannot get their needs met, they will either take from the resources of others or exchange current resources for different resources. Work, for example, is an exchange of resources.

The question becomes: How much choice did the individual have in this situation? If it's a child who must go without resources because of the behaviors of an adult or the lack of resources of the adult, then the child's choices are very limited. Because of child labor laws, the child cannot work. The child does not have voting rights and has few legal rights. There are many poverty households where the needs of the children are met before the needs of the adults. There are also households, however, where the children cannot get their needs met because of the *choices* and *resources* of the adult(s). This then makes the situation dysfunctional for the child because the child cannot get basic needs met—needs of love, food, and shelter.

What Does This Information Mean in the School or Work Setting?

- Resources of students and adults should be analyzed before dispensing advice or seeking solutions to the situation. What may seem to be very workable suggestions from a middle-class point of view may be virtually impossible given the resources available to those in poverty.

- Educators have tremendous opportunities to influence some of the non-financial resources that make such a difference in students' lives. For example, it costs nothing to be an appropriate role model.

Chapter 2

Language and Story: How They Impact Thinking, School, and Work

To better understand poverty, one must understand four aspects of language: registers of language, discourse patterns, story structure, and specificity of vocabulary. Many of the key issues for schools and businesses are related to these patterns, which often are different in poverty than they are in middle class.

Registers of Language

Every language in the world has five registers.[25] These registers are the following:

Register	Explanation
Frozen	Language that is always the same. For example: Lord's Prayer, wedding vows, etc.
Formal	The standard sentence syntax and word choice of work and school. Has complete sentences and specific word choice.
Consultative	Formal register when used in conversation. Discourse pattern not quite as direct as formal register.
Casual	Language between friends, characterized by a 400- to 800-word vocabulary. Word choice general and not specific. Conversation dependent on nonverbal assists. Sentence syntax often incomplete.
Intimate	Language between lovers or twins. Language of sexual harassment.

Source: *The Five Clocks* by M. Joos.

RULE: Joos found that one can go down one register in the same conversation, and that is socially accepted. However, to drop two registers or more in the same conversation is to be socially offensive.

How then does the preceding five-part register impact students from poverty? First of all, the work of Dr. Maria Montaño-Harmon found that most students from less educated households and students from poverty don't hear formal register at home.[26] As a matter of fact, these students generally cannot use formal register. The problem is that all the state and national tests—SAT, ACT, etc.—are in formal register. Further complicating the matter is that to get a well-paying job, one is expected to be able to use formal register. The ability to use formal register is a hidden rule of middle class. The inability to use it will knock one out of most interviews in two or three minutes. The use of formal register, on the other hand, allows one to score well on tests and do well generally in school and higher education.[27] Furthermore, because generational poverty is so isolating, the more generations one is in poverty, the less access one has to formal register. The one exception is if the family/individual has a strong religious background; the exposure to written religious texts provides both frozen and formal register.

Intergenerational Transfer of Knowledge

Increasingly, research is looking at the intergenerational transfer of knowledge. An Australian study—which followed the children of 8,556 women (mostly from poverty) from their first clinic visit for pregnancy, again at age 5 and again at age 14—found that the child's maternal grandfather's occupational status independently predicted the child's verbal comprehension levels at age 5 and nonverbal reasoning scores at age 14.[28]

Why would the maternal grandfather's *occupation* be so predictive? The occupation would tell you the level of stability in the household and be a predictor of the family's level of education. Because the mother is so instrumental in the early nurturing of the child and the vocabulary that the child hears, it would follow that the mother's access to knowledge and vocabulary would be based on her own childhood experiences. Therefore, the maternal grandfather's occupation would be a key predictor of achievement.

Furthermore, the amount of language differs tremendously. As was initially pointed out in Chapter 1, researchers Hart and Risley put tape recorders in the homes of people from different economic classes.[29]

Research About Language in Children, Ages 1 to 4, in Stable Households by Economic Group

Number of words exposed to	Economic group	Affirmations (strokes)	Prohibitions (discounts)
13 million words	Welfare	1 for every	2
26 million words	Working class	2 for every	1
45 million words	Professional	6 for every	1

Source: *Meaningful Differences in the Everyday Experience of Young American Children* by B. Hart & T. R. Risley.

In fact, Hart and Risley found that by age 3, children from professional, educated families have heard at least 30 million more words than children from less educated, welfare families.[30]

Based on this work, a number of researchers have studied the relationship of school outcomes to early language experience. They found that early language exposure predicted subsequent verbal ability, receptive and spoken language, and academic achievement through the third grade.[31]

The use of formal register is further complicated by the fact that these students don't have the vocabulary or the knowledge of sentence structure and syntax to use formal register. When student conversations in casual register are observed, much of the meaning comes not from the word choices but from the nonverbal assists. To be asked to communicate in writing without the nonverbal assists is a formidable, even overwhelming, task, which most students from poverty tend to avoid. Writing, at least initially, has very little meaning for them.[32]

Discourse Patterns in Formal and Casual Register

The pattern of registers is connected to the second issue: the patterns of discourse. Discourse will be discussed here with two different meanings. The first meaning is the manner in which the information is organized. In the formal register of English, the pattern is to get straight to the point.[33] In casual register, the pattern is to go around and around and finally get to the point. For students who have no access to formal register, educators become frustrated with the tendency of these students to meander almost endlessly through a topic. But this is simply the manner in which information is organized in casual register.

Language Acquisition in Primary and Secondary Discourse

The other meaning associated with discourse is the notion of primary and secondary discourse issues. Primary discourse is the language an individual first acquired. Secondary discourse is the language of the larger society that the individual must be able to use to function in the larger society. For example, if students have as their primary discourse the casual register of Spanish or the casual register of English, then they must also learn the formal register of English in order to fully negotiate and participate in the larger U.S. society. Gee points out that students do much better in school when their primary discourse is the same as their secondary discourse.[34]

Ramifications

Gee proceeds to make a distinction between acquisition and learning. Acquisition is the best and most natural way to learn a language and is simply the immersion in, and constant interaction with, that language. Learning is the direct-teaching of a language and usually is at a more metacognitive level. What Gee doesn't talk about, however, is the following: In almost all cases, acquisition of language occurs primarily when there is a significant relationship. Just think … Would you learn to use sign language well if there were no significant relationship that called for that usage? Would you learn to speak Chinese well if there were no significant relationship? This, then, leads to the next question: To what extent can an educational institution create significant relationships?

It follows, therefore, that when educators ask students to move from casual to formal register, we need to direct-teach it. Natural acquisition of formal register would require a significant relationship. Many students resist—saying, in effect, *You are asking me to learn "white talk."*[35] We tell them, *No, it's "green talk"— the language of money, and it's used in the workplace as well.* Add Wheeler and Swords:

> While the traditional approach attempts to correct, repress, eradicate, or subtract student language which differs from the standard written target, once we recognize that language comes in different varieties and styles and that each is systematic and rule-governed, a different response to language becomes possible. Instead of seeking to correct or eradicate styles of language, we may add language varieties to the child's linguistic toolbox, bringing a pluralistic vantage to language in the classroom. Such an approach allows us to maintain the language of the student's home community, all the while adding the linguistic tools needed for success in our broader society—the tool of Mainstream American English.[36]

Montaño-Harmon found that for students to move from casual-register English to formal-register English required them to *translate* because the word choice, sentence syntax, and discourse pattern are different.[37] This translation becomes much more meaningful if there is a significant relationship. If there is not a significant relationship, however, then the instruction must be more direct.

Patterns of Discourse

In the oral-language tradition in which casual register operates, the pattern of discourse is quite different. Discourse is defined as the organizational pattern of information (see the following graphic representations).

Formal-Register Discourse Pattern

Speaker or writer gets straight to the point.

Casual-Register Discourse Pattern

Speaker or writer goes around the issue before finally getting to the point.

How does this make a difference for students and teachers? First of all, parent/teacher conferences tend to be misunderstood on both sides. Teachers want to get right to the point; parents, particularly those from poverty, often need to talk around the issue first. When teachers cut the conversation short and get directly to the point, parents view that as being rude and uncaring. Second, writing becomes especially difficult for students from poverty because they tend to use a circular pattern of discourse and not adhere to the organizational schema of getting to the point. This discourse pattern is coupled with a third pattern, that of story structure (see the next two diagrams).

Story Structure

Formal-Register Story Structure

The formal-register story structure starts at the beginning of the story and goes to the end in a chronological narrative pattern. The most important part of the story is the plot.

Casual-Register Story Structure

The casual-register story structure begins with the chronological end of the story or the part with the greatest emotional intensity. The story is told in vignettes, usually with audience participation in between. The story ends with a comment about the character and the character's value. The most important part of the story is the characterization.

To help you understand this story structure better, the following is the transcript of an actual student telling a story in a Houston, Texas, middle school—and then what the story would be if it were told in formal register.

Casual-Register Version

Interviewer asked what happened. Male student said:

"Well, when I was in Ms. Ortiz's office I was already wrote up. I think it was dumb the reason I got wrote up … and I looked down, and I wasn't even speaking to her, and I was like, 'Man, y'all be trippin',' and it made it to another write-up … and that didn't matter 'cause … I was like talking to myself, and like I looked down and was like, 'Man, y'all teachers be trippin'.'"

At this point, the interviewer asked the student to tell the story from the beginning. The student said:

"OK, I went to the nurse's office, and he wouldn't let me stay in there for five minutes, and I wanted to rest because I really didn't feel good … and he kept tellin' me, 'Leave,' and I was like, 'Can I just stay five more minutes?' … and then he wouldn't let me. He wrote me up anyways, even though I got up and left. Then when Ms. Ortiz called me to the office, she told me I was in a lot of trouble with the nurse, and I told her OK and that she had gave me too much for just … for that little write-up … she had gave me too much because I had got DMC [in-school suspension] too … and then that's when I looked down, and I said that, and then she added like a couple more days to DMC."

Formal-Register Version

A student went to the nurse's office because he didn't feel good. The nurse repeatedly asked the student to leave and go back to class. The student requested another five minutes in the nurse's office. The nurse said no. The student didn't leave. Then the student told the nurse, "Ya'll be trippin'." At that point, the nurse sent the student to the office. The student received in-school suspension for the argument with the nurse. The student protested that the punishment was too much for the incident, whereupon the principal added two more days to the in-school suspension.

The casual-register story structure is far more entertaining, more participatory, and exhibits a richness of character, humor, and feeling that is absent from the formal version. The formal version uses sequence, order, cause and effect, and a conclusion—skills necessary for problem solving, inference, etc., all of which also are skills that are tested on state and national assessments.

Cinderella

To help you understand formal versus casual story structure better, the story of Cinderella will be told both ways.

Formal-Register Version

(The story is abbreviated because of familiarity.)

Once upon a time, there was a girl named Cinderella. She was very happy, and she lived with her father. Her father remarried a woman who had two daughters. When Cinderella's father died, her stepmother treated Cinderella very badly and, in fact, made her the maid for herself and her two daughters.

At the same time in this land, the king decided that it was time for the prince to get married. He sent a summons to all the people in the kingdom to come to a ball. Cinderella was not allowed to go but was forced to help her stepsisters and stepmother get ready for the ball. After they left for the ball, and as Cinderella was crying on the hearth, her fairy godmother came and, with her magic wand, gave Cinderella a beautiful dress, glass slippers, and a stagecoach made from pumpkins pulled by horses made from mice. She then sent Cinderella to the ball in style. There was one stipulation: She had to be back home by midnight.

At the ball, the prince was completely taken with Cinderella and danced with her all evening. As the clock began striking midnight, Cinderella remembered what the fairy godmother had said and fled from the dance. All she left was one of her glass slippers.

The prince conducted a big search using the glass slipper as a way to identify the missing woman. He finally found Cinderella; she was the only one the glass slipper fit. He married her, and they lived happily ever after.

Casual-Register Version

(*Italicized type* indicates the narrator; plain type indicates audience participation.)

Well, you know Cinderella married the prince, in spite of that old nasty stepmother.

Pointy eyes, that one. Old hag!

Good thing she had a fairy godmother, or she never woulda made it to the ball.

Lucky thing! God bless her ragged tail! Wish I had me a fairy godmother.

And to think she nearly messed up big time by staying 'til the clock was striking 12. After all the fairy godmother had done for her.

Uh-huh. She shoulda known better. Eyes too full of the prince, they were. They don't call him the prince for no reason.

When she got to the ball, her stepsisters and stepmother didn't even recognize her she was so beautiful without those rags.

Served 'em right, no-good jealous hags.

The prince just couldn't quit dancing with her, just couldn't take his eyes off her. He had finally found his woman.

Lucky her! Lucky him! Sure wish life was a fairy tale. Kinda like the way I met Charlie. Ha ha.

The way she arrived was something else—a coach and horseman—really fancy. Too bad that when she ran out of there as the clock struck 12 all that was left was a pumpkin rolling away and four mice!

What a surprise for the mice!

Well, he has to find her because his heart is broke. So he takes the glass slipper and hunts for her—and her old wicked stepmother, of course, is hiding her.

What a prize! Aren't they all?

But he finds her and marries her. Somebody as good as Cinderella deserved that.

Sure hope she never invited that stepmother to her castle. Should make her the maid!

Cognitive studies indicate that story structure is a way that the brain stores memories. Given the first story structure, memories would be stored more sequentially, and thinking patterns would follow story structure. Feuerstein describes episodic, nearly random memory and its effects on thinking.[38]

Teachers in DeKalb County, Georgia, helped young speakers of minority dialects explicitly contrast their mother tongue with the standard. Thus, when a fifth-grader answered a question with a double negative ("not no more"), the teacher prompted the student to "code switch," to which the student replied, "Not anymore." The children learned to switch from their home speech to school speech at appropriate times and places. They also learned that "the dialect they might use at home is valuable and 'effective' in that setting, but not for school, for work—or for American democracy." This program has been designated a "center of excellence" by the National Council of Teachers of English.[39]

Specificity of Vocabulary

Why is specificity of vocabulary so critical to school success? In poverty, when something falls on the floor, the adult says, "Get that." In middle class when something falls on the floor, the adult says, "Please pick up the fork from under the table." Someone in wealth might say, "Please pick up that Queen Anne fork from under the Chippendale table." Specificity of language tends to be higher in wealth than in middle class. (Even the relative "crowdedness" of a household impacts children's early language exposure. Evans et al. found that parents in crowded homes speak in less complex, less sophisticated ways with their children compared with parents in uncrowded homes.)[40]

Specificity of vocabulary is important because it indicates two things—the amount of shared vocabulary a person has and the ability to think critically about something.[41] Shared vocabulary means that you and I have words around which there is a common understanding. For example, if I ask how far it is to the next town and you say, "a far piece," I really have no idea what that means. But if you say, "five miles up the road," I know what that means. Writing has meaning only to the extent there is shared vocabulary. Furthermore, the specificity of language indicates the detail in which something can be examined. Virtually all compare-and-contrast activities are based on specificity of language.

What Can Schools Do to Address Casual Register, Discourse Patterns, Story Structure, and Specific Vocabulary?

Because there is such a direct link between achievement and language, the matter must be addressed. The following suggestions are not exhaustive, but rather a place to begin.

1. Have students write in casual register, then translate into formal register. (To get examples of casual register down on paper, ask them to write the way they talk.)

2. Establish as part of a discipline plan a requirement that students learn how to express their displeasure in formal register and therefore not be reprimanded as readily.

3. Use graphic organizers to show patterns of discourse.

4. In the classroom, tell stories both ways. Tell the story using the formal-register story structure, then tell the story with the casual-register structure. Talk about the stories: how they stay the same, and how they're different.

5. Encourage participation in the writing and telling of stories.

6. Use stories in math, social studies, and science to develop concepts.

7. Make up stories with the students that can be used to guide behavior.

8. Use casual register to build relationships and to translate meaning between formal register and casual register.

9. Tell students that just as there are different rules for different sports, so there are different ways of expressing ourselves at home and at school.

What Does This Information Mean in the School or Work Setting?

- Formal register needs to be direct-taught.
- Casual register needs to be recognized as the primary discourse pattern for many students, particularly those from poverty.
- Discourse patterns need to be direct-taught.
- Both story structures need to be used as a part of classroom instruction.
- Discipline that occurs when a student uses the inappropriate register should be a time for instruction in the appropriate register.
- Students need to be told how much formal register affects their ability to get a well-paying job.

Chapter 3

Hidden Rules Among Classes: How They Impact Relationships with People Different from You

Hidden rules are the unspoken cues and habits of a group. Distinct cueing systems exist between and among groups and economic classes. Generally, in the United States, that notion is recognized for racial and ethnic groups, but not particularly for economic groups.[42] There are many hidden rules to examine.

How and Where Do You Learn Hidden Rules?

Hidden rules come out of one's situated-learning environment and are learned both by being in that environment and by being taught. Some of the hidden rules one learns come from the hidden rules the parents use. So if one parent came from poverty and the other from middle class, then there is a mixed set of rules.[43] Sociologists refer to this as social learning.

How you spend your time impacts your knowledge base and resources—and therefore the hidden rules you follow.

When we work with adults in poverty, we tell them they are problem solvers but don't necessarily have all the information that other people have. We ask them to tell us how they spend their time. The following "Mental Model for Poverty" diagram summarizes what many individuals in poverty indicate as their time allocations.

Similar "time" charts are presented for middle class and wealth. Please remember that these charts are about what a person tends to spend time doing. In wealth, for example, chemical dependency is generally "outsourced" to paid individuals who spend time with that issue—e.g., a clinic, a law firm, etc.

Mental Model for Poverty

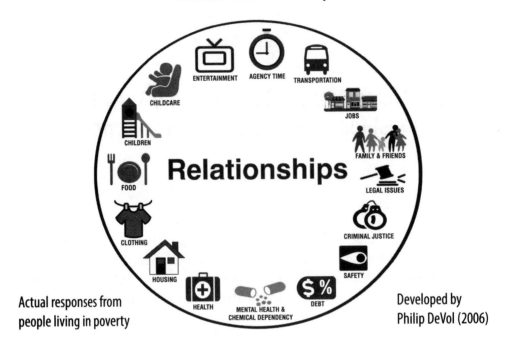

Actual responses from
people living in poverty

Developed by
Philip DeVol (2006)

Next is what people in middle class say they spend their time doing. Middle class in many ways is about stability.

Mental Model for Middle Class

Developed by
Philip DeVol (2006)

Below is what individuals in wealth say they spend their time doing.

Mental Model for Wealth

This applies to the top 1% of households in the United States—a net worth of $10.4 million or more

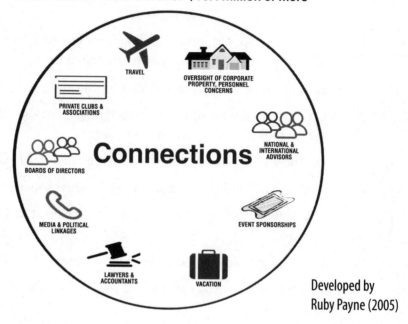

Developed by
Ruby Payne (2005)

Making the Transition Along the Continuum

When individuals move from poverty to middle class or middle class to wealth as their resource base grows and stabilizes, they use some of the rules they grew up with and some of the rules they are moving to. When individuals have been in a given group for two generations or more, that group's rules tend to be the only rules they know.[44]

Hidden rules are important because they impact relationships. One of the key issues in making the transition from poverty to middle class or middle class to wealth is to develop bridging social capital—in other words, developing relationships with people different from you. When hidden rules are broken, offense is frequently taken, and then the relationship doesn't get a chance to develop.[45]

Before going farther, let's take …

A Little Quiz

You're invited to take the following three-part quiz, putting a check mark by all the things you know how to do.

Could You Survive in Poverty?

Put a check by each item that applies to you.

☐ 1. I know which churches and sections of town have the best rummage sales.

☐ 2. I know when Walmart, drug stores, and convenience stores throw away over-the-counter medicines with expired dates.

☐ 3. I know which pawn shops sell DVDs for $1.

☐ 4. In the courts in my town, I know which judges are lenient, which ones are crooked, and which ones are fair.

☐ 5. I know how to physically fight—and defend myself physically.

☐ 6. I know how to get a gun without doing the legal paperwork.

☐ 7. I know how to keep my clothes from being stolen at the laundromat.

☐ 8. I know what problems to look for in a used car.

☐ 9. I/my family use a payday lender and don't have a checking account (cash only).

☐ 10. I know how to live without electricity and a phone.

☐ 11. I know how to use a knife as scissors.

☐ 12. I can entertain a group of friends with my personality and my stories.

☐ 13. I know which churches will provide assistance with food and/or shelter.

☐ 14. I know how to move in half a day.

☐ 15. I know how to get and use food stamps or an electronic card for benefits.

☐ 16. I know where the free medical clinics are.

☐ 17. I am very good at trading and bartering.

☐ 18. I can get by without a car.

☐ 19. I know the ways to keep my car from being repossessed if I get behind on the payments.

☐ 20. We pay our cable bill before we pay our rent.

☐ 21. I know which sections of town "belong" to which gangs.

☐ 22. I buy prepaid minutes for my cell phone.

☐ 23. I know at least one person in jail and one person on probation.

☐ 24. At least one person in my household smokes.

☐ 25. I know which grocery stores have dumpsters where I can get discarded food—and the best times to go.

Could You Survive in Middle Class?

Put a check by each item that applies to you.

☐ 1. I know how to get my children into Little League, piano lessons, soccer, etc.

☐ 2. I have an online checking account and monitor my bills online.

☐ 3. Every bedroom has its own TV and DVR.

☐ 4. My children know the best name brands in clothing.

☐ 5. I know how to order in a nice restaurant.

☐ 6. I know how to use a credit card, checking account, and savings account—and I know what an annuity is. I understand term life insurance, disability insurance, and 80/20 medical insurance, as well as house insurance, flood insurance, and replacement insurance.

☐ 7. I talk to my children about going to college and how to pay for it.

☐ 8. I know how to get one of the best interest rates on my new-car loan.

☐ 9. I understand the difference among the principal, interest, and escrow statements on my house payment.

☐ 10. I know how to help my children with their homework and don't hesitate to call the school if I need additional information.

☐ 11. I know how to decorate the house for the different holidays.

☐ 12. I/my family belong to an athletic or exercise club.

☐ 13. I know how to use most of the tools in the garage.

☐ 14. I repair items in my house almost immediately when they break—or know a repair service and call it.

☐ 15. We have more than one computer in our home.

☐ 16. We plan our vacations six months to a year in advance.

☐ 17. I contribute to a retirement plan separate from Social Security.

☐ 18. I am billed monthly for my cell phone.

Could You Survive in Wealth?

Put a check by each item that applies to you.

☐ 1. I can read a menu in at least three languages.

☐ 2. I have several favorite restaurants in different countries. I use a concierge to book the best restaurants as I travel throughout the world.

☐ 3. During the holidays, I know how to hire a decorator to identify the appropriate themes and items with which to decorate the house.

☐ 4. I know who my preferred financial adviser, legal firm, certified public accounting firm, designer, florist, caterer, domestic employment service, and hairdresser are. In addition, I have a preferred tailor, travel agency, and personal trainer.

☐ 5. I have at least two residences that are staffed and maintained.

☐ 6. I know how to ensure confidentiality and loyalty from my domestic staff.

☐ 7. I have at least two or three "screens" that keep people whom I do not wish to see away from me.

☐ 8. I fly in my own plane, the company plane, or first class.

☐ 9. I know how to enroll my children in the preferred private schools.

☐ 10. I know how to host the parties that "key" people attend.

☐ 11. I am on the boards of at least two charities.

☐ 12. I contribute to at least four or five political campaigns.

☐ 13. I support or buy the work of a particular artist.

☐ 14. I know how to read a corporate financial statement and analyze my own financial statements.

☐ 15. I belong to at least one private club (country club, yacht club, etc.) and carefully scrutinize my bill each month.

☐ 16. I own more vehicles than there are drivers.

☐ 17. I "buy a table" at several charity events throughout the year.

☐ 18. I can cite the provenance (historical documentation) of all of my original art, jewelry, antiques, and one-of-a-kind items.

☐ 19. I have no trouble translating exchange rates for currency between and among different countries.

Another Quiz: Hidden Rules in Relationships

Not only do the hidden rules impact schools, work, and organizations, they also impact personal relationships. The next three-part quiz is about how these rules show up in relationships.

Could You Cope with a Spouse/Partner Who Came from Generational Poverty (or Had That Mindset)?

It would bother me if my spouse or partner:

☐ Repeatedly gave money to a relative who would not work.

☐ Left household bills unpaid in order to give money to a relative.

☐ Loaned the car to a relative who doesn't have insurance and cannot be insured.

☐ Allowed a relative to move in and stay with us.

☐ Didn't pay attention to time (e.g., missed dates, was extremely late, didn't show).

☐ Quit jobs without having another one because they didn't like the boss.

☐ Cursed at their boss in public.

☐ Physically fought—fairly frequently.

☐ Didn't think education was important.

☐ Left numerous items in the house unrepaired.

☐ Used physical punishment on the children as part of discipline.

☐ Self-identified as a "fighter" or a "lover" who works hard physically.

☐ Served food from the stove and ate most meals in front of the TV.

☐ Almost always had the TV and/or radio on—and often loudly.

☐ Kept the house dark on the inside: poorly lit and with window coverings closed.

☐ Kept organizational patterns of the household chaotic.

☐ Bought clothing from secondhand stores, garage sales, and so on.

☐ Bought designer clothing or shoes for our children, but didn't pay an urgent household bill.

☐ Made a big deal about the quantity of food.

☐ Viewed me as a possession.

☐ Had family members who made fun of me for having a college degree.

☐ Bragged about me by talking badly about me.

☐ Often spent time with relatives, rather than spending time with me.

☐ Purchased alcoholic beverages for entertainment before paying for necessities (e.g., car insurance, utilities, rent).

Could You Cope with a Spouse/Partner Who Came from Middle Class (or Had That Mindset)?

It would bother me if my spouse or partner:

☐ Spent long hours at the office.

☐ Required our household to run on a budget.

☐ Planned out our week in advance.

☐ Started a college fund at the birth of our child.

☐ Hired a plumber to do a needed repair.

☐ Fixed the plumbing without help.

☐ Played golf every weekend with his friends.

☐ Kept a job that they hated for financial reasons.

☐ Rigidly adhered to time demands—and was often early.

☐ Was organized, keeping a paper trail on everything.

☐ Refused to give money to relatives who weren't working.

☐ Refused to allow a relative to come live with us.

☐ Planned vacations 6–12 months in advance.

☐ Spent evenings taking graduate courses.

☐ Devoted considerable time to a community charitable event.

☐ Shopped for high-quality clothing/shoes/accessories, then charged those items.

☐ Withdrew screen time and other privileges from the children as part of discipline.

☐ Paid for our child's college expenses and tuition.

☐ Paid for tennis, golf, dance, swimming, and other types of lessons for our child.

☐ Often made a big issue over the quality of food.

☐ Bought reprints and numbered artwork as part of our home's décor.

☐ Purchased furniture for its practicality and match to the décor.

☐ Had family members who discounted me because of my lack of education or achievement.

Could You Cope with a Spouse/Partner Who Came from Old Money (or Had That Mindset)?

It would bother me if my spouse or partner:

☐ Spent money on private club memberships.

☐ Had a trust fund from birth.

☐ Insisted on the artistic quality and merit of household items, clothing, accessories, and so on.

☐ Had a personal assistant to help with purchases of clothing and accessories.

☐ Spent money on a personal tailor and physical trainer.

☐ Spent a great deal of time on charitable activities and did not make or take money for that time.

☐ Often placed our children in the care of a nanny.

☐ Insisted that our children be placed in private boarding schools at the age of 6.

☐ Talked a lot about the presentation of food.

☐ Staffed and maintained homes in more than one country.

☐ Spent money on a private airplane and/or yacht.

☐ Established trust funds for our children at birth.

☐ Maintained social and financial connections with individuals I didn't like.

☐ Had family members who looked down on me because of my bloodline or pedigree (or lack thereof).

☐ Kept an accountant, lawyer, domestic service agency, and investment broker on retainer.

☐ Was adamant about details, insisting on perfection in virtually everything.

☐ Wanted to have nothing further to do with a decent individual who didn't have a suitable connection.

☐ Spent $1 million-plus on an original piece of art—and would purchase only original works of art.

☐ Graduated from an Ivy League college or university.

☐ Appeared to value me largely for the social connections I had.

☐ Reviewed family assets and liabilities on a monthly basis.

☐ Purchased furniture and furnishings for their artistic merit or designer designation.

☐ Kept almost no food in the house.

The first point about these exercises is that if you fall mostly in the middle class, the assumption is that "everyone knows" these things. However, if you didn't know a number of the items for the other classes, the exercise points out how many of the hidden rules are taken for granted by a particular class, which assumes they are a given for everyone. What, then, are the hidden rules? The following chart gives an overview of some of the major hidden rules among people from poverty, middle class, and wealth.

First, however, some background information and stories may help explain parts of the preceding quizzes and the ensuing chart. The bottom line or driving force against which decisions are made is important to note.[46] For example, in one school district, the faculty had gone together to buy a refrigerator for a family that didn't have one. About three weeks later, the children in the family were gone for a week. When the students returned, the teachers asked where they had been. The answer was that the family had gone camping because they were so stressed. What had they used for money to go camping? Proceeds from the sale of the refrigerator, of course. The bottom line in generational poverty is entertainment and relationships. In middle class, the criteria against which most decisions are made relate to work and achievement. In wealth, it is the ramifications of the financial, social, and political connections that have the weight.

Being able physically to fight or have someone who is willing to fight for you is important for survival in poverty. Yet, in middle class, being able to use words as tools to negotiate conflict is crucial. Many times one's *fists* are used in poverty because words are neither available nor respected.

The one deep experience that distinguishes the social rich from the merely rich and those below is their schooling, and with it, all the associations, the sense and sensibility, to which this education routine leads throughout their lives.

As a selection and training place of the upper classes, both old and new, the private school is a unifying influence, a force for the nationalization of the upper classes.

–C. Wright Mills, *The Power Elite*[47]

Hidden Rules Among Classes

	Poverty
Possessions	People
Money	To be used, spent
Personality	Is for entertainment; sense of humor is highly valued
Social emphasis	Social inclusion of people who are liked
Food	Key question: Did you have enough? Quantity important
Clothing	Valued for individual style and expression of personality
Time	Present most important; decisions made for moment based on feelings or survival
Education	Valued and revered as abstract but not as reality
Destiny	Believes in fate; cannot do much to mitigate chance
Language	Casual register; language is about survival
Family structure	Tends to be matriarchal
Worldview	Sees world in terms of local setting
Love	Love and acceptance conditional, based on whether individual is liked
Driving forces	Survival, relationships, entertainment
Humor	About people and sex

Middle Class	Wealth
Things	One-of-a-kind objects, legacies, pedigrees
To be managed	To be conserved, invested
Is for acquisition and stability; achievement is highly valued	Is for connections; financial, political, social connections are highly valued
Emphasis is on self-governance and self-sufficiency	Emphasis is on social exclusion
Key question: Did you like it? Quality important	Key question: Was it presented well? Presentation important
Valued for its quality and acceptance into norm of middle class; label important	Valued for its artistic sense and expression; designer important
Future most important; decisions made against future ramifications	Traditions and history most important; decisions made partially on basis of tradition and decorum
Crucial for climbing success ladder and making money	Necessary tradition for making and maintaining connections
Believes in choice; can change future with good choices now	*Noblesse oblige*
Formal register; language is about negotiation	Formal register; language is about networking
Tends to be patriarchal	Depends on who has the money
Sees world in terms of national setting	Sees world in terms of international view
Love and acceptance conditional and based largely on achievement	Love and acceptance conditional and related to social standing and connections
Work, achievement	Financial, political, and social connections
About situations	About social *faux pas*

It should be noted that this chart indicates only patterns that may be seen. Many individuals use combinations or parts of the chart. If this chart is used to stereotype—i.e., assuming that everyone in a given group uses these rules—then the chart is misunderstood.

One of the biggest difficulties in getting out of poverty is managing money—and the general information base around money. How can you manage something you've never had? Money is seen in poverty as an expression of personality and is used for entertainment and relationships.[48] The notion of using money for security is grounded in the middle and wealthy classes.

The question in the quiz about using a knife as scissors was put there to illustrate the lack of tools available to those in poverty. Tools in many ways are one of the identifiers of middle class—from the kitchen to the garage. Therefore, the notion of maintaining property and repairing items is dependent on having tools. When they aren't available, things aren't repaired or maintained. Students sometimes don't have access to scissors, pens, paper, pencils, rulers, etc., which may be part of an assignment.

A major difference among the classes is how "the world" is defined for them. Wealthy individuals view the international scene as their world. As one told me, "My favorite restaurant is in Brazil." Middle class tends to see the world in terms of a national picture, while poverty sees the world in its immediate locale. Several fourth-grade students from poverty told us when they were writing to the prompt, *How is life in Houston different from life in Baytown?* (Baytown is 20 minutes from Houston): "They don't have TVs in Houston."

In wealth, to be introduced or accepted, one must have an individual already approved by that group make the introductions. Yet to stand back and not introduce yourself in a middle-class setting is not the accepted norm. And in poverty it isn't unusual to have a comment made about the person before the person is ever introduced.

Additional Hidden Rules in Wealth

Old money and new money don't think alike. Very rarely are students from old money in public schools. Typically it is new-money students in public schools. It has been my experience that many middle-class educators have more difficulty with students from affluence than they do with students from poverty. There is no place in the world more competitive to live than new money because the financial resources are there to pursue opportunities, but the connections are not. Therefore, the only way your children can have those opportunities is to be better than everyone else. The level of competition in new money is extremely high.

Here are additional hidden rules that operate in wealth.

1. It's not OK not to be perfect. That would seldom be articulated, but it is rigidly followed.

2. If you don't have connections or wealth, then you may be respected for your expertise.

3. Social exclusion is the weapon of choice; you simply aren't invited.

4. Time is more important than money (particularly true in new money).

5. Details are *very* important. One word in a legal document can transfer assets. Details are critical to success.

6. A paper protocol exists (including the paper itself) for invitations, responses, and thank yous.

7. A key role of a parent in wealth is to ensure that the child has access to the appropriate connections and schooling.

8. Personal concerns of an emotional nature are not openly shared in a social setting but rather with the appropriately paid, credentialed professional.

9. Humor is most often about social *faux pas*.

10. Indiscretion (disclosing information gained through social connections) to media or others not in the social set is rarely forgiven.

NOTE: *Addiction and drug use occur in all classes. The impact of addiction and the level of stability are more about the available support systems and resources to address the addiction, and those vary by class.*

When You Move from One Class to Another, Which Hidden Rules Do You Keep, and Which Ones Do You Release?

Which rules you keep and which ones you discard as you make the transition to another class depends on the survival issues you had growing up. The hidden rules that individuals keep usually have to do with identity or deep emotional issues.[49]

Key Point About Hidden Rules

The key point is that hidden rules govern a great deal of our immediate assessment of individuals and their capabilities. Not understanding the hidden rules of the next class often is the key factor in keeping an individual from moving upward in a career—or even getting the position in the first place. Many times, key relationships with someone different from you are (bridging social capital) don't occur because a hidden rule is broken, leading the other person to think the one who broke the rule is either stupid or rude, as indicated above. In reality, they just didn't know the rules.

Why Is It That Many Who Are Raised in Middle Class Will Often Take on a Number of the Hidden Rules of Poverty?

Adult personality is not considered to be formed until around age 29.[50] From early adolescence until about that age, such factors as early pregnancy, drug/biochemical/addiction issues, learning disabilities, abuse, and social isolation (virtually no friends) can impact individuals and have them using the hidden rules of poverty, even though they may have been raised middle class.

What Does This Information Mean in the School or Work Setting?

- Assumptions made about individuals' intelligence and approaches to the school and/or work setting may relate in large measure to their understanding of hidden rules.

- Students need to be taught the hidden rules of middle class—not in denigration of their own hidden rules but rather as another set of rules that can be used if they so choose.

- Many of the attitudes that students and parents bring with them are an integral part of their culture and belief systems. Middle-class solutions should not necessarily be imposed when other, more workable, solutions might be found.

- An understanding of the culture and values of poverty will lessen the anger and frustration that educators may periodically feel when dealing with these students and parents.

- Most of the students in poverty I have talked to don't believe they are poor, even when they're on welfare. Most of the wealthy adults I have talked to don't believe they're rich; they will usually cite someone who has more than they do.

Chapter 4

The 'Situated Learning' Reality of Generational Poverty: How It Impacts Navigation of One's Life

Life is lived in common, but not in community.

–Michael Harrington, "The Invisible Land"
in *Four Horsemen*[51]

Generational poverty is defined as having been in poverty for at least two generations; however, the patterns begin to surface much sooner than two generations if the family lives with others who are from generational poverty.

Situational poverty is defined as a lack of resources due to a particular event (e.g., a death, chronic illness, divorce, etc.). Unlike generational poverty, it is focused largely on monetary resources and can be a temporary situation. Individuals in situational poverty usually have other resources intact, including cultural and social capital, along with the ability to use formal register.

Generational poverty, in contrast, has its own culture, hidden rules, and belief systems.[52] A culture tends to be self-reinforcing—and includes a set of values transmitted from parent to child.[53]

One of the key indicators of whether it's generational or situational poverty is the prevailing attitude. Frequently the attitude in generational poverty is that society "owes me a living." In situational poverty the attitude is often one of pride and a great reluctance (sometimes refusal) to accept charity.

What, then, makes generational poverty so different from the middle class? How is it that school is such an unsatisfactory experience for so many students from poverty?

Allison Boisvert, social justice minister, Pax Christi Catholic Community, Eden Prairie, Minnesota, goes so far as to say, "The generationally poor are usually as confined by their poverty as if they lived in a maximum security prison."[54]

What Is Often Part of the Reality of Generational Poverty?

- Instability of housing
- Violence
- Food insecurity
- Unemployment/underemployment
- Unaddressed health issues
- Frequent exposure to addiction
- Predators (both inside and outside the group)
- Periodic homelessness
- Crowded housing/lack of personal space
- Incarceration
- Lots of time at agencies getting assistance
- Uneducated/undereducated adults
- Limited knowledge bases
- Death[55]

To examine the differences, a case study will be used.

Case Study: Walter (white male)

The following was an actual court case heard in Houston, Texas, in March 1995. *Italicized type* indicates what came out in the trial; plain print indicates the kinds of comments that might be made by others in generational poverty. Names have been changed to protect the girl.

As the Story Would Be Told in Poverty ...
Probably by a Relative or Neighbor

Well, you know Walter got put away for 37 years. Him being 48 and all. He'll probably die in jail. Just couldn't leave his hands off that 12-year-old Susie.

Dirty old man. Bodding's gonna whup his tail.

Already did. You know Bodding was waiting for him in jail and beat the living daylights out of him.

In jail?

Yeah, Bodding got caught for possession. Had $12,000 on him when they arrested him.

Golly, wish I had been there to cash in! (laughter) A man's gotta make a living!

Susie being blind and all—I can see why Bodding beat the daylights out of Walter. Lucky he didn't get killed, old Walter is.

Too bad her momma is no good.

She started the whole thing! Susie's momma goes over there and argues with Bodding.

Ain't they divorced?

Yeah, and she's got Walter working for her, repairing her house or something.

Or something, I bet. What's she got in her house that's worth fixing?

Anyway, she goes over to Bodding's house to take the lawnmower ...

I reckon so as Walter can mow the yard? I bet that's the first time old Walter has ever broken a sweat! Reminds me of the time I saw Walter thinking about taking a job. All that thinking, and he had to get drunk. He went to jail that time, too—a felony, I think it was. So many of those DWIs. Judge told him he was egregious. Walter said he wasn't greasy—he took a bath last week! (laughter)

Bodding and Susie's momma got in a fight, so she tells Walter to take Susie with him.

Lordy, her elevator must not go all the way to the top! Didn't she know about him getting arrested for enticing a minor?

With Susie blind and all. And she sends Susie with Walter?

She sure don't care about her babies.

Well, Walter's momma was there 'cause Walter lives with his momma, seeing as how he can't keep no job.

Ain't his other brother there?

Yeah, and him 41 years old. That poor momma sure has her burdens to bear. And then her 30-year-old daughter, Susie's momma, at home too. You know Susie's momma lost custody of her kids. Walter gets these videos, you know. Those adult videos. Heavy breathing! (laughter)

Some of them are more fun to listen to than look at! (laughter) Those people in the videos are des-per-ate!

Anyway, he puts those on and then carries Susie to his room and tells her she wants him—and describes all his sex-u-al exploits!

Golly, he must be a loooooooooover. (laughter) He should be shot. I'd kill him if he did that to my kid!

Then he lets his fingers do the walking.

Kinda like the Yellow Pages! (laughter)

I guess he didn't do anything with his "thang," according to Miss Rosie who went to that trial every day. And Susie begging him to stop so many times.

Probably couldn't do anything with it; that's why he needs to listen to that heavy breathing! Pant! Pant! (laughter) What a no-count, low-down creep. I'll pay Bodding to kill him!

Bodding says the only way Walter is coming out of jail is in a pine box.

Don't blame him myself.

Yeah, Miss Rosie said Walter's momma said at the trial that the door to Walter's room was open, and there ain't no way Walter could have done that. That she is a good Christian momma and she don't put up with that.

Oh Lordy, did God strike her dead on the spot, or is she still alive? I'd be afraid of ending up in eternal damnation for telling a story like that!

Miss Rosie said her 12-year-old nephew testified that the door was closed and his grandma told him to say it was open!

Ooo! Ooo! Oooo! That poor baby tells the truth? His grandma's gonna make him mis-er-a-ble!

And then Walter's momma tells that jury that she never allows those adult videos in her house, leastways not that she pays for them! (lots of laughter)

I bet the judge bit on that one! How is Walter gonna get videos except for her money? Mowing yards? (more laughter) No, I bet he saves his pennies! (laughter)

All these years she has covered for Walter. Guess she just couldn't cover no more.

Remember that time Walter got drunk and wrecked her car, and she said she was driving? And she was at the hospital at the time with a broken leg. And the judge asked her how she could be driving and in the hospital "simultaneously." And she said that's just how it was—simultaneously—she had never felt so excited in her life. (laughter) Who turned Walter in?

Well, it wasn't Susie's momma. She was busy with Skeeter, her new boyfriend. I hear he's something.

Remember that one boyfriend she had? Thought he was so smart?

Speaking of smart, that Susie sure is. Her blind and all, and she won the district spelling bee for the seventh grade this year. I hear she's in National Honor Society, whatever that is.

Wonder if it's kinda like the country club. Instead of playing golf, you just spell! (laughter)

Susie calls this friend of hers who tells her mother and they come and get her and take her to the police and hospital.

Some rich lady, not minding her own business, that's for sure.

Well, it was a good thing for Susie, 'cause that momma of hers sure ain't good for Susie. She don't deserve a kid like Susie. SHE oughta be the one who's blind.

Ain't that the truth. Way I see it, she already is. Just look at Skeeter! (gales of laughter)

What Actually Happened Is This:

Walter is the uncle of Susie, a 12-year-old, very intelligent, blind girl. Walter is Susie's mother's brother. Bodding is not Susie's biological father but a stepfather. Bodding and Susie's mother get into an argument over a lawnmower. Susie's mother sends Susie to her mother's house (Grandma) so that Walter and Bodding won't get into a fight. At the house, Walter takes Susie into his bedroom, shuts the door, and molests her.

Knowing that her grandma will take Walter's side, Susie waits until the next day when Walter takes her and her two cousins to the Houston Zoo. She makes a phone call to a girlfriend. The girlfriend's mother comes and picks her up at the zoo. The girlfriend's mother reports the incident to the police who pick up Walter.

In the meantime, Bodding has been arrested for having $12,000 in cash on him, as well as drugs. When Walter gets put in jail, Bodding arranges to have Walter surrounded by men, and Bodding beats him up before jail security can break up the fight.

In the trial, the lawyer for Walter states that Susie liked Walter's advances because she didn't report the assault until the next day at the zoo. Susie had no way to get to safety at Grandma's, so she had to wait until the next day to report it. Walter was sentenced to 37 years in prison.

NOTE: Many middle-class readers of this story have been offended at the humor involved and the seemingly crass acceptance of the situation. Actually the humor is a way to mask the deep pain and disgust for what happened.

What Patterns Are Often Present in Generational Poverty?

NOTE: The following items constitute patterns; they certainly wouldn't apply in every household of generational poverty.

- [ ] **Background "noise":** Almost always the TV is on, no matter what the circumstances. Conversation is participatory, often with more than one person talking at a time.[56]

- [ ] **Importance of personality:** Individual personality is what one brings to the setting—because money is seldom brought. The ability to entertain, tell stories, and have a sense of humor are highly valued.

- [ ] **Significance of entertainment:** When one is merely surviving, then respite from survival mode is important. Indeed, entertainment brings that respite.

- [ ] **Importance of relationships:** One has only people on whom to rely, and those relationships are important to survival. One often has favorites.[57]

- [ ] **Matriarchal structure:** The mother has the most powerful position in generational poverty, especially when she functions as a caretaker.[58]

- [ ] **Oral-language tradition:** Casual register is used for just about everything.[59]

- [ ] **Survival orientation:** There tends to be little room for the abstract and minimal discussion of academic topics; most conversations center around people and relationships. A job is about making enough money to survive. A job is not about a career (e.g., "I was looking for a job when I found this one").[60]

- [ ] **Identity for men tied to lover/fighter role:** The key issue for males is to be a "man." The rules are rigid, and a man is expected to work hard physically— and be a lover and a fighter.[61]

- [ ] **Identity for women tied to rescuer/martyr role:** A "good" woman is expected to take care of and rescue her man and her children as needed.

- [ ] **Importance of nonverbal/kinesthetic communication:** Touch is used to communicate, as are space and nonverbal emotional information.[62]

- [ ] **Ownership of people:** People are possessions. There's a great deal of fear and comment about leaving the neighborhood/culture and "getting above your raisings."

- [ ] **Negative orientation:** Failure at anything is the source of stories and numerous belittling comments.

- [ ] **Discipline:** Punishment is usually about penance and forgiveness, not change.

- [ ] **Belief in fate:** Destiny and fate are the major tenets of the belief system. Choice is seldom considered.[63]

- [ ] **Polarized thinking:** Nuanced options on the continuum are hardly ever examined. Just about everything is polarized; it is one way or the other. The concept of "gray areas" seldom enters the picture. These kinds of statements are common: "I quit," "I can't do it," and "He's just plain no good."

- ☐ **Mating dance:** The mating dance is about using the body in a sexual way, as well as verbally and nonverbally complimenting (or criticizing) body parts. If you have few financial resources, the way you sexually attract someone is with your body.

- ☐ **Time:** Time occurs only in the present. The future doesn't exist—except as a word. Time is flexible and not measured. Time is often assigned on the basis of the emotional significance and not the actual measured time.

- ☐ **Sense of humor:** A sense of humor is highly valued, as entertainment is one of the key aspects of poverty. Humor is almost always about people— either situations that people encounter or things people do to other people.

- ☐ **Lack of order/organization:** Many of the homes/apartments of people in poverty are unkempt and cluttered. Devices for organization (files, planners, etc.) scarcely exist.[64]

- ☐ **Living in the moment:** Being proactive, setting goals, and planning ahead are not part of generational poverty. Most of what occurs is reactive and in the moment. Future ramifications of present actions are seldom considered.[65]

> Even in telling me some of those stories
> that involve a great deal of humiliation at
> the hands of hospital or welfare personnel,
> she usually manages to find something
> that's funny in the madness of it all and
> keeps on saying things that make both of
> us laugh [in describing Mrs. Washington].
>
> —Jonathan Kozol, *Amazing Grace*[66]

The following story is told by Sandy Smith (not her real name), who successfully completed the Getting Ahead in a Just-Gettin'-By World training.[67] She gave permission to use her case study in this book.

Sandy's Story

"My name is Sandy Smith, and today I'm going to share a little bit about my life … Before I go into the details I first must give you a description of my parents. My father was a sergeant in the Vietnam War and a Black Panther in the civil rights movement. My family says before he went to Vietnam he was a man of strong integrity, values, and work ethic. When my father came home he wasn't the same. My father felt abandoned by his country, and since he was African-American, he blamed a lot of it on his color. My mother at 12 had the burden of raising her brother and little sister. My mom never bonded with her mother. She has spent most of her life wanting to be loved and accepted and, most of all, she did not want to be like her family. She privately carried the guilt of having me with a married man. Truthfully, my father's family hated my mother because she was white and young—and because she had me.

"I learned quickly to please both sides of my family. When I was with my father, he would get mad and tell me horrible things about my mother to get me not to love her. My mom had many boyfriends, and because she didn't fit in with her family, she felt that black men accepted her better. I often wondered, since the only thing she really said about her own mother was that she hated black people. My father acted like I was his friend and confided in me like I was an adult. He had nothing to hide, whether it was sharing his violent Vietnam stories or his drug addiction. He often had me in an environment where I helped pass the pipe around. Instead of having dreams of the first day of school, I was wondering where we would sleep and eat.

"I was around 8 years old when my father kidnapped me and fled to California, and I quickly learned how to commute across San Francisco by myself. I learned the true meaning of Christmas at 9, homeless in the back seat of a car. My dad was constantly trying to find a girlfriend to take care of me, but the more disappointments that came our way, the more drugs he used. I remember when my real mother finally found me, I was furious! I mean, I just got used to the situation. I started to miss my father. Even as a kid I could understand her side, but deep down I knew that it would make her mad if I told her. So I held it in and went on; my mother tried her best to give me what I wanted. Naturally she couldn't afford this lifestyle, so I picked up on her schemes and scams, along with a few of my own. So then I started to talk back and stay out late. I'll be honest: I was terrible, and I probably deserved to be disciplined, but she was just too busy to discipline me; 70% of the time my mother was at work. So I then felt I could come and go and do as I pleased.

"When I moved back with my mother it seemed that being introduced to the gang life was inevitable to a kid growing up in Elgin, Illinois, close to Chicago. The whole town was gang infested. There are a lot of rules and regulations in gang life. Respect and pride are a must to survive where I come from. I know through life that you can't let people see your weakness, as my parents modeled for me firsthand. To look at me I was built pretty tough, and I can give someone a look that will keep them up at night. But it's all an act that I learned to survive in my environment.

"My environment was chaotic; we were constantly struggling, hungry almost every night, isolated, and in constant pain from fighting, jumping in [gang initiation], and drive-bys. Even though the gang wanted us to do bad things to one another, they always undeniably showed me love, support, and acceptance. You can always find someone to relate to in the gang; it's the parents who are addicts and deadbeat dads, with sexual and/or physical abuse in the home (you name it, you'll find someone who has been affected by it). I eventually pushed my mother farther and farther away with my violent gangbanger attitude. Despite my tough attitude, I've always felt the closest to my sister; after all, she was in the same situation as I was. 'Different deadbeat dad, same situation,' I would always say.

"I eventually ended up pregnant by another gang member. I remember when my mother got so sick of my actions, she rented an apartment for me in the neighborhood that I used to bang in. She told me that she and Brittany were moving back to Ohio. I was so happy. I got an apartment, and I could finally do what I wanted to do, I thought. The day before my mother was supposed to go back to Ohio, I was walking to the local 7-Eleven when one of my rivals jumped out of a car and put a gun to my head. I was about six months pregnant at the time. I still can hear the guy screaming, representing his gang and disrespecting mine.

"He pointed the gun to my head and said, 'Are you ready to die?' and I screamed, 'Go ahead and do what you gotta do.' I remember as I said those words I thought of the innocent life that was in my stomach and I knew that I was done with the gang life. It wasn't about me anymore; I had someone else to take care of. It took one of the older girls to check him. She hated me, but she was about seven years older than me. She told him that he was going too far. I was pregnant and the baby didn't deserve to die. If it hadn't been for Taylor in my stomach, I wouldn't be able to write this story right now, and this I know for sure. So he told me to go home, and when he caught me in nine months my child would not have a mother. As I was walking away, I felt like the world was spinning around me. I had certain life events flash in my head, and I began to break down. By the time I hit my front door I don't think I had ever needed my mother so badly before—ever. I started packing all my stuff in her already packed U-Haul and told her that I was coming to Ohio also. I promised to go back to school and stay out of trouble.

"So we moved back to Ohio, and I went back to high school but eventually dropped out. My mother placed me in an abuse shelter with my daughter. She felt she could do no more for me or my child. I have been the victim of abusive relationships all my life, and when it came time for romance, I accepted what was available to me. I was 17 and had an apartment, and I was a perfect target for every hustla, playa, and drug dealer around. I was abused physically, sexually, and mentally on a daily basis. I ended up pregnant again and again and again and again. I found myself alone, used up, with five hungry mouths to feed. I would be so afraid to leave because I thought I couldn't make it financially—or the fear of my kids never having any father figure would hold me back. In fact, most of my pregnancies were forced on me just to keep me in the relationship.

"People often say they don't know how I could raise five children, and I smile because honestly people probably would not like the reality of how we survived for so long. Being around all those unsavory people taught me a lot. I was exploited and terrorized, so eventually I did the same back. I even married the first nice man that came my way just to get out of the abusive relationship that I was in. I didn't realize until I wanted a divorce after only nine months that I was living the same way my mother was. I was simply 'looking for love in all the wrong places.' I didn't want my mistakes to be repeated through my children. I always had a job, but the pay barely allowed me to make it from month to month.

"I enrolled in college full-time while working, and I would do great when I could get there, but often I couldn't. Whether it was the car breaking down, sick kids, or abuse from a relationship … you name it, it probably happened to me. Not only did I have virtually no family support, but then people in my neighborhood thought I was a threat to them (that is, haters, thinking I was acting white or better than them). Just because I was doing something with my life they assumed I had money and was acting better than them. Most days I wanted to just give up and go back to the street life. After all, it seems a lot easier to survive, especially when that's all you really know.

"I encountered a [support] group through my local job and family services. I was given a mandatory interview. My childcare was only for my employment. For it to cover my schooling, I would have to work full-time. Now, I'm not the smartest person in the world, but I know the only way out of poverty is to complete my education." [Sandy graduated with an associate's degree.]

Lack of Understanding of Money in Generational Poverty

I have heard Al Silva, general manager and COO of Labatt Food Service, say that when you grow up in poverty, it's like growing up in a foreign country—nobody explains the rules to you—especially the rules about money. When Silva spoke to a class at Texas Lutheran University, he "encouraged the audience to be lifelong learners. In the process, it is important to 'know what you don't know.'"[68]

In work and in middle-class life, money is handled as an abstract representational construct. For example, a teenage girl I knew got a checking account. She started writing checks. They were bouncing everywhere. When I asked her what she was doing, the girl said she had all these checks, and she was going to use them. I told her that checks represent money, but they aren't cash.

Organization of Space and Paper in Generational Poverty

Space is where your body goes and how you keep track of things. In middle-class households, the space is often assigned a function. For example, *This is the bedroom where people sleep.* When there are 14 people in four rooms, space is used for everything. Furthermore, in middle-class households, space serves as an organizing function. Another example: *This drawer will have the silverware; this drawer will have plates.* But when you move every three to six months, there is little organization of space. Consequently, to do well in school and at work, the expectation is that you will be able to stay organized, know where your papers are, etc. This is an acquired skill that may or may not have been learned.

Family Patterns in Generational Poverty

One of the most confusing things about understanding generational poverty is the family patterns. It should be noted that there is family structure and family function. Family structure is the configuration(s) of the relationships within the household, whereas family function is the extent to which a child is cared for and nurtured. The two should not be confused. A child can be in an unusual structure that still has family function. However, when both the family structure and the family function are unstable, then the child suffers.

Distribution of U.S. Children Ages 6–11 by Family Structure

Family structure: two-parent families	Percentage of U.S. 6- to 11-year-olds in each type
Nuclear family	54%
Stepparent	9%
Adoptive family	2%
Grandparents alone	2%
Two same-sex parents	<1%

Family structure: single-parent families	Percentage of U.S. 6- to 11-year-olds in each type
Single mother (never married)	10%
Single mother (divorced, separated, or widowed)	13%
Grandparent alone	1%
Single father	4%

Family structure: more than two adults	Percentage of U.S. 6- to 11-year-olds in each type
Extended family	5%
Polygamous *	0%

* In some nations (not the United States) men can legally have
more than one wife.

Source: *The Developing Person Through the Life Span* by K. S. Berger.

In most middle-class families, even with divorce, lineage is fairly easy to trace because of legal documents. In generational poverty, on the other hand, many marital arrangements are common-law. Marriage and divorce in a legal court are important only if there's property to distribute or custody of children to decide. When you were never legally married to begin with and you have no property, why pay a lawyer for something you don't have, don't need, and don't have the money to purchase?

In middle class, family diagrams tend to be drawn as shown in the first diagram that follows. The notion is that lineage is traceable and that a linear pattern can be found.

In generational poverty (second diagram), the mother is the center of the organization, and the family radiates from that center. Although it can happen that the mother is uncertain of the biological father, most of the time the father of the child is known.[69] The second family diagram is based on a real situation. (Names have been changed.)

In this pattern, Jolyn has been legally married three times. Jolyn and Husband #1 had no children. Jolyn and Husband #2 had one child, Willy. They divorced. Husband #2 eventually married the woman he lived with for several years, and they had a child together. She also had a son from a previous marriage. Willy has a common-law wife, Shea; Shea and Willy have a daughter. Jolyn and Husband #3 lived together several years before they were married, and they have a son named M. J. When M. J. was 13 he had a child with a 13-year-old girl, but that child lives with the girl's mother. Husband #3 and Jolyn divorced; Jolyn is now living with a woman in a lesbian relationship. Husband #3 is living with a younger woman who is pregnant with his child.

Diagram of Middle-Class Family

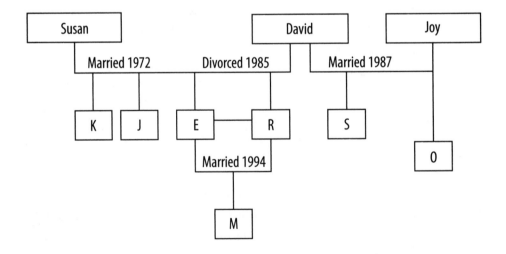

Diagram of Family from Generational Poverty

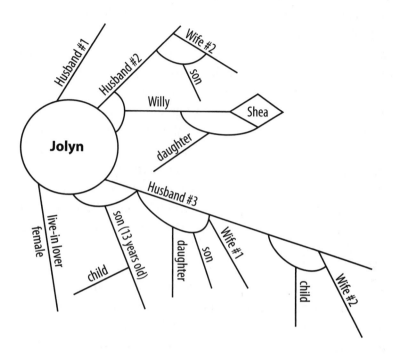

As noted, *the mother is invariably at the center,* though she may have multiple sexual relationships. Many of her children also will have multiple relationships, which may or may not produce children. The basic pattern is the mother at the heart of things, with nearly everyone having multiple relationships, some legally recognized and some not. Eventually the relationships become intertwined. It wouldn't be out of the question for your sister's third husband to become your brother's ex-wife's live-in boyfriend. Also in this pattern are babies born out of wedlock to children in their early teens; these youngsters are often raised by the grandmother as her own children. For example, the oldest daughter has a child at 14. This infant becomes the youngest child in the existing family. The oldest daughter, who is actually the mother of the child, is referred to as her sister—and the relationship is a sibling one, not a mother-daughter one.[70]

But the mother or maternal grandmother tends to keep her biological children. Because of the violence in poverty, death tends to be a prominent part of the family history. But it's also part of the family present because the deceased play such a role in the memories of the family. It's important to note when dealing with the family patterns who is alive and who is dead—because in the discussions they are often still living (unless you, the listener, know differently).[71]

Frequently, in the stories that are brought to school officials, the individual will tell the story in the episodic, random manner of the casual-register story structure. Key individuals are usually not referred to during the story because making reference to them isn't part of the story structure. *The most important keys to understanding the story are often the omissions.* For example, when someone says, "He left," you can pretty much predict who "he" will go stay with when there is trouble. If he is having trouble with his mother, he will go stay with an ex-wife or a girlfriend. If he is having trouble with his current wife, he will go stay with his mother. Women tend to go stay with their sisters and sometimes their mother. Whether or not a mother or ex-wife is mentioned in the story, if the family is in generational poverty you can be fairly certain that these are key players. You also can be fairly sure that the males are in and out—sometimes present, sometimes not, but not in any predictable pattern. Furthermore, you can know that as the male temporarily or permanently changes residences, the allegiances will change also.[72]

Additionally within these families there tend to be multiple internal feuds. Allegiances may change overnight; favoritism is a way of life. *Whom children go to stay with after school, who stays with whom when there is trouble, and who is available to deal with school issues are dependent on the current alliances and relationships at that moment.* For example, Ned comes home drunk and beats up his wife, Susan. She calls the police and escapes with the three kids to her mother's house. He goes to his mother's because she arranges to get him out of jail. His mother is not speaking to Susan because she called the cops on him and put him in jail. But Ned's mother usually keeps his kids after school until Susan gets home. Now it's Monday, and Susan doesn't have anyplace to send the kids. So she tells them to go to her mother's house after school, which means they must go on a different bus because she doesn't know if Ned will show up at the house and be waiting for her. On Tuesday the kids again go to Susan's mom's house. But on Wednesday Ned's mom calls Susan and tells her that that no-good Ned got drunk last night and she kicked him out of her house. So now Susan and Ned's mother are good friends, and Ned is on the hot seat. So Ned goes to the apartment of his ex-wife, Jackie, because last week she decided she'd had enough of Jerry, and she was very glad to see Ned ... And so the story continues.[73]

The key roles in these families are fighter/lover, caretaker/rescuer, worker, storyteller, and "keeper of the soul" (i.e., dispenser of penance and forgiveness). The family patterns in generational poverty are different from middle class. *In poverty the roles, the multiple relationships, the nature of the male identity, the ever-changing allegiances, the favoritism, and the matriarchal structure result in different patterns.*[74]

The economic traits which are most characteristic of the culture of poverty include the constant struggle for survival, unemployment and underemployment, low wages, a miscellany of unskilled occupations, child labor, the absence of savings, a chronic shortage of cash, the absence of food reserves in the home, the pattern of frequent buying of small quantities of food many times a day as the need arises, the pawning of personal goods, borrowing from local money lenders at usurious rates of interest, spontaneous informal credit devices (tandas) organized by neighbors, and the use of second-hand clothing and furniture.

—Oscar Lewis, "The Culture of Poverty"
in *Four Horsemen*[75]

How These Characteristics May Surface with Adults and Students from Poverty

They ...

- Get mad and quit their job/work. If they don't like the boss/teacher, they will quit. The emphasis is on the current feeling, not the long-term ramifications.

- Will work hard if they like you.

- Either use humor as a conflict-resolution tool or physical assault.

- Use survival language, tending to operate out of casual register.

- More openly display feelings and emotion. They don't have the reserve of wealth or the caution of middle class.

- Have an extreme freedom of speech, enjoy a sense of humor, use the personality to entertain, have a love of stories about people.

- Are very independent. They won't take kindly to the "parent" voice. If their full cooperation is sought, the boss/employer needs to use the "adult" voice.

- Periodically need time off or late arrival due to family emergencies.

- Need emotional warmth from colleagues, the boss, and/or teacher(s) in order to work/learn from them.[76]

- Require a level of integrity from management, actively distrusting organizations and the people who represent the organizations. They see organizations as basically dishonest.

- Exhibit a possessiveness about the people they really like.

- Show favoritism for certain people and give them preferential treatment.

Also …

- Men socialize with men and women with women. Men tend to have two social outlets: bars and work. Women with children tend to stay at home and have only other female relatives as friends, unless they work outside the home. Men tend to be loners in any other social setting and avoid those social settings. When a man and a woman are together, it is usually about a private relationship.

Role and Gender Identity/Rite of Passage

In generational poverty, as noted, the primary role of a real man is to physically work hard, to be a physical fighter, and to be a lover. In middle class, a real man is a provider. If one follows the implications of male identity as one who is a fighter and a lover, then one can understand why the male who takes this identity (of fighter and lover) as his own can seldom have a stable life. Of the three responses to life—to flee, flow, or fight—he can only fight or flee. So when the stress gets high, he fights, then flees from the law and the people closest to him, leaving his home. Either way he's gone. When the heat dies down, he returns—to an initial welcome, then more fights. The cycle begins again.

Is Generational Poverty's Family Structure Synonymous with Dysfunctionality?

Not necessarily. In generational poverty, people are the possession and resource. So when one person leaves, another comes into the household. Middle class wants to assign a moral judgment to that. In reality it is a survival mechanism.

Dysfunctionality will be defined here as the extent to which individuals cannot get their needs met. And it is common sense that the fewer the resources, the greater the chance that there will be dysfunctionality simply because of the scarcity of resources. Again, it's possible to have many financial resources and have a very dysfunctional household because other resources are not available, such as emotional resources or relationships and role models.

A Demographic Shift Is Under Way in the United States

One of the reasons it's getting more and more difficult to conduct school in the United States as we have in the past is that the students who bring the middle-class culture with them are decreasing in numbers, and the students who bring the poverty culture with them are increasing in numbers. As in any demographic shift, the prevailing rules and policies eventually give way to the group with the largest numbers.

In order to better serve these students from generational and situational poverty, the next several chapters have ideas about ways in which we can work with students—and adults—from poverty. But to do so, we must fundamentally rethink the notions we have traditionally assigned to relationships and achievement.

What Does This Information Mean in the School or Work Setting?

- *Education* is the key to getting out of, and staying out of, generational poverty. And as stated in the Introduction, individuals leave poverty for one of four reasons:
    1. A situation that is so painful that just about anything would be better
    2. A goal or vision of something they want to be or have
    3. A specific talent or ability that provides an opportunity for them
    4. Someone who "sponsors" them (e.g., an educator or spouse or mentor or role model who shows them a different way or convinces them that they could live differently)

- Being in poverty is rarely about a lack of intelligence or ability.

- Many individuals stay in poverty because they don't know there is a choice—and if they do know that, they have no one to teach them hidden rules or provide resources.

- Schools are virtually the only places where students can learn the choices and rules of the middle class.

The culture of poverty has some universal characteristics which transcend regional, rural-urban, and even national differences ... There are remarkable similarities in family structure, interpersonal relations, time orientations, value systems, spending patterns, and the sense of community in lower-class settlements in London, Glasgow, Paris, Harlem, and Mexico City.

–Oscar Lewis, "The Culture of Poverty"
in *Four Horsemen*[77]

Chapter 5

Role Models and Emotional Resources:
How They Provide for Stability and Success

To understand the importance of role models and their part in the development of emotional resources, we must first briefly look at the notion of functional and dysfunctional systems. The following definitions will be used:

A system is a group in which individuals have rules, roles, and relationships.[78]

Dysfunction is the extent to which individuals cannot get their needs met within a system.[79]

Using these definitions, families and schools are both systems, as are peer groups, neighborhoods, gangs, etc.[80] All systems are, to some degree, dysfunctional. A system is not equally functional or dysfunctional for each individual. The extent to which individuals must give up meeting their needs in order to meet the needs of another person is the extent to which the situation is dysfunctional for those individuals.[81]

Michael Dumont gives a case study of a girl named Ellie that demonstrates a family situation that appears to be functional for some family members, while it's clearly dysfunctional for others.

Ellie

Ellie's mother, Victoria, is bedridden with multiple sclerosis, and her father, Larry, is a small storekeeper. Victoria, in her rage at the disease and her distrust of Larry, attempts suicide when Ellie is 9 years old. It is Ellie's job each day when she comes home from school to count her mother's pills to make certain they are all there—and to check to see if her mother is alive. Ellie tells Mr. Dumont that the worst part of her day is when she comes home from school and must check on her mother's well-being. When he tells Ellie that she is smart and asks her what she wants to be, she tells him she would like to be a secretary. At 13 Ellie becomes pregnant and drops out of school.

The situation is dysfunctional for Ellie because she must subordinate her needs to address the needs of her mother. In order for Ellie to have an appropriate developmental process emotionally, she needs to be a child, then an adolescent, then an adult. By being forced to take on an adult role earlier, she must in essence put her emotional development on hold while she functions in an adult role. Therefore, for the rest of her life, Ellie will seek to have her emotional needs met that were not met during her childhood. She almost certainly will not have the emotional resources and stamina necessary to function as an interdependent adult.[82]

Dependence

Independence

Interdependence

To become a fully functioning adult, one moves developmentally from being dependent to being independent to being interdependent. Stephen Covey calls it the maturity continuum, John Bradshaw refers to it as becoming whole, and Lev Vygotsky terms it the "zone of proximal development."[83] Regardless of the terminology, the process involves moving from being dependent on others to being able to work together with other adults, each independent of the other, but jointly, as equal partners.

Simply put, an individual operating in a dysfunctional situation is often forced to assume an adult role early and then, as an adult, is literally caught between being dependent and independent. So one will see this fierce independence coupled with a crippling dependence that weakens people to the point that they have few emotional resources. This roller-coaster ride up and down between dependence and independence takes a heavy toll. Bradshaw and others describe this constant fluctuation between dependence and independence as codependency.[84]

As Ellie's case study illustrates, the emotional resources come in part from the role models who are present for the child. When appropriate role models are present, the child can go through the developmental stages at appropriate times and build emotional resources. Emotional resources are built in this fashion: The child watches the adult for emotional responses to a given situation and notes the continuum of behaviors that go with those responses. In Ellie's situation, her mother's response to her husband's infidelity was to create an even greater level of dependence—and to use the emotional ploy of guilt to manipulate Ellie. So what does Ellie do when she gets old enough? She creates a level of dependence on others as well (e.g., through pregnancy and going on welfare).

A child may decide that the role-model responses are not appropriate. Often what occurs then is that the child selects—in understandable reaction—the opposite extreme from which to operate. What becomes problematic for the child, then, is recognizing what is "normal"; an appropriate adult response is rarely seen as one of the options. The child, in essence, is forced to guess at what "normal" or appropriate is.

Question: Why would emotional resources have such importance in school and at work?

Answer: Emotional responses dictate much of one's behavior and, eventually, determine achievement.

Furthermore, in order to move from poverty to middle class or from middle class to wealth, one must usually trade off some relationships for achievement, at least for a period of time. To do this, one needs emotional resources and stamina.[85]

Emotional resources are collected over time, through experience, and stored in the brain in what essentially is an "emotional memory bank." The emotions that are accessed habitually and reinforced become those that "feel right" and therefore become the person's natural responses and reactions.[86]

When a relationship is traded off for achievement, the emotional memory bank must be held in abeyance until the new "feel right" feeling can be accessed through new experiences. That process sometimes takes years.

Emotional resources and stamina allow the individual to live with feelings other than those in the emotional memory bank. This allowance provides the individual the opportunity to seek options and examine other possibilities. As the case study shows, Ellie stays with her emotional memory bank and creates situations that "feel right."

How Do You Provide Emotional Resources When the Individual Has Not Had Access to Appropriate Role Models?

1. Through support systems

2. By using appropriate discipline strategies and approaches

3. By establishing long-term relationships (apprenticeships, mentorships) with adults who are appropriate

4. By teaching the hidden rules

5. By identifying options

6. By increasing individuals' achievement level through appropriate instruction

7. By teaching goal setting

8. By developing a future story

The Role of Positive Self-Talk in Building Emotional Resources

What many educators don't know is how essential self-talk is in building emotional resources and learning. According to cultural anthropologist Angeles Arrien, emotional resources are evident in self-esteem, which she defines as self-love, self-trust, and self-respect. Self-esteem is not available when fear, control issues, fixation, or stubbornness are present. She further indicates that self-esteem has these characteristics:

1. Ability to set limits and boundaries

2. Flexibility and openness

3. Ability to give and receive love—follow the heart

4. Capacity for staying in one's truth or integrity

5. Communication skills

6. Sense of honor and respect about oneself[87]

In the Hart and Risley study (cited in Chapters 1 and 2), not only did they find that the amount of vocabulary was significantly less in poverty, they also found that, in welfare households, negative comments were 2 to 1. In other words, a child heard twice as many negative comments/prohibitions as positive comments. But in a professional household, a child heard six positives for every negative.[88]

One of the most valuable tools that educators can provide to students is positive affirmations. Completing tasks and learning something new is tied to your ability to self-talk your way through the task. If ... then ... statements are recommended. Find something the student can already do, and then say, "If you can do this, then you can pass this test."

I was working with three high school boys who had all failed the state exit test four times. I gave them skills tests. They all had the skills. So I asked them if they had finished the test. All of them had quit in the middle. I asked them what they said to themselves before they quit. They told me things like "This test is dumb," "I'm tired," and "I've already failed it, so what's the point?"

I then asked them if they had driver's licenses. All of them did. So I told them, "When you start taking that test, you say to yourself, 'If I can get a driver's license, then I can pass this test.'" I also told them how many questions they could miss and still pass. They all passed the test—because they persisted. For more on persistence, see Gladwell.[89]

Development of Appropriate Boundaries

Emotional resources additionally are linked to appropriate boundaries. Boundaries signify the ability to say "no" to being "used." In other words, boundaries allow you to maintain self-respect. The closer you get to survival, the fewer the boundaries. Spaces are crowded, resources are scarce, one has to "give" in order to "get." These factors over time lead to abuse, manipulation, codependence, and servitude. The response to a lack of boundaries frequently is to become over-controlling, manipulative, and fixated. Options are seldom considered, and thinking becomes polarized; it's "either/or." Psychologists also call this "black or white thinking."[90]

The easiest way to start this discussion in the classroom is to identify physical boundaries:

- How much space in the room is actually theirs?

- How do you keep someone out of your space?

- How do you stay in your space?

This discussion of physical boundaries is the beginning of setting emotional boundaries.

To establish boundaries, it's important to understand the Karpman triangle.

Karpman Triangle

Source: "Fairy Tales and Script Drama Analysis" by S. Karpman.

The same person can take all three roles in different situations. In one setting the person is a bully, in another setting the person is a rescuer, and in another setting the person is a victim. Once you are in the triangle, you will eventually take on all three roles—and boundaries disappear because ownership isn't taken by anyone. To stay out of the triangle, you can ask questions.

Here's an example (of using questions to avoid the triangle):

When my son was in second grade, he came home from school and told me he was "bored." I asked him, "Whose problem is that?" He said, "The teacher's." He was presenting himself as a victim and asking me to go to school and "rescue" him. So I asked him, "Is the teacher bored?" He said, "No, I am." So I said, "Then it isn't the teacher's problem. It's your problem. Since it's your problem, how can you solve it?"

Had I gone to the school and "bullied" the teacher in order to "rescue" my son who was a "victim," chances would have been very good that the teacher would've felt like a "victim" and gone to the principal to be "rescued." The principal likely would've called me and "bullied" me for being so insensitive to the teacher and blaming the teacher for my son's problems. And then I would have felt like a "victim" and told my husband so that he would "rescue" me and go to school and "bully" the principal. The cycle would continue.

In other words, once a person is in the triangle, that person can be expected to take on all three roles eventually. Most importantly, the problem won't get solved, and boundaries will disappear. The best way to stay out of the triangle is to ask questions and clarify the issues—so that the problem can be solved.

How Do Role Models and Emotional Resources Contribute to Stability?

When individuals have emotional resources, they are much less likely to engage in destructive or self-destructive behaviors, they can function reasonably well in school even if they don't like certain teachers or administrators, they can keep a job in spite of difficult personalities at work, and they can maintain stable relationships. Because role models teach through example the many ways to address difficult situations, if individuals haven't experienced those examples, they cannot maintain stable, long-term relationships or work. That means they move more often and spend more time in "survival mode." The more time one spends simply surviving, the less time one can devote to abstract learning.

What Does This Information Mean in the School or Work Setting?

- Teachers and administrators are much more important as role models than is generally recognized.

- The development of emotional resources is crucial to student success. The greatest free resource available to schools is the role modeling provided by teachers, administrators, and staff.

Chapter 6

Support Systems and Parents: How They Impact the Ability to Do Homework and to Navigate School and Work

Support systems are the friends, family, and backup resources that can be accessed in times of need. Support systems (sometimes also termed social capital) tend to fall into seven general categories.

1. Coping Strategies

Coping strategies are ways in which one copes with daily living: the disappointments, the tragedies, the triumphs. Coping strategies are attitudes, self-talk, strategies for resolving conflicts, problem-solving techniques, the avoidance of needless conflicts, and ways to think about things. Coping strategies are also ways of approaching tasks, setting priorities, and determining what one can live with and what one can live without.[91]

2. Options During Problem Solving

Options are all the ways to solve a problem. Even very capable adults often talk over a problem with another adult just in order to consider other options they haven't thought about.[92]

3. Information and Know-How

This is a key aspect of a support system. When a child has homework, who in the support system knows enough math to help the child? Who knows the research process? Who knows the ropes for going to college or getting a new-car loan? Who knows how to talk to the insurance agent so the situation can be clarified? Who knows how to negotiate difficult situations with a teacher and come to a resolution? Who understands the court system, the school system? Information and know-how are crucial to success.[93]

4. Connections to Other People and Resources (Bonding and Bridging Social Capital)

When you are upset, who provides relief for you? When you aren't sure how you will get everything finished, who helps you? Who takes your children when you're desperate for a break? These people are all part of a support system.[94]

5. Temporary Relief from Emotional, Mental, Financial, and/or Time Constraints

When you don't have the information and know-how, who are the people you turn to for assistance? Those people are your connections. Connections to people and resources are an integral part of a healthy support system.[95]

6. Positive Self-Talk

Everyone has a little voice inside their head that talks to them all the time. This little voice can give encouraging messages. These encouraging messages help one finish tasks, complete projects, and get through difficult situations. If an individual doesn't listen to this encouraging little voice, the success rate is much lower.[96]

7. Procedural Self-Talk

Procedural self-talk is the voice that talks an individual through a task. It is key to success. Many individuals in poverty have a very limited support system—and particularly missing is procedural self-talk. Many tasks are never finished. In numerous dealings with students, teachers and other school officials find that self-talk is simply not available to the student.[97]

The following case study identifies what aspects of a support system would be beneficial to a student—and would promote success.

LaKeitha

You are a high school social studies teacher in inner-city Houston. One of your students, LaKeitha, was so rude in your 10th-grade class that you told her she couldn't return until you had a conversation with her mother. She calls her mother and tells you that her mom will be there at 7:30 a.m. the next day to meet with you. You are at school the next morning at 7:15 a.m. LaKeitha's mother doesn't show up.

The next day LaKeitha is waiting for you before school. She is crying. She apologizes profusely for her behavior in class and tells you the following: Her dad is in prison. She is the oldest of five children. Her mother works two jobs, and LaKeitha works from 5 to 9 p.m. at Burger King every day to bring in money. Yesterday her mother was on her way to school to see you, but she got stopped by the police for an expired inspection sticker. Because she didn't have a driver's license, she was put in jail. Her mother is still in jail, and LaKeitha is all alone with the children. She is 15 years old.

LaKeitha asks to be allowed back into your class, and she asks you to help get her mother out of jail.

Debriefing the LaKeitha Case Study

One of LaKeitha's issues is simply time. She doesn't have any extra time. One of the things the teacher can have LaKeitha do is identify when, given her schedule, she can get things done. The teacher needs to provide flexibility for LaKeitha to finish her assignments (maybe an extra day) and be flexible about the almost inevitable interruptions that are part of her life. The teacher also can give LaKeitha phone numbers and addresses of organizations (churches, social service agencies, etc.) that can help provide some relief to her: mentally, emotionally, financially, and physically. Someone needs to spend five minutes with LaKeitha explaining how to access the adult voice—and how using that voice will help her negotiate her difficulties with authority figures and be a better caretaker of her siblings. Of great importance to LaKeitha is the acceptance and understanding of her situation by the teacher.

What Support Systems Can Be Accessed to Help LaKeitha—and Students Like Her?

Here is a sample list of the support systems some schools use to help students like LaKeitha.

Support Systems Schools Can Use

1. **Schoolwide homework support.** A very successful middle school in Texas schedules the last 45 minutes of every day for homework support. Students who didn't get their homework done must go to the cafeteria where tutors are available to help them with their homework. The students must stay until their homework is finished. School officials have arranged

for a late bus run to take students home. Many students from poverty don't have access to adults who have the knowledge base to help them with homework. The school has built this into the school day. Another middle school has arranged for students to have two sets of textbooks—one set at home and one at school. This school doesn't have lockers. The school has eliminated several problems and also has provided support for students.

2. **Supplemental schoolwide reading programs.** Many schools have gone to the concept of using a computer-based management program that provides tests for students to take regarding the book(s) they have read. Students are encouraged to read more because the programs are designed so that students aren't penalized for what their parents don't know or cannot provide for them.

3. **Keeping students with the same teacher(s) for two or more years and having a school within a school** are other options. Both of these concepts are designed to build longer-term relationships between teachers and students. Also, much less time is spent at the beginning of the year establishing relationships with the students and their parents.

4. **Teaching coping strategies** can be done in several ways. One is to address each issue as a student needs assistance. Many schools have small groups that meet with the counselor, principal, or a teacher during lunch to work on coping strategies in a number of areas. This ongoing group support allows students to discuss issues and ways to deal with those issues. For example, one elementary school divided all its sixth-graders into groups of eight. Then school officials took these students and met with them for four weeks, twice a week over lunch, to discuss the issues they would face the next year when they went on to junior high school. Another school has a similar group of students who are physically aggressive get together; the discussion centers on ways to lessen the aggression at school. Advisory groups are yet another way to address issues of support.

5. **Schoolwide scheduling that puts students in subgroups by skill for reading and math** can be a way of providing support. One concern with heterogeneous groupings is the teacher's difficulty in addressing all the diverse instructional needs in the classroom simultaneously. One elementary school scheduled the hour for math at the same time in grades 1 through 3, as well as 4 through 6. Students were then pretested and moved to the appropriate group for that particular unit of instruction. Within two years, the math scores in that building made a considerable gain.

6. **Parent training and contact through video is invaluable,** particularly in communities with high poverty rates. One pattern in poor communities is that virtually everyone has a TV because of the value placed on entertainment. An Illinois principal whose school had 95% of its parents on welfare started a very successful program of parental education and contact through videos. Each teacher in the building made a 15-minute video. During those 15 minutes, the teacher made a personal introduction, gave an overview of the instruction for the year, identified the expectations of the class, and encouraged the parents to visit or call. Copies of each video were made, and during the first month of school, each student could take a copy home and have an adult view the video. This was very successful for several reasons: (1) Parents who were not literate could understand, (2) it provided a kinesthetic view and feel for what kind of teacher the child had, (3) the parent was not dependent on transportation to have contact with the school, and (4) it prevented unnecessary miscommunications early in the year. It's a low-cost intervention, and other short videos could be made for parents about school rules, appropriate discipline, etc.

7. **The direct-teaching of classroom survival skills** makes a difference, according to the research. What are classroom survival skills? Many of these skills are referred to as study skills, but there are also the cognitive strategies that are discussed in Chapter 9 on instruction. These include such simple hidden rules as how to stay in your seat, how to participate appropriately, where to put your things, etc.

8. **Requiring daily goal setting and procedural self-talk** would move many of these students light years ahead. In the beginning, goal setting would focus on what a student wants to accomplish by the end of each day and by the end of the week. Goals would be in writing. At the end of the school day, five minutes would need to be taken with the class to see if the goals were met or not. Procedural self-talk would begin in written form; most students likely would need assistance. Procedural self-talk has value only when tied to a specific task. Procedures vary with tasks.

9. **Team interventions** are a way to provide support to students. This happens when all the teachers of a student meet with the parent(s) to make a plan for helping that student be more successful. This works as long as the intervention with the parent(s) is positive and supportive.

Working with Parents: What Happens When They Move from Stability to Instability Because of Job Loss, Health Issues, Divorce, a Recession, Etc.?[98]

During the long-term recession in the United States, many principals and teachers were reporting to me the growing number of students and parents seeking assistance through the school, as well as increasing numbers of homeless students. There is a great reluctance on the part of people who have been in the middle class to admit that their resource base is becoming unstable or even nonexistent.

The first thing that happens in a severe economic downturn is that hope and choice are replaced with fear and a sense of scarcity. When fear and scarcity come into one's thinking, the brain is less able to seek options or see possibilities. The negative "parent voice" takes over the internal conversation with the self. For adults who have never experienced unemployment, insufficient funds to pay the mortgage, or the need to sell things for cash, there's considerable confusion because the knowledge base isn't available to know what the choices are. Furthermore, in middle class it's usually seen as a personal failing to lose a job or not be able to pay the mortgage. So it often isn't shared with others right away. Making things worse, credit cards frequently are used as a short-term borrowing mechanism to avoid the possibility of losing one's house, which then exacerbates the financial issues.

As adults begin to assess the reality of their situation, most go through the five stages of grief as outlined by Elisabeth Kübler-Ross. These five stages are denial, anger, bargaining, depression, acceptance.[99] A person tends to move back and forth along this continuum. Middle class generally makes its decisions about time and money against these three factors: work, achievement, and material security. But when you've lost your job, you've lost two of the three—work and material security. It then impacts your identity: Who are you if you don't have work? If you cannot keep your house? If your material security is breached? And how do you make decisions about all this? Furthermore, the two rules about money that middle class uses are now out the window: (1) "I don't ask you for money, and you don't ask me" and (2) "If you borrow money, you have to pay it back." Personal pride and the deeply ingrained hidden rules about money are now challenged. Further, it's typically taboo in middle class to tell people that you're in financial trouble. Middle class has yet another hidden rule about personal money, and it's simply that you don't talk about it. So asking a middle-class person to participate in a group sharing session about finances usually isn't going to happen—particularly for the men because male identity in middle class is, first and foremost, about being a provider. And the majority of middle-class men won't talk very freely about what's most important to them.

The adults then are moving through the stages of grief as the resource base becomes less predictable and stable. For example, as the financial resources disappear, the emotional resources become less predictable. The spiritual resources of hope and optimism tend to be replaced with fear and scarcity. Relationships become strained. Support systems either are not accessed or become thin. And the hidden rules don't work anymore for this new situation. Life becomes about day-to-day survival. More time is spent accessing fewer resources—e.g., food, shelter, money.

And you lose social capital. You find out in a hurry who your real friends are. You say things that are less than fully accurate. For example, when money is tight, you don't go out to eat as part of a social group. You say things like, "I need to help my daughter with her homework" or "That evening doesn't work for us." In time, the very individuals who could provide support have been pushed away. *And,* when they find out you've lost your job, there's reluctance on their part to ask you to join their group because they don't want to embarrass you. So the support systems become thinner.

Three times in my marriage of 31 years, my former husband lost his job because of recessions. I can tell you from personal experience that it's not only financially difficult but emotionally devastating. It impacts identity, self-worth, and personal value. The stages of grief are so palpable that you can touch them on virtually a daily basis. Furthermore, the resource base that you worked so hard to develop erodes before your eyes—much faster than it took to develop it. Even if the words are there, you can't talk about it every day. Anxiety is the cousin of fear. Anxiety produces cortisol, which causes anxiety to increase. So less is said every day, and certain topics are avoided. Eventually, each person goes to their own corner to worry, to work through the fears—*alone.*

This in turn impacts children. Often middle-class parents don't want to burden their children with fear, or they don't tell the children. But the child usually knows when things aren't right. And so students may become withdrawn, act out, or get involved in substance abuse.

How does the school help students deal with the grieving and the shift in resources?

1. Journal writing. Give students questions or topics to write about. For example: What do you think it feels like to lose a job? Should the government give money and provide support for those who have lost their homes? How does it feel when you can't have many of the same things your friends have? Which is more important—things or love? Why?

2. Have teachers look for "red flag" behaviors:

- ☐ Truancy

- ☐ Patterns of tardiness

- ☐ "Acting out" or withdrawn behaviors

- ☐ Knowledge of, or conversation about, sex and drugs inappropriate for the child's age or stage of development

- ☐ Delays in common adaptive-behavior skills

- ☐ Lower than expected academic performance

- ☐ Inability to build or maintain appropriate peer and/or adult relationships

- ☐ Anxiety, fearfulness, flinching

- ☐ Inability to cope with transitions during the school day

- ☐ Lethargy, sleeping at school

- ☐ Hunger

- ☐ Poor hygiene

- ☐ Encopresis, enuresis, or other unusual toileting habits

- ☐ Unusual eating habits or patterns

- ☐ Somatic complaints

- ☐ Lack of parental interest in child's basic health or school performance[100]

Refer to the counselor or office if any of these behaviors show up. Provide coping strategies and access to community resources.

3. All of us orient ourselves to daily life through space, time, and ritual. For example, I get up most mornings at 5 a.m., use the bathroom, make coffee, go online, and check my emails. All of these activities involve space, time, and ritual. When you are homeless or in a highly unstable living situation, all of these are disrupted. You don't know where your things are, routines aren't predictable—nor is time. There are other people in the bathroom, you can't go to the computer (the house or apartment doesn't have one), you have only a few things … what you can carry with you. So for students who are homeless or moving frequently, provide them with a place in the classroom that is their own space to put their things where they can find

them. Allow them to keep a couple of extra things there if they aren't dangerous, such as mementos, stickers, etc. Give them a morning routine when they come into the class—e.g., "Do these three things first." Routine often has a way of calming and orienting people.

How does the school help parents deal with the grieving and the shift in resources?

1. Encourage parents to talk to their children about their personal economic situation. Assure the children that it won't last forever. Provide an analogy for children to help them understand. For example, remember when you were riding your bicycle and you had to pedal hard to get up the hill, and you stopped and took a rest to get to the top, and then you got to coast down the other side of the hill? Well, right now we're riding the bicycle up the money hill, and we're having to stop and take a rest. So we aren't going to buy this or this or this; those will come later when we're coasting down the hill.

2. Put the situation in a long-term perspective. Ask these questions: Will this situation last forever? No. Have I lost the people I love? No. What am I learning from this situation that will help me in the future? How has this situation changed my thinking?

3. In the research, if you are homeless, religious social capital does more to move you out of being homeless than any other form of assistance. Link the homeless family with a church, synagogue, mosque, or other religious organization.[101]

4. Pair men together (but don't put them in groups): "A father came in yesterday about the same type of situation … Would you be willing to talk to him?"

5. Provide a list of places where food and other forms of assistance are available.

6. Share this material with parents. This may be their situation or that of their siblings or their neighbors. When people understand that they aren't going through a tough time alone, there is more ability to name the experience and deal with it.

7. Develop a plan to address the current situation (sometimes termed situational poverty), along with a future story that includes what you will do when this crisis has passed.

8. Provide a list of books that you have read or staff has read that talk about what it's like to go through difficult times. This could include autobiographies/biographies of individuals who have gone through very hard times—for example, Lincoln or Einstein or Michelangelo. Sometimes someone else's story puts our own in perspective, for example: "I cried because I had no shoes until I met a man who had no feet."

9. *Do not engage in pity.* That is humiliating for the persons receiving it. If they have the courage to tell you about their situation, accept it, and give them time to talk about their thoughts and feelings. Focus the conversation on what they will do next. Having a plan usually helps with anxiety.

It isn't the school's responsibility to provide physical resources or money for students and parents. It is, however, the school's responsibility to provide high expectations, insistence, and support for students academically and behaviorally. To do that, some understanding of the students' personal situation needs to be acknowledged. In other words, a relationship with the students is pivotal to their academic and behavioral progress. Greenspan and Benderly assert that all learning is double-coded—both cognitively *and* emotionally.[102] The emotional component of learning is often predicated on a relationship.

When I was principal of an elementary school, a sixth-grader was determined to come to school the morning after his father was killed in an auto accident at 2 a.m. A neighbor brought the boy to school, and the neighbor said to me, "I don't understand why he insisted on coming to school." I said to the neighbor, "I do. It's the one place in his life that is still the same, that is predictable, and he knows what is going to happen. There's a routine. The rest of his life is up for grabs. He needed to know that one place in his life is stable." I took the boy into my office and said to him, "I can't bring your life before your father died back for you. But I can help you cope. Go on to class. If you need to leave, tell your teacher to let you come back to the office—and then you and I can figure out how to handle the rest of your day."

Education can give you the language, the tools, and the options to move beyond a situation. That is a gift we can give to our students and, sometimes, their parents. Schools can be a tremendous source of stability and routine for children, even when their own world seems to be falling apart.

Differences in Parenting by Class and Race

In a landmark study, *Unequal Childhoods: Class, Race, and Family Life,* Annette Lareau studied the difference between middle-class and working-class/poor households and how they raised their children. She also looked at black and white households. What she found was that in middle-class households, regardless of race, the children experienced "concerted cultivation" while in poor and working-class households the approach was one of "accomplishment of natural growth."

This chart indicates some of the findings of the study.

	Concerted cultivation	Accomplishment of natural growth
Key elements	▪ Parent actively fosters and assesses child's talents, opinions, and skills	▪ Parent cares for child and allows child to grow
Organization of daily life	▪ Multiple child leisure activities orchestrated by adults	▪ "Hanging out," particularly with kin, by child
Language use	▪ Reasoning, directives ▪ Child contestation of adult statements ▪ Extended negotiations between parents and child	▪ Directives ▪ Rare questioning or challenging of adults by child ▪ General acceptance by child of directives
Interventions in institutions	▪ Criticisms and interventions on behalf of the child ▪ Training of child to take on this role	▪ Dependence on institutions ▪ Sense of powerlessness and frustration ▪ Conflict between child-rearing practices at home and school
Consequences	▪ Emerging sense of entitlement on the part of the child	▪ Emerging sense of constraint on the part of the child

Source: *Unequal Childhoods* by A. Lareau.

What Lareau found in her study was that poor and working-class parents usually didn't know how to negotiate with the schools, while most middle-class parents taught their children to frequently question and negotiate with adults.[103]

Much of the middle-class children's ability to negotiate at school was learned from their parents. It means that the school must provide language and tools students can use to negotiate on their own behalf.

What Does This Information Mean in the School or Work Setting?

- By reorganizing the school day and schedule—and often by making minor adjustments—educators can build support systems into the school day without additional cost.

- Support systems need to include the teaching of positive self-talk, procedural self-talk, planning, goal setting, coping strategies, appropriate relationships, options during problem solving, access to information and know-how, and connections to additional resources.

Chapter 7

Creating Relationships: How and Why One Is Motivated to Learn and Change

Locate a resilient kid and you will also find a caring adult—or several—who has guided him.

–J. P. Shapiro et al., "Invincible Kids"[104]

The key to achievement for students from poverty is in creating relationships with them. Because relationships are essential for survival in poverty, the most significant motivator for these students is relationships.[105]

The question becomes *How does a formal institution create relationships?* Several sources provide some answers to this question. These sources are (1) research in various scientific fields, (2) the work Stephen Covey has done with personal effectiveness, (3) Ron Ferguson's work with student achievement, (4) Steven and Sybil Wolin's research on resiliency, and (5) Stanley Greenspan and Beryl Benderly's work that identifies that all learning is double-coded— emotionally and cognitively.[106] The emotional coding of the learning is based on the relationship. This also was previously addressed in the book in the material on support systems.

Margaret Wheatley, in her book *Leadership and the New Science* (1992), puts it this way:

> Scientists in many different disciplines are questioning whether we can adequately explain how the world works by using the machine imagery created in the 17th century, most notably by Sir Isaac Newton. In the machine model, one must understand parts. Things can be taken apart, dissected literally or representationally … and then put back together without any significant loss … The Newtonian model of the world is characterized by materialism and reductionism—a focus on things rather

than relationships … The quantum view of reality strikes against most of our notions of reality. Even to scientists, it is admittedly bizarre. But it is a world where *relationship is the key determiner* of what is observed and of how particles manifest themselves … Many scientists now work with the concept of fields—invisible forces that structure space or behavior [emphasis added].[107]

Wheatley goes on to say that, in the new science of quantum physics, physical reality is not just tangible, it is also intangible. Fields are invisible, yet:

[They are the] substance of the universe … In organizations, which is the more important influence on behavior—the system or the individual? The quantum world answered that question: It depends … What is critical is the relationship created between the person and the setting. That relationship will always be different, will always evoke different potentialities. *It all depends on the players and the moment* [emphasis added].[108]

Teachers and administrators have always known that relationships, often referred to as "politics," make a great deal of difference—sometimes all the difference—in what could or could not happen in a building. But since the 1980s we have concentrated our energies in schools on "achievement" and "effective teaching strategies." We used the Newtonian approach to teaching, dissecting it into parts. Yet the most important part of learning seems to be related to relationships, if we listen to the data and the potent metaphors emerging from the disciplines of biology and physics.[109]

When students who have been in poverty (and have successfully made it into middle class) are asked how they made the journey, the answer nine times out of 10 has to do with a relationship—a teacher, counselor, or coach who gave advice or took an interest in them as individuals.[110]

Covey uses the notion of an emotional bank account to convey the crucial aspects of relationships. He indicates that in all relationships one makes deposits to and withdrawals from the other individual in that relationship. The following chart lists some of these deposits and withdrawals.[111]

Relationships Bank Account

DEPOSITS	WITHDRAWALS
Seek first to understand	Seek first to be understood
Keeping promises	Breaking promises
Kindnesses, courtesies	Unkindnesses, discourtesies
Clarifying expectations	Violating expectations
Loyalty to the absent	Disloyalty, duplicity
Apologies	Pride, conceit, arrogance
Open to feedback	Rejecting feedback

Source: *The 7 Habits of Highly Effective People* by S. Covey.

The first step in creating relationships with students and adults is to make the deposits that are the basis of relationships. Relationships begin as one individual to another. First and foremost in relationships with students is the relationship between each teacher and student, then between each student and each administrator, and finally, among all of the players, including student-to-student relationships.[112]

What, then, is meant by relationship? (Should students become my personal friends? Usually not. Should I go out with them? Probably not.) A successful relationship in the school setting occurs when emotional deposits are made to the student, emotional withdrawals are avoided, and students are respected. Are there boundaries to the relationship? Absolutely—and that's what is meant by clarifying expectations. But to honor students as human beings worthy of respect and care is to establish a relationship that will provide for enhanced learning.

What are the deposits and withdrawals with regard to students and adults from poverty? (See the following chart.) By understanding deposits that are valued by students from poverty, the relationship is stronger.

Relationships Bank Account—Poverty

DEPOSITS MADE TO INDIVIDUAL IN POVERTY	WITHDRAWALS MADE FROM INDIVIDUAL IN POVERTY
Appreciation for humor and entertainment provided by the individual	Put-downs or sarcasm about the humor or the individual
Acceptance of what the individual cannot say about a person or situation	Insistence and demands for full explanation about a person or situation
Respect for the demands and priorities of relationships	Insistence on the middle-class view of relationships
Using the adult voice	Using the parent voice
Assisting with goal setting	Telling individuals their goals
Identifying options related to available resources	Making judgments on the value and availability of resources
Understanding the importance of personal freedom, speech, and individual personality	Assigning pejorative character traits to the individual

How does an organization or school create—and build—relationships? Through support systems, through caring about students, by promoting student achievement, by being role models, by insisting on successful behaviors for school. Support systems are simply networks of relationships.[113]

Will creating healthy relationships with students make all students successful? No. But if we make a difference for 5% more of our students the first year and 5% more each year thereafter, we will have progressed considerably from where we are right now.

In the final analysis, as one looks back on a teaching career, it is the relationships one remembers.

What Does This Information Mean in the School or Work Setting?

- For students and adults from poverty, the primary motivation for their success will be in their relationships.

- If your school or work setting presently affords few opportunities for building relationships, find ways to establish natural connections that will enable this vital resource to take root and grow.

Chapter 8

Discipline: How to Manage Personal Behavior So One Can 'Win' in a Given Environment

What allows a person to "win" in one environment is not necessarily the same in another environment. Many educational problems that can be understood through the lens of poverty come to light as "discipline" or "classroom management" issues. Students from poverty enter school with an entirely different understanding of what rules are, and this causes a lot of frustration in school because of the mismatch. In school, a middle-class definition of discipline is used (along these lines): Discipline is a punishment used to address inappropriate behavior—in order to change that behavior.

In poverty, discipline tends to be about penance and forgiveness, not necessarily change.[114] Getting in trouble also may be a way of escaping classroom work.[115]

Because love tends to be unconditional in generational poverty, and because the time frame is the present, the notion that discipline should be instructive/redemptive and change behavior isn't part of the culture. In matriarchal, generational poverty, the mother has the most powerful position and is, to a considerable degree, "keeper of the soul." So she dispenses the judgments, determines the amount and price of penance, and offers forgiveness. When forgiveness is granted, behaviors and activities usually return to the way they were before the incident.[116]

Penance/Forgiveness Cycle

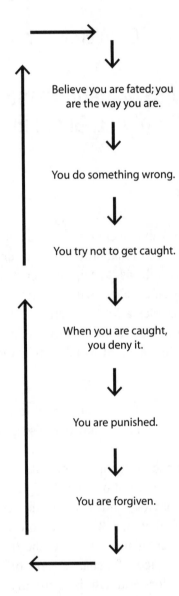

Believe you are fated; you are the way you are.

You do something wrong.

You try not to get caught.

When you are caught, you deny it.

You are punished.

You are forgiven.

It's important to note that the approach to discipline advocated in this book is to teach a separate set of behaviors. Many of the behaviors that students bring to school are necessary to help them survive outside of school. Just as students learn to use various rules, depending on the video game or sport they're playing, they also need to learn to use certain rules to be successful in school settings and circumstances. If students from poverty don't know how to fight physically, they are going to be in danger on the streets.[117] But if fighting is virtually their only method for resolving a problem, then they will have difficulties in school.[118]

Being successful in middle-class school and work settings requires self-control concerning behavior. What, then, do schools need to do to teach appropriate behavior?[119]

Structure and Choice

The two anchors of any effective discipline program that moves students to self-governance are structure and choice.[120] The program must clearly delineate the expected behaviors and the probable consequences of not choosing those behaviors. The program also must emphasize that the individual always has a choice: to follow or not to follow the expected behaviors. With each choice then comes a consequence—either desirable or not desirable. Many discipline workshops use this approach and are available to schools.[121]

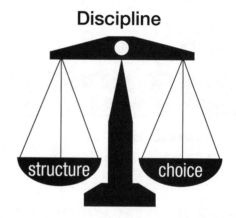

When the focus is "I'll tell you what to do and when," the student is much less able to move from dependence to independence, remaining at the level of dependence.

Behavior Analysis

Before responding to classroom misbehavior mentally or in writing, the educator is advised to first answer certain questions about the behavior. When these questions are answered, they lead to the strategies that will most help the student. The purpose of this analysis is not to excuse the behavior but rather to identify an appropriate response based on understanding the behavior.

Behavior Analysis

1. What kinds of behaviors does a student need to be successful?

2. Does the student have the resources to develop those behaviors?

3. Will it help to contact parent(s)?

   Are resources available through them?

   What resources are available through the school/district?

4. How will behaviors be taught?

5. What are other choices the student could make?

6. What will help the student repeat the successful behavior?

The following chart indicates possible explanations of behaviors, along with suggested interventions.

Explanations of Student Behavior and Suggested Interventions

Students' behavior related to poverty	Intervention
Laugh when disciplined: A way to save face in matriarchal poverty.	Understand the reason for the behavior. Tell students three or four other behaviors that would be more appropriate.
Argue loudly with the teacher: Poverty is participatory, and the culture has a distrust of authority. Many see the system as inherently dishonest and unfair.	Don't argue with students. Use the four-part sheet later in this chapter and have students write the answers to the questions. Model respect for students.
Angry response: Anger is usually based on fear. Question what the fear is: Loss of face? Or something else?	Respond in the adult voice. When students cool down, discuss other responses they could have used.
Inappropriate or vulgar comments: Reliance on casual register; may not know formal register.	Have students generate (or teach students) other phrases that could be used to say the same thing.
Physically fight: Necessary to survive in poverty. Only know the language of survival. Don't have language or belief system for conflict resolution. See themselves as less than a man or woman if they don't fight.	Stress that fighting is unacceptable in school. Examine options that students could live with at school other than fighting. One option is not to settle the business at school, for example.

continued on next page

continued from previous page

Students' behavior related to poverty	Intervention
Hands always on someone else: Poverty has a heavy reliance on nonverbal data and touch.	Allow them to draw or doodle. Have them hold their hands behind their back when in line or standing. Give them as much to do with their hands in a constructive way as possible.
Cannot follow directions: Little procedural memory used in poverty. Sequence seldom used or valued.	Write steps on the board. Have them write at the top of the paper the steps needed to finish the task. Have them practice procedural self-talk.
Extremely disorganized: Lack of planning, scheduling, or prioritizing skills. Seldom taught in poverty. Also, probably don't have a place at home to put things so they can be found.	Teach a simple, color-coded method of organization in the classroom. Use the five-finger method for memory (assign one thing to remember for each finger) at the end of the school day. Have each student give a plan for organization.
Complete only part of a task: Very little if any procedural self-talk. Don't "see" the whole task.	Write on the board all the parts of the task. Require each student to check off each part when finished.
Disrespectful to teacher: Have a lack of respect for authority and the system. May not know any adults worthy of respect.	Tell students that disrespect is not a choice. Identify for students the correct voice tone and word choice that are acceptable. This allows students to practice.
Harm other students, verbally or physically: This may be a way of life. Probably a way to buy space or distance. May have become a habitual response.	Tell students that aggression is not an option. Have students generate other alternatives that are appropriate choices at school. Give students phrases that can be used instead of the one(s) used.
Cheat or steal: Indicative of weak support system, weak role models/emotional resources. May indicate extreme financial need. May indicate little instruction/guidance during formative years.	Use a metaphor story (see example later in this chapter) to find the reason or need behind the cheating or stealing. Address the reason or need. Emphasize that the behavior is illegal and not an option at school.
Talk incessantly: Poverty is very participatory.	Have students write five questions and responses on a notecard two days a week. Tell students that each of them gets up to five comments a day. Build participatory activities into the lesson.

Participation of the Student

While the teacher or administrator is analyzing, the student must analyze as well. To help the student do so, this four-part questionnaire is given to the student for completion. This has been used with students as young as second semester of first grade. Children in poverty have the most difficulty with Question #3. Basically, they see no other choices available than the one they have made.

In going over the sheet with the student, the educator is urged to discuss other choices that could have been made. Students often know only one choice. They don't have access to another way to deal with the situation. For example, if I slam my finger in the car door, I can cry, swear, hit the car, be silent, kick the tire, laugh, stoically open the car door, groan, etc. I have a wide variety of choices.

Name: _____

1. What did you do? _____

2. When you did that, what did you want? _____

3. List four other things you could have done instead of the choice you made.

   1) _____

   2) _____

   3) _____

   4) _____

4. What will you do next time? _____

The Language of Negotiation

One of the biggest issues with students from poverty is the fact that many children in poverty must function, in effect, as their own parents. They parent themselves and others—often younger siblings. In some instances they also act as parent to the adult in the household.

Inside virtually everyone's head are three internal voices that guide the individual. These voices are the child voice, the parent voice, and the adult voice. It has been my observation that individuals who have become their own parent quite young seldom have an internal adult voice. They have a child voice and a parent voice, but not an adult voice.[122]

An internal adult voice allows for negotiation. This voice provides the language of negotiation and allows issues to be examined in a nonthreatening way.

Educators tend to speak to students in a parent voice, particularly in disciplinary situations. To the student who is already functioning as a parent, this is unbearable. Almost immediately, the situation is exacerbated beyond the original incident. The tendency for educators to use the parent voice with students who are poor is based on the assumption that a lack of resources must indicate a lack of intelligence. Students and parents in poverty are very offended by this.

When the parent voice is used with a student who is already a parent in many ways, the outcome is anger. The student is angry because anger is based on fear. What the parent voice forces the student to do is use either the child voice or the parent voice. If the student uses the parent voice, which could sound sarcastic in this context, the student will get in trouble. If the student uses the child voice, the student will feel helpless and therefore at the mercy of the adult. Many students choose to use the parent voice because it's less frightening than memories connected with being helpless.

Negotiation is generally not part of the reality of poverty because negotiation takes place only when a surplus exists. The reality of poverty is scarcity and the language of survival. There simply aren't enough resources for people in poverty to engage in a discussion of them. For example, if there are five hot dogs and five people, the distribution of the food is fairly clear. The condiments for the hot dogs are going to be limited, so the discussion about their distribution will be fairly limited as well. Contrast that, for example, with a middle-class household where the discussion will be about how many hot dogs, what should go on the hot dog, how much of each ingredient, etc. Thus the ability to see options and to negotiate among those options is not well developed in poverty.

To teach students to use the "language of negotiation," which is necessary for them to see alternative choices, one must first teach them phrases they can use. Especially beginning in fourth grade, have them use the adult voice in discussions. Direct-teach the notion of an adult voice, and give them phrases to use. Have them tally each time they use a phrase from the adult voice. There will be laughter. However, over time, if the teacher also models that voice in interactions with students, one will hear more of those kinds of questions and statements.

In addition to this strategy, several staff-development programs are available to teach peer negotiation. It's important that, as part of the negotiation, the students' culture of origin is not denigrated, but rather that the ability to negotiate is seen as an additional survival tool for the school and work setting.

Three Voices

Adapted from the work of Eric Berne[123]

The Child Voice *

Defensive, victimized, emotional, whining, losing attitude,
strongly negative nonverbal

☐ Quit picking on me.

☐ You don't love me.

☐ You want me to leave.

☐ Nobody likes (loves) me.

☐ I hate you.

☐ You're ugly.

☐ You make me sick.

☐ It's your fault.

☐ Don't blame me.

☐ She, he, _____ did it.

☐ You make me mad.

☐ You made me do it.

* The child voice is also playful, spontaneous, curious, etc. The phrases listed often
occur in conflictual or manipulative situations and impede resolution.

The Parent Voice * **

Authoritative, directive, judgmental, evaluative, win-lose mentality,
demanding, punitive, sometimes threatening

☐ You shouldn't (should) do that.

☐ It's wrong (right) to do _____ .

☐ That's stupid, immature, out of
line, ridiculous.

☐ Life's not fair. Get busy.

☐ You are good, bad, worthless,
beautiful (any judgmental,
evaluative comment).

☐ You do as I say.

☐ If you weren't so _____ , this
wouldn't happen to you.

☐ Why can't you be like _____ ?

* The parent voice also can be very loving and supportive. The phrases listed usually
occur during conflict and impede resolution.
** The internal parent voice can create shame and guilt.

The Adult Voice

Not judgmental, free of negative nonverbals, factual, often in question format, attitude of win-win

- ☐ In what ways could this be resolved?
- ☐ What factors will be used to determine the effectiveness, quality of _____ ?
- ☐ I would like to recommend _____ .
- ☐ What are choices in this situation?
- ☐ I am comfortable (uncomfortable) with _____ .
- ☐ Options that could be considered are _____ .
- ☐ For me to be comfortable, I need the following things to occur _____ .
- ☐ These are the consequences of that choice/action _____ .
- ☐ We agree to disagree.

Using Metaphor Stories

Another technique for working with students and adults is to use metaphor stories.[124] A metaphor story will help an individual voice issues that affect subsequent actions. A metaphor story doesn't have any proper names in it and goes like this:

A student keeps going to the nurse's office two or three times a week. There is nothing wrong with her. Yet she keeps going. Adult says to Jennifer, the girl, "Jennifer, I am going to tell a story and I need you to help me. It's about a fourth-grade girl much like yourself. I need you to help me tell the story because I'm not in fourth grade.

"Once upon a time there was a girl who went to the nurse's office. Why did the girl go to the nurse's office? (Because she thought there was something wrong with her.) So the girl went to the nurse's office because she thought there was something wrong with her. Did the nurse find anything wrong with her? (No, the nurse did not.) So the nurse didn't find anything wrong with her, yet the girl kept going to the nurse. Why did the girl keep going to the nurse? (Because she thought there was something wrong with her.) So the girl thought something was wrong with her. Why did the girl think there was something wrong with her? (She saw a TV show …)"

The story continues until the reason for the behavior is found, and then the story needs to end on a positive note: "So she went to the doctor, and he gave her tests and found that she was OK."

This is an actual case. What came out in the story was that Jennifer had seen a TV show in which a girl her age had died suddenly and had never known she was ill. Jennifer's parents took her to the doctor, he ran tests, and he told her she was fine. So she didn't go to the nurse's office anymore.

A metaphor story is to be used one-on-one when there is a need to understand the existing behavior and motivate the student to implement the appropriate behavior.

Reframing

Reframing is a technique used to identity the behavior that will be compatible with identity. It requires the adult voice. It doesn't work if the person has a biochemical issue or addiction, and it must be framed against the individual's identity. An example is physical fighting. Many students physically fight because it is seen as a position of strength. If you reframe it this way—"It takes more strength to stay out of a fight than get into it"—you have reframed it. When parents tell me that they have told their child to fight, I thank them for giving the child necessary survival skills for their environment. Then I ask them this question: "Do you fight at work?" What you are trying to get the parent to see is that there is an appropriate place to physically fight, and it isn't school or work.

Statements to help reframe a situation include:

- This behavior (not fighting) will help you win more often.

- This will keep you from being cheated.

- This will help you be tougher or stronger.

- This will make you smarter.

- This will help keep the people you love safe.

- This will give you power, control, and respect.

- This will keep you safer.

A coach south of Houston told me this story: The coaches had a rule that anyone who was late to class owed them a minute of pushups for every minute late. A 10th-grade boy was late. The coach said, "Give me a minute of pushups." The boy said "No way." The boy got sent to the office and received 45 minutes of detention. The next day the coach said to the boy, "I didn't understand why you gave up a minute for 45 minutes." The boy was confused. So the coach said, "Yesterday, you could have done a minute of pushups, but you chose 45 minutes of detention. I didn't understand." The day after that the boy came to the coach and said, "I'll do pushups next time." The coach had reframed the situation not as power and control but as use of time.

Teaching Hidden Rules

Many times students from poverty don't respond the way a teacher expects or considers appropriate. This is because the student's hidden rules conflict with the teacher's hidden rules. One tool for determining the student's hidden rules is the behavior analysis earlier in this chapter. For example, if a student from poverty laughs when disciplined, the teacher needs to say, "Do you use the same rules in basketball that you use in football? No, you don't, because you would lose. The same is true at school. There are street rules, and there are school rules. Each set of rules helps you be successful where you are. So, at school, laughing when being disciplined is not one of the options. It doesn't help you be successful. It only buys you more trouble. Keep a straight face and look sorry, even if you don't feel that way."

This is an example of teaching a hidden rule. It can be even more straightforward with older students: "Look, there are hidden rules on the streets and hidden rules at school. What are they?"

After the discussion, detail the rules that make students successful where they are.

What Does This Information Mean in the School or Work Setting?

- Students from poverty need to have at least two sets of behaviors from which to choose—one for the street and one for the school and work settings.

- The purpose of discipline should be to promote successful behaviors at school.

- Teaching students to use the adult voice (i.e., the language of negotiation) is important for success in and out of school and can become an alternative to physical aggression.

- Structure and choice need to be part of the discipline approach.

- Discipline should be seen and used as a form of instruction.

Chapter 9

Instruction and Improving Achievement: How to Live in the Abstract Representational World of School and Work

One of the overriding purposes of this book is to improve the achievement of students from poverty. *Low achievement is closely correlated with lack of resources, and numerous studies have documented the correlation between low socioeconomic status and low achievement.*[125] To improve achievement, however, we will need to rethink our instruction and instructional arrangements.[126]

Traditional Notions of Intelligence

> The [children of the poor] are catalogued, measured,
> and deemed wanting the moment they enter school;
> they are tested before they are instructed. The teacher
> becomes a judge; the class's standing in reading
> and arithmetic is a yardstick of collective failure;
> and the fear of inadequacy pervades the classroom,
> suffocating teacher and pupil alike.
>
> –Vera John and Eleanor Leacock,
> *Transforming the Structure of Failure*[127]

Genetic determinism is the notion that nearly all intelligence is inherited; "geniuses are born, not made." In fact, the book *The Bell Curve* purports that individuals in poverty have on the average an IQ of nine points lower than individuals in the middle class.[128] That might be a credible argument if IQ tests really measured ability, an idea that has been disputed by reputable scholars.[129] What IQ tests largely measure is acquired information.[130]

Genetic determinism was the theory upon which IQ tests were designed to predict success in school. However, they don't predict ability or basic intelligence. They are mostly about an acquired knowledge base; if your parents are educated, chances are you will have a greater acquired knowledge base. In fact, recent research suggests that a huge part of intelligence is the intergenerational transfer of knowledge. As mentioned previously, in an Australian study that followed 8,556 children for 14 years, the researchers found they could predict with reasonable accuracy the verbal reasoning scores of 14-year-olds based on the maternal grandfather's occupation.[131] It stands to reason that intelligence is developed. A better approach to achievement is to look at teaching and learning.

Differentiating Between Teaching and Learning

The emphasis in education has generally been on teaching. The theory has been that if you teach well enough, then learning will occur. But we all know of individuals, including ourselves, who decided in a given situation not to learn. And we have all been in situations where we found it virtually impossible to learn because we didn't have the background information or the belief system to accept it, even though it was well-taught and presented.

Teaching is what occurs outside the head.
Learning is what occurs inside the head.

Traditionally in education in the United States, we have presented the research on teaching to teachers and the research on learning to counselors and early-childhood teachers. It is the research on learning that must be addressed and utilized if teachers are to work successfully with students from poverty. In order to learn, an individual must have certain cognitive skills to take in and process information—and must have a structure (a schema) inside the head to organize and store the information; picture a file cabinet or a piece of software.

In U.S. schools furthermore, we have traditionally assumed that the cognitive skills and structures—the schema—are in place when a child enters school. We assume the child is "ready to learn." If the student is not, we test and place the student in a special program or give the student a label: special education, dyslexia, Title I, ADHD, 504, etc. Little attempt is made to address the cognitive strategies because we believe that to a large extent they are not remediable— that "intelligence" is unchangeable.[132] The truth is that we can no longer pretend this arrangement works, no matter how well or how hard we teach. Increasingly, students (mostly from poverty) are coming to school without the concepts, but more importantly, without the cognitive strategies.[133] We simply can't assign them all to special education. What are these cognitive strategies, and how do we build learning structures inside the heads of students?

Cognitive Strategies

Compelling work in this area has been done by Reuven Feuerstein, an Israeli. He began in 1945 working with poor, disenfranchised Jewish youths who settled in Israel after World War II. He had studied under Jean Piaget and disagreed with Piaget in one major way. Piaget believed that an environmental stimulus led to a response. Feuerstein felt that between the environmental stimulus and the response should be mediation (i.e., the intervention of an adult).[134]

Mediation

Identification of a stimulus **What**	Assignment of meaning **Why**	Identification of a strategy **How**
Don't cross the street without looking.	You could get hit by a car.	Look both ways twice.

Mediation is basically three things: identification of the stimulus, assignment of meaning, and identification of a strategy. For example, we say to a child, "Don't cross the street without looking. You could get hit by a car. So if you must cross the street, look both ways twice."

Why Is Mediation So Important?

Mediation builds cognitive strategies, and those strategies give individuals the ability to plan and handle new information in an organized way.[135]

> If an individual depends on a random, episodic story structure for memory patterns, lives in an unpredictable environment, and has not developed the ability to plan, then …
>
> If individuals cannot plan, *they cannot predict.*
>
> If individuals cannot predict, *they cannot identify cause and effect.*
>
> If individuals cannot identify cause and effect, *they cannot identify consequence.*
>
> If individuals cannot identify consequence, *they cannot control impulsivity.*
>
> If individuals cannot control impulsivity, *they have an inclination toward criminal behavior.*

Reuven Feuerstein identified *cognitive strategies* as the missing links that occur in the mind when mediation had not occurred. The young people with whom Feuerstein worked would have been identified by any standard as special education students. Yet, with his program, many of the students who came to him even in mid-adolescence went on to be very successful, some even completing their doctorate. To teach these strategies, Feuerstein developed more than 50 instruments.[136]

Feuerstein's work has been validated by recent brain research. A University of California, Berkeley study released in 2008 used EEG (electroencephalogram) scans of 9- and 10-year-old children in poverty and middle class. The study, led by Mark Kishiyama, found that patterns in the brains of most children from poverty were very similar to those of adults who have had strokes—showing lesions in the prefrontal cortex. This is the part of the brain that handles executive function: impulse control, planning, and working memory. The researchers went on to state that the problem is remediable, but there must be direct intervention.[137] In other words, the prefrontal cortex is heavily involved in the input strategies of cognition.

There is a great deal of research, however, to show that these strategies can be taught.[138]

Missing Links

What are these missing cognitive strategies?[139]

1. **"Mediated focusing"**—Ability to focus attention and see objects in detail. Opposite of blurred and sweeping perceptions.

2. **"Mediated scheduling"**—Based on routine. Ability to schedule and plan ahead. Ability to represent the future abstractly and therefore set goals.

3. **"Mediation of positive anticipation"**—Ability to control the present for a happy representation of the future.

4. **"Mediation of inhibition and control"**—Ability to defer gratification, think before acting, control impulsiveness.

5. **"Mediated representation of the future"**—Ability to construe imaginatively a future scenario based on facts.

6. **"Mediation of verbal stimulation"**—Use of precise language for defining and categorizing the environment.

7. **"Mediated precision"**—Ability to precisely define situations, things, people, etc. and use that precise thinking for problem solving.

In short, missing links/mediations result in cognitive issues.

What Are These Cognitive Issues?

Blurred and sweeping perceptions and the lack of a systematic method of exploration mean that these students have no consistent or predictable way of getting information. They see only about 50% of what is on a page. If you watch these students in a new setting, they will rapidly go from object to object, touching everything. Yet when you ask them what they have seen, they cannot tell you. This area is related to the use of the casual-register story structure, which is episodic and random in the details or information presented. They simply don't have cognitive methodology for doing tasks or a systematic way to finish tasks.

Impaired verbal tools mean they don't have the vocabulary to deal with the cognitive tasks. Vocabulary words are the building blocks of the internal learning structure. Vocabulary is also the tool to better define a problem, seek more accurate solutions, etc. Many students who rely solely on casual register don't use or have many prepositions or adverbs in their speech.

Impaired spatial orientation is simply the inability to orient objects, people, etc. in space. Directions, location, object size, object shape, etc. are not available to them. They have neither the vocabulary nor the concepts for spatial orientation.

Impaired temporal orientation is the inability to organize and measure in time. One of Feuerstein's observations was that these students assign time to incidents on the basis of the emotional intensity of the experience, not the measured time that is part of educated thinking. I find among students from poverty that time is neither measured nor heeded. Being somewhere on time is seldom valued. And time itself is not seen as a thing to be used or valued.

Impaired observations of constancies are the inability of the brain to hold an object inside the head and keep the memory of the object constant. In other words, when there are impaired observations of constancies, objects change shape and size in the mind. If this is the case, then learning alphabet letters, retaining shapes, etc. is problematic. It is also the inability to know what stays the same and what changes. For example, east and west are constant; left and right change based on the orientation of the moment.

Lack of precision and accuracy in data gathering is another cognitive issue. It's related to several of the above issues. Problem solving and other tasks are extremely difficult because students from poverty seldom have the strategies to gather precise and accurate data.

Another cognitive issue is the inability to hold two objects or two sources inside the head while comparing and contrasting. *(According to brain research, this is what working memory is.)* If a student is unable to do this, the student cannot assign information to categories inside the brain. If a student cannot assign information to categories, then the student cannot retrieve the information except in an associative, random way.

These issues explain many student behaviors. How do we make interventions? We build cognitive strategies.

What Are These Cognitive Strategies That Must Be Built?

Feuerstein identified three stages in the learning process: "input, elaboration, and output."[140]

1. Input Strategies

Input is defined as the "quality and quantity of the data gathered."

1. Use planning behaviors.
2. Focus perception on a specific stimulus.
3. Control impulsivity.
4. Explore data systematically.
5. Use appropriate and accurate labels.
6. Organize space with stable systems of reference.
7. Orient data in time.
8. Identify constancies across variations.
9. Gather precise and accurate data.
10. Consider two sources of information at once.
11. Organize data (parts of a whole).
12. Visually transport data.

2. Elaboration Strategies

Elaboration is defined as "use of the data."

1. Identify and define the problem.
2. Select relevant cues.
3. Compare data.
4. Select appropriate categories of time.
5. Summarize data.
6. Project relationships of data.
7. Use logical data.
8. Test hypotheses.
9. Build inferences.
10. Make a plan using the data.
11. Use appropriate labels.
12. Use data systematically.

3. Output Strategies

Ouput is defined as "communication of the data."

1. Communicate clearly the labels and process.
2. Visually transport data correctly.
3. Use precise and accurate language.
4. Control impulsive behavior.

Mediation builds these strategies. When these strategies are not present, they can be built, and they must be present before children can work at the elaboration level. Typically in school, we begin teaching at the elaboration level (i.e., use of the data). When students don't understand, we reteach these strategies, but we don't revisit the quality and quantity of the data gathered—the input.

Input Strategies (Quality and Quantity of Data)

Now let's take each of the dozen input strategies and look at them separately.

1. **Use planning behaviors** includes goal setting, identifying the procedures in the task, identifying the parts of the task, assigning time to the task(s), and identifying the quality of the work necessary to complete the task.

2. **Focus perception on a specific stimulus** is the strategy of seeing every detail on the page or in the environment. It is the strategy of identifying everything noticed by the five senses.

3. **Control impulsivity** is the strategy of stopping action until one has thought about the task. There is a direct correlation between impulse control and improved behavior and achievement.

4. **Explore data systematically** means that a strategy is employed to procedurally and systematically go through every piece of data. Numbering is a way to go systematically through data. Highlighting each piece of data can be another method.

5. **Use appropriate and accurate labels** is the use of precise words and vocabulary to identify and explain. If a student doesn't have specific words to use, then the ability to retrieve and use information is severely limited. It isn't enough that a student can do a task; the student must also be able to label the procedures, tasks, and processes so that the task can

be successfully repeated each time and analyzed at a metacognitive level. Metacognition is the ability to think about one's thinking. To do so, labels must be attached. Only when labels are attached can the task be evaluated and, therefore, improved.

6. **Organize space with stable systems of reference** is crucial to success in math. It means that up, down, right, left, across, horizontal, vertical, diagonal, etc., are understood. It means that an individual can identify with labels the position of an item. It means that a person can organize space. For example, if an individual doesn't have this strategy, then it's virtually impossible to tell the letters *p, b,* and *d* apart. The only differentiation is the orientation in space.

7. **Orient data in time** is the strategy of assigning abstract values to time and the measurement of time. This strategy is crucial for identifying cause and effect, for determining sequence, and for predicting consequences.

8. **Identify constancies across variations** is the strategy of knowing what always remains the same and what changes. For example, if you don't know what makes a square a square, you cannot identify constancies. This allows one to define things, to recognize a person or an object, and to compare and contrast. The strategy allows cursive writing to be read in all of its variations. I once asked this question of a group of fifth-grade students with whom I was working: "If you saw me tomorrow, what about me would be the same, and what would be different?" Many of the students had difficulty with that concept.

9. **Gather precise and accurate data** is the strategy of using accurate labels, identifying the orientation in time and space, knowing the constancies, and exploring the data systematically.

10. **Consider two sources of information at once** is the strategy of visually transporting data accurately, identifying the constancies and variations, and exploring the data systematically. When that is done, then precise and accurate labels need to be assigned.

11. **Organize data (parts of a whole)** involves exploring data systematically, organizing space, identifying constancies and variations, and labeling the parts and the whole with precise words.

12. **Visually transport data** is when the eye picks up the data, carries it accurately to the brain, examines it for constancies and variations, and labels the parts and the whole.

Elaboration and Output Strategies

These tend to be fairly well understood in schools because this is where the teaching tends to occur.

Abstract Representational Systems

Most of the approaches to teaching and learning address issues of instruction or the teaching part. This chapter is focusing on the learning part. In other words, what must a student do inside the head to learn—and then be able to use the information?

In order to survive in school, a learner must be able to negotiate the abstract representational world, which is the paper world or the world as represented on a computer screen. This takes a different skill set because of the requirement that sensory information be represented on paper. For example, an apple in three dimensions does not look like a two-dimensional drawing of an apple. The drawing only represents the apple on paper. Words represent a feeling, but they are not the feeling. A photo represents a person, but it is not the person. Numbers represent an amount, but they are not the actual item being counted.

What Is the Paper World?

The paper world is how information and understandings are conveyed in formal schooling. Words, symbols, etc., are used to convey the meaning. Paper doesn't have nonverbals, emotions, or human interaction. Paper depends on a shared understanding of vocabulary in order to communicate. If you grew up in a household where there were very few books, calendars, clocks, etc., the concept of information on paper is difficult. It has to be learned.

Abstract, decontextualized, representational symbols, ideas, etc. are on paper to represent a tangible, sensory reality. Here are some examples:

Abstract Items and Their Concrete Representations

Abstract item	Represents
Grades	The "ticket" to get into college, a better job, more money
House deed	The physical property
Address	The physical location
Social Security number	The person (a way to keep track of people on paper)
Daily to-do list	Tasks to be accomplished that day
Clock or calendar	Abstract time
State assessment	Knowledge base and personal vocabulary; a representation of shared understandings for communication
Homework	Ability to complete a task in a given time frame in order to establish understandings
Insurance papers	An external support system that provides money, assistance, and expertise for unusual circumstances, health, etc.
Driver's license	The right to physically operate a vehicle
TV guide	The shows or programs
Photograph	The person (a photo doesn't breathe; it's a two-dimensional representation of the person)
Letters in alphabet	Symbols that represent physical sounds that together make up words
Numbers	Symbols that represent quantity
Musical notations	Symbols that represent sounds and timing
Road map	Objects, roads, etc. in physical space
Sonogram	A three-dimensional representation of an object
MRI (magnetic resonance imaging)	A three-dimensional representation of a body, body part, etc. (it isn't the body, but it represents the body)
Trust document	A legal entity (has its own Social Security number) that pays taxes, owns property, and identifies how assets will be held and distributed over time
Student handbook	Paper version of the appropriate behaviors that are to be used
Teacher contract	A legal document that establishes expectations for teachers' compensation, benefits, terms of employment, etc.
Menu	The food choices in a restaurant (it isn't the food itself)

Continuum of Paper Documents

As your resources grow and become more complex, the amount of paper documents in a household indicates to some extent your familiarity and comfort with the paper world.

birth certificates
immunization records
driver's license
rental agreements
money orders
paycheck stubs
bills

wills
magazines/newspapers
payment records
credit card and bank statements
mortgage papers
calendars
planners
to-do lists
tax returns
books
coupons
passports

corporate financial statements
prenuptial agreement
stock certificates/personal investments
provenance
property deeds
charity events/invitations
board of directors minutes/records
club memberships
trusts

What Do We Need to Do Instructionally? Focus on Eight Key Issues[141]

Key Issue #1: Use Mental Models

A. Mental models are how the mind holds abstract information, i.e., information that has little or no sensory representation.

Each of us carries much abstract information around in our head every day. How do we do this? We carry it in mental models.

Just as a computer has a file manager to represent the structure of the software content, so does the human mind.

B. There are generic mental models.

In addition to having mental models for subject areas or disciplines, there also are mental models for occupations. To be successful in school or work one must have four generic mental models. They are:

- Space
- Time
- Part to whole
- Formal register

These mental models are fundamental to all tasks.

Space

Space becomes important because your body operates in space. The mind must have a way to keep track of your body. One way is to touch everything. Another way is to assign a reference system to space using abstract words and drawings. For example, we talk about east, west, north, south, up, down, etc. Because math is about assigning order and value to the universe, we tend to do it directionally. Another illustration: We write small to large numbers from left to right. To read a map, one must have a reference for space. To find things in your office or desk, there must be an abstract referencing system for space.

Time

A mental model for abstract time (days, minutes, weeks, hours, etc.) is crucial to success in school and work. One way to keep time is emotionally (how it feels), but another is abstractly with a calendar or a clock. Past, present, and future must be in the mental model because, without these, it isn't possible to sequence. Examples of mental models for time would be a timeline, calendar, schedule, or clock.

Part to Whole

Part to whole means that one can identify the parts, as well as the whole. For example: Chapters make a book. Words make a sentence. Writing a term paper has multiple steps. You cannot effectively analyze anything unless you can break it down and understand part to whole.

Formal Register

Because formal register is the language currency of school and work, it becomes crucial to have an understanding of it.

Key Issue #2: Build Vocabulary—or the 'What'

Vocabulary becomes the tool with which the mind categorizes information (like and different), sorts the information, assigns the information to a pattern or group, and then communicates shared meaning. One of the misunderstandings of constructivism was that as long as students made meaning inside their heads, they were OK. But meaning has value only to the extent that it can be shared and communicated. This requires a collective understanding of what a word means. Vocabulary literally is the key tool for thinking.

Key Issue #3: Direct-Teach the Processes—or the 'How'

To do any task requires a "how" component that is the process. Unless the "how" is directly taught, a student doesn't have a key tool for completing the task. One of the reasons generic study skills have not been as successful as the researchers would like is that processes are specific to tasks.

Key Issue #4: Have the Students Develop Questions

Question making has a huge payoff in learning. Question making is the tool that allows you to get inside your brain and know what you know and what you don't know. When students say to you, "I don't understand," and you ask them what part they don't understand, and they say, "All of it," then you know the student doesn't know how to ask questions syntactically. Anne Marie Palincsar found in her research that if you cannot ask questions, you rarely get past the third-grade reading level.[142] The good news is that question making can be taught.

> **I think the most beneficial strategy I have used in the classroom has been question making. At our middle school we have a semester-long competition playing "Jeopardy!" The students have really enjoyed it, and they have actually gotten into writing their own questions. It has paid off in terms of their comprehension. Also, I have extensively used mental models … This strategy really enables the students to connect some of the things they're learning and to remember material so much easier. In this way they can really make it their own knowledge.**
>
> –Brian Conner, Middle School Science Teacher[143]

A quick approach is to give students the question stems and then have them use the rules to develop a multiple-choice question. Creating multiple-choice questions develops critical-thinking skills.

Key Issue #5: Change Our Approach to New Learning by Making It Relational

**The key process to educate now is autonomous and competitive.
It needs to change to be relational learning.**

What is relational learning? It is when the learning occurs in a context of mutual respect, and the student has a group to which the student belongs for learning. This becomes a support system.

When adults are learning something new, rarely do they make the learning autonomous and competitive. For example, several years ago I went to Europe for the first time with a friend. Neither of us had been to Europe, so we learned together. We didn't say, *OK, let's make this trip a competition and see who does the best and then we'll grade ourselves and see who has the best grade!* No, we relied on each other to make it through the trip.

All learning occurs within a social context and relationships and has since the beginning of time. Many people in the school business have seemingly tried very hard to make learning a separate endeavor from relationships. The students who succeed in school have the ability to establish relationships and belong to a group. Why not create the processes so they're available to all students?

In addition, many of the students who fail don't have a support system—i.e., adults and resources outside the school system that provide the support to succeed in school. Mentors and email buddies with outside sources are two ways to do that. For more information on support systems, please review Chapter 6.

Key Issue #6: Enhance Content Comprehension

Another critical piece of achievement is content comprehension. Just as reading comprehension means you understand the reading passage, so content comprehension means you understand the content at a level that you can manipulate it and use it.

To use and manipulate content, in addition to knowing the meaning of vocabulary, you also must know the *purpose, structures, patterns,* and *processes* used in that particular discipline or content. These four things tell you what is important and not important as you sort information in order to use it.

For example, the purpose of language arts is to study how structure and language are used to influence a reader. It is basically about writers and readers. The structures are the genres (short story, drama, poetry, biography, novel, etc.), grammar, organizational patterns of text, syllables, phonics, etc. The patterns then become units of study. The processes include reading, writing, speaking, filmmaking, and listening. So an expert teacher in language arts is going to help students understand that language arts is always about the relationship between the reader and writer—the manipulations of structure, word choice, and organization.

For example, math is about assigning order and value to the universe. We use numbers, space, and time as primary structures to do that. Patterns that are taught include fractions (part to whole of space), decimals (part to whole of numbers), and measurement (assigning the value of space and time). Processes are addition, subtraction, multiplication, and division. So an elementary teacher would facilitate a discussion with students about how to know how much space is theirs in a classroom *before* introducing fractions. The class would measure the room, divide it with masking tape, and calculate space using fractions. The teacher could do the same thing by dividing pizza. The students would then understand why each student needs to know about measurement *and* fractions.

For example, the purpose of chemistry is to understand chemical bonding. The periodic table provides the rules or patterns for bonding. The process used to figure out the bonding is equations. The structure theory has varied from shell theory, to vapor-cloud theory, to string theory.

When the teacher has content comprehension, the teacher spends the majority of the time teaching what is critical to understanding the use and manipulation of the content. For example, in language arts in high school, the teacher doesn't test by asking what color the girl's dress was in the story, but rather: What specific techniques did the writer use to make the reader feel empathetic in relation to the girl? Or how would the reader have felt differently if this short story had been told in the form of a poem?

Lee Shulman found that content comprehension is a critical issue in excellent teaching and, furthermore, that graphic visual representations (mental models) used by the teacher came out of this understanding. He indicated that teachers then could determine when a student had a slight misunderstanding versus no understanding at all.[144]

Quite simply, if the teacher doesn't understand the content against these four criteria—purpose, structures, patterns, and processes—the teacher will have difficulty facilitating or developing high achievement. It isn't possible to teach what you don't know.

Key Issue #7: Evaluate and Calibrate Student Work

When the emphasis moves to student *learning*—as opposed to teaching—then monitoring and observing teachers isn't nearly as important as monitoring and evaluating student work. Expertise rubrics to measure the growth of student expertise are critical, as are rubrics and assignments calibrated to standards.

Another tool is curriculum calibration. This simply means that the assignments given to students are calibrated against the standards for that grade level. In one study, researchers found that while 100% of kindergarten assignments were on grade level, only 2% of fifth-grade assignments were on grade level. To calibrate assignments, simply take the standards and look at the given assignments to see if the assignment matches the standard.

Curriculum Calibration

Grade	Mathematics GLS * %						Average Grade Level	Language Arts GLS %						Average Grade Level
	* grade-level standards													
	K	1	2	3	4	5		K	1	2	3	4	5	
K	100						K	100						K
1st		100					1.0		100					1.0
2nd		23	77				1.8		20	80				1.8
3rd			45	55			2.6		2	14	84			2.8
4th			40	40	20		2.8		2	30	35	33		3.0
5th		2	35	59	2	2	2.7			28	60	10	2	2.9

Source: *Explicit Direct Instruction* by J. R. Hollingsworth & S. E. Ybarra.

Teacher and Student Artifact Analysis

Artifacts are the products of the classroom. They often reflect the pedagogy and/ or curriculum. This checklist is a tool to assess artifacts—particularly student assignments. Many students drop out of school because it's "boring," which usually means that the assignments aren't interesting.

Artifact Analysis

Teacher artifacts	Student artifacts
EXAMPLES: lesson plans, project guidelines, classroom guidelines/procedures, rubrics, tests, homework assignments	EXAMPLES: completed projects, research papers, tests, homework, writing samples, rubrics used for self-assessment, student notes
Questions to ask about the teacher artifacts	**Questions to ask about the student artifacts**
1. Is the process clearly identified (procedures, steps)?	1. Did the student complete the assignment?
2. Are student evaluation tools given (rubrics, grading guidelines, etc.)?	2. What was the level of difficulty of the assignment for the student?

continued on next page

continued from previous page

Questions to ask about the teacher artifacts	Questions to ask about the student artifacts
3. Is the assignment relevant to the student in any way (linked to a personal experience, a future story, a creative option)?	3. Was the quality of the student work sufficient to assess student understanding of the task/content?
4. Is the purpose of the assignment to develop automaticity? If so, how much automaticity is required?	4. Was the finished project/assignment on grade level?
5. Is the assignment tied to grade-level standards (GLS) and expectations?	5. Is the student able to demonstrate the use of the self-evaluation tool?
6. How often is the same kind of assignment given? Is there variation in the week?	6. Did the student follow directions?
7. Does the assignment require thought?	
8. Is it a "beginning learning" assignment? If so, what are the opportunities to do the assignment with a peer or a group?	
9. Does it involve media/technology? If so, is that accessible to the student?	
10. Is the timeframe given to do the assignment reasonable for the majority of students?	
11. What is the motivation for the student? (tied to a future story, a work environment, a personal interest, an understanding of the content, the relationship with the teacher, personal expertise/knowledge)	
12. Does the assignment provide any choice(s) for demonstrating understanding?	
13. To what extent is the assignment dependent on memory versus utilization of information sources?	

Learning new cognitive structures is difficult, and students may resist. We know they have the ability to learn, since research shows that intelligence is changeable. But direct-teaching the cognitive strategies discussed in this chapter is not sufficient. We must not only support students, we must insist that they can, and will, learn.

- If the research on improving student achievement had to be summed up in three points, these are the three: insistence, support, and high expectations. They appear repeatedly in the research.[145] Traditionally in U.S. schools we have provided insistence, and since the mid-1970s we have added expectations as part of the equation. It is, however, the notion of support that must be provided to students now.

- What is appropriate support? I'm not talking about a warm, fuzzy, feel-good notion of support; I'm talking about what girders are to a bridge. The supports these students need are cognitive strategies, appropriate relationships, coping strategies, goal-setting opportunities (a future story), and appropriate instruction both in content and discipline. The true discrimination that comes out of poverty is the lack of cognitive strategies. The lack of these unseen attributes disadvantages in every aspect of life the individual who does not have them.

- Last but not least, to have high achievement, there also has to be a buildingwide approach.[146]

In conclusion, as we adapt and flex our instruction to meet the needs of these students, cognitive strategies and support need to be integrated with insistence and high expectations.

Key Issue #8: Create a Future Story

Future Story

A "future story" is a plan for the future. Without it, neither schooling nor work has purpose or significance.

Future story	Name:
You are 10 years older than you are now. You are the star of a movie. What are you doing? Who is with you? Circle any of these that are in your future story: children, job, career, marriage/partnership, health, wealth, travel, living in a city, town, rural area, another country, vehicles, hobbies, sports, music, movies, college, technical school, military, church/religion, Internet, video games, friends, family, other.	
For which of these reasons do you want to graduate from high school? Keep track of money, I will know I am getting paid correctly, so I can go on to college or military or technical school, to get a better job, to take care of my parents or siblings, to afford my hobbies, to pay for my vehicle, to take care of my children, other.	
What do you enjoy doing and would do even if you did not get paid for it? What do you need to do so you can do that and get paid for doing it?	
Who are the friends and adults who will help you get your future story?	
Write out your future story and include how education will help you get it. 	
Signature:	DATE:

For more on these eight key issues/strategies, see the books *Under-Resourced Learners* and *Research-Based Strategies*.

What Does This Information Mean in the School or Work Setting?

- The focus in schools needs to be on learning and on evaluation of student work.

- Make 80% of the grade based on content and 20% based on the processes the student must use or steps the student must take to do the assignment.

- Staff development would do well to focus on a diagnostic approach rather than a programmatic approach.

- Efforts to promote learning must pay greater heed to what is in the student's head.

- Insistence, support, and high expectations with a relationship of mutual respect need to be guiding lights in our decisions about instruction.

Chapter 10

Poverty and Intersectionality: How Poverty Intersects with Race, Health, Immigration

Intersectionality is the way that different kinds of discrimination overlap—the ways they intersect. Classism, or discrimination based on poverty, intersects with many other kinds of discrimination: ageism, racism, sexism, and discrimination based on disability and health issues, immigration status, etc.—to name a few.

> In the late 1980s, the legal scholar Kimberlé Williams Crenshaw ... introduced the theory of intersectionality, the idea that when it comes to thinking about how inequalities persist, categories like gender, race, and class are best understood as overlapping and mutually constitutive rather than isolated and distinct.[147]

Our lives are like a rich fabric woven from many threads. We all have racial and ethnic threads, and we have other threads that may or may not open us up to discrimination—economic class, sexual orientation, religion, and all the other factors that make a person an individual. While this book looks at poverty as its own thread in the cloth, it does not dismiss the intersecting issues that exacerbate poverty and discrimination based on poverty. The purpose of this book is to address the impact of poverty on classroom interactions.

This chapter briefly addresses the layered, myriad issues that students, parents, and other stakeholders may bring into the classroom, issues that increase the complexity of building and sustaining the emotional resources of a student in the classroom.

The chapter reviews a lot of statistics, and it is important to remember that the statistics are the results of intersectionality—they are not the intersectionality itself. Furthermore, the statistics used here illustrate barriers faced by marginalized groups, but intersectionality also creates positive opportunities.

When one is marginalized for any reason, the concept of being "less than" or "separate from" comes into reality and impacts the emotional well-being of the individual. This creates issues for learning and for building relationships of mutual trust, and it can hinder the development of a strong inner self. For more on the importance of emotional well-being and a strong inner self, see my book *Emotional Poverty.*

What Are the Actual Numbers and Percentages of Children in Poverty by Race?

There is often confusion about the difference between numbers and percentages. In this chart, you can see both.

Percent of Children in Poverty by Age and Race/Ethnicity*, 2016

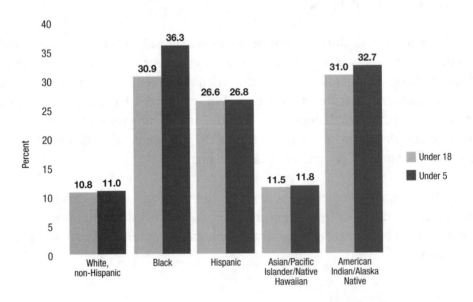

* Data for all racial groups exclude Hispanic ethnicity

Source: Children's Defense Fund, "Child Poverty in America 2016."

The number of white children in poverty is second only to the number of Hispanic children in poverty. But even though there are more than 4 million white children in poverty, they represent only 10.8% of all white children in the United States. By contrast, there are nearly 5 million Hispanic children in poverty, and those children represent 26.6% of all Hispanic children. The representation is disproportionate: In most marginalized groups, the percentage of people living in poverty is greater than the percentage of the U.S. population as a whole. Black and Native American populations have the highest rates of child poverty at 30.9% and 31%, respectively. Overall, the greatest percentages and numbers of children in poverty are from marginalized groups.[148]

The intersectionality of race and poverty is multifaceted, as the following story illustrates.

Black, White, and Green: A Story of Racism and Classism in Elementary School

by Dr. Chestin Auzenne-Curl

When I was in the second grade, I attended a school that was for the most part white and for the most part solidly upper middle class—the kind of middle class that appreciates name-brand clothing and ribbons and bows that match socks and shoes. And there was one little girl in class who didn't fit the bill: Amy. She was usually alone, but she was very nice, so I befriended her.

We would sit together at lunch and play together at recess. Then one day she said she wanted to visit my home. I told her that I wouldn't be able to ask my mother if she could come over until I had met her mother. She got excited because her mother was going to be attending the class's Valentine's Day party.

I waited for the day to come.

When it did, I saw her mother enter the room and immediately approached her, introduced myself, and extended my hand. She did not extend her hand in return. She told me that she was sick.

I recognized the lie.

I walked back across the room to the table where Amy was sitting, and we continued our routine and enjoyed the Valentine's Day party together. However, I scanned the room and followed Amy's mother periodically. I watched her as she shook hands with and hugged other classmates. I wondered why I wasn't worthy of a handshake. What had I not done correctly? I almost asked Amy, but I didn't think she knew.

It would be our last day of friendship.

She went home, and something happened. When she returned to school the following day, she came up to me and said, "We can't be friends anymore because brown people are not allowed at my house."

Even at the age of 8, I was more concerned for Amy than I was for myself. I learned two lessons from that relationship: Lesson #1 was that some people placed value on race, on color, on class. Coming from a family of many different colors, many different textures of hair, and many different sets of beliefs, I never thought about the differences being weighted. I was taught to appreciate differences and to accept them.

The second lesson wasn't as clear to me at first, but as time went on, I understood more and more about Amy's mother. She had been ostracized by all of the other mothers who felt they were higher class than was she. She needed to shield her shame by feeling better than someone, and so she chose me. More specifically, she chose my blackness.

In her eyes I was just a little brown child, but I know she found it hard to ignore my long pigtails crowned with bows, top-brand clothing, and other material things that she couldn't afford to provide for her daughter. I wondered if she knew that the other kids in class referred to Amy as poor white trash. Was it better for her to endure that alone than to have a friend of color?

After that I would still see Amy on the playground, but from a distance I noticed things I didn't notice when we were playing together. I noticed her dirty T-shirts and her tennis shoes with frayed shoestrings. I noticed that she wore the same blue jeans every day. And I noticed that she was alone.

The shame she would carry for the rest of our school years was apparent. We passed one another in the halls in high school, and she looked at the lockers instead of me. Or down at the ground when it was time for lunch. I saw her many times. And every time, she was alone.[149]

Reflections on 'Black, White, and Green'

Many African Americans have a story like the one above. Dr. Auzenne-Curl's background and strong family support system assisted her in developing a future story in which racism did not limit her goals. However, she knew that racism would impact her pursuit of those goals:

> You just don't stop there. My parents reminded me all the time that whether it be race, gender, class, whatever ... there was going to be something that people would find "not to love" about you. They loved me, and so I loved myself enough to not let racism or sexism limit my pursuits. I encounter them both to this day—more often than some would believe. People who say that racism is dead or who say they don't see color, that isn't helpful. It isn't true. It's not productive to take ownership or authorship of another's experiences.

> There are many ways teachers can acknowledge the very real ways that students of color experience marginalization and ostracism while supporting the establishment of a future story that is not bound by those negative experiences. For this, teachers must be willing to listen to their students' stories and to look further into issues of community.[150]

Racism

As we saw in the numbers and percentages chart, there may be more white children than black children in poverty in the United States, but a greater percentage of black children are in poverty. In other words, black children are disproportionately represented in poverty, as are most other marginalized groups. Depending upon where you are in the world or which part of the United States you are in, the race that is most heavily impoverished may be different. No matter which marginalized group has the highest percentage of people in poverty, structural racism is one of the causes of that poverty.

> There are at least two distinct phases in the sociology of racism, demarcated by the changing nature of race and racism as constructed by social actors and social forces after World War II. The first phase—from the late nineteenth to the mid-twentieth century—typically considered racism as a set of overt individual-level attitudes; the second phase— from the mid-twentieth century to the present—considers racism as not simply explicit attitudes but also implicit biases and processes that are constructed, sustained, and enacted at both micro- and macro-levels.

While the first phase focused on the direct relationship between racism and racial inequality, the second phase considers diffuse relationships between these concepts and the ways in which historical, unconscious, institutional, and systemic forms of racism interact with other social forces to perpetuate racial inequality.[151]

The second phase looks at structural racism, which is also often called systemic racism. This systemic racism intersects with classism and every other kind of discrimination. The following examples are some of the ways that structural racism intersects with classism and shows up in schools:

- Forty percent of poor and minoritized students have an Algebra I teacher who is not certified in math.

- Many poor and minoritized students never have a teacher who has more than three years of experience. In many districts, beginning teachers are assigned to the schools with the highest levels of poverty and the largest populations of minoritized students. The way contract agreements are written with most districts, teachers can transfer to a different position after three years of teaching. This means they often teach for three years in a high-poverty area until they can transfer to another higher-income district or school, usually one with more white and affluent students than the school they're coming from.

- Seventy percent of students assigned to special education come from poverty, and a great percentage of those students are racially minoritized. It should be noted that in poverty, many parents request and sometimes demand that their children be placed in special education because they want to receive Supplemental Security Income (SSI) payments from the federal government.[152] In 2018 the government payment per month per SSI recipient was $750.[153]

- The percentage of racially minoritized individuals and individuals from poverty in gifted/talented programs is very small.

- A disproportionate number of suspensions and discipline referrals are from poor, minoritized males.

- A curriculum may focus heavily on the dominant cultural group to the exclusion of all others. For example, in history, the two canons that are studied are military and political. The other history canons—art, music, social, ethnic, etc.—are ignored. An African-American woman told me that her son refused to learn to read. When she finally got to the bottom of the issue, he said to her, "There aren't any books in my classroom with pictures of people who look like me."

- Minoritized students are also less likely to see teachers and administrators who look like them.

- Schools/districts may not offer advanced placement courses.

- Maintenance of school facilities may be inadequate, and textbooks may be damaged and/or outdated.

To address systemic racism, it is also important to understand how racism has been influential throughout history. James Loewen's *Lies My Teacher Told Me* is a good book on this topic.

Racism can also come into play when dealing with immigrant students. Along with race, immigration intersects with issues related to language, hidden rules, and more.

Intersectionality of Poverty and Immigration

As I write this, immigration and anti-immigrant attitudes are hot-button issues in the U.S. No matter what your personal and political feelings are on immigration, as an educator it is a professional responsibility to offer an equitable education to all of your students.

There are many issues that impact the ability of immigrant students to adapt to the K–12 setting:

- The amount of schooling the parent had in the country of origin

- The amount of trauma the student had before, during, and after the immigration process

- The level of the support system to which the student belongs (how strong and intact is the family?)

- The familiarity with the predominant language of the place to which the student is moving

- The number of hours that the parent or parents work

- The age of the student at the time of immigration

Often when immigrants come into the new country, unless they were wealthy in the country of origin, they tend to live in areas of high poverty because that is what is affordable. This may create more trauma for the student who has immigrated both in terms of limited resources and in terms of having a very different set of hidden rules than the ones the student is used to.

I was at a high school in Arizona that had just gotten two refugee sisters from a country in Africa where there had been ethnic cleansing. The district placed one girl in ninth grade and one in seventh grade. The girls were there without their parents and were staying with a relative. The younger sister would not leave the older sister without a huge, traumatic event. Finally, the school district allowed the girls to be together so the seventh-grader was with the ninth-grader all day, every day. The principal said to me, "Neither of them is going to pass the state assessment in Algebra I, even though they are both in the class. They are dealing with so many emotional issues related to the trauma of immigration and what occurred before immigration that they can barely function."

Maria Montaño-Harmon, a linguist at California State University, Fullerton, stated that in her research she found that if an immigrant family stayed in a high-poverty neighborhood for three generations, the third generation had less formal-register language than the original immigrant generation had.[154] In other words, the casual register of poverty becomes the daily language.

There is a big difference in how first-generation, second-generation, and third-generation immigrants think about their country of origin and the country in which they are now living. First-generation immigrants tend to have very tight family structures, relationships, support systems, etc. They may not have financial resources, but the other resources provide a great deal of stability to the family.

Dealing with Discrimination Related to Immigration

by Rickey Frierson

Sayar is a new refugee student from another country who has fled due to civil war. Everything is different. Sayar does not say much due to his unfamiliarity with the English language. He does not feel a sense of community because many of the students do not talk to him.

Sayar believes that the students are completely disrespectful in class with their side chats, passing notes, and asking questions without first being acknowledged by the teacher. Sayar is confused about why the teacher never calls on him to answer questions, while his teacher is concerned about why Sayar does not speak out more.

Sayar is hoping that gaining appreciation from his teacher will help him be better liked by his classmates. His teacher is hoping Sayar will become more social in class to build friendships and help with his adjustment.

Sayar is also confused by the political statements about immigrants made by other students. Sayar does not see himself as a threat to others, but rather as a person whose family is trying to avoid a life-threatening situation. Sayar hopes through his relationship with his teacher that he can help change the mindset of his classmates through his input, but the teacher never calls on him. Classroom dynamics are making it hard for Sayar to fit in and gain friends. His unfamiliarity with this new country makes him wonder how others view him without knowing anything about him.

If you have ever lived in another country and had to speak a new language for any length of time, you know how difficult the transition can be.

Adding a difference in language, along with possible racial, ethnic, and even religious differences, to the reality of survival makes the transition very lonely, layered with unknown hidden rules and riddled with self-doubt. *Can I do this? Will this work? Do I have a choice?*

On Health, Race, and Class

Healthcare disparities can be seen in the social determinants of health, which include access to healthcare, diet, exercise, prenatal care, environmental pollutants, and dental care, as well as preventive care for early recognition of health issues.

According to the Centers for Disease Control and Prevention:

> Understanding the demographic and socioeconomic composition of U.S. racial and ethnic groups is important because these characteristics are associated with health risk factors, disease prevalence, and access to care, which in turn drive health care utilization and expenditures ... Hispanic individuals are often found to have quite favorable health and mortality patterns in comparison with non-Hispanic white persons and particularly

with non-Hispanic black persons, despite having a disadvantaged socioeconomic profile—a pattern termed the epidemiologic paradox. The Department of Health and Human Services defines a racial or ethnic health disparity as 'a particular type of health difference that is closely linked with social, economic, and/or environmental disadvantage. Health disparities adversely affect groups of people who have systematically experienced greater obstacles to health based on their racial or ethnic group.'[155]

Please note that government data tends to be 2–3 years behind the current year, as it takes them that amount of time to track the data accurately.

At the intersection of race, poverty, and health are the following issues and statistics:

1. The better educated you are, the healthier you are. Education is a major social determinant of health.

2. The poorer you are, the worse your health is. Bad health reduces income and may lead to poverty. Seventy-five percent of personal bankruptcies are related to health issues.

3. Poorer people have less access to medical care. There are several ZIP codes in the U.S. that have no doctors. In rural areas it is not unusual for a visit to a doctor to require a drive of 2–3 hours.

4. Rates of cigarette smoking are higher among those who are less educated and have lower incomes.[156]

5. Suicide rates are higher in rural areas; homicide rates are higher in urban areas.

6. There are fewer dental visits in poverty.[157]

7. Obesity and diabetes rates are higher in poverty.

8. Levels of stress are much higher in marginalized populations (poor, minority, disability). "Certain stressful experiences—such as living in a disordered, impoverished neighborhood—are associated with the shortening of the telomeres, structures that sit on the tips of our chromosomes, which are bundles of DNA inside our cells. Often compared to the plastic caps on the ends of shoelaces, telomeres keep chromosomes from falling apart … Some researchers think stress shrinks telomeres, until they get so short that the cell dies, hastening the onset of disease."[158]

9. Access to parks and areas for physical activity is more limited in high-poverty areas.

10. There are more "food swamps" (areas where fast food restaurants outnumber healthier choices) and "food deserts" (areas where grocery stores are not available) in higher poverty areas and in racially segregated areas. More than 23 million people in the U.S., including 6.5 million children, live in food deserts that are more than a mile away from a supermarket.[159]

11. Poor diets and hunger lead to poor cognitive functioning and greater difficulties in learning. "In 2008, an estimated 49.1 million people, including 16.7 million children, experienced food insecurity (limited availability to safe and nutritionally adequate foods) multiple times throughout the year."[160]

Two School Nurses, Two Very Different Realities

The following stories are about two school nurses who are in very different settings dealing with very different students—and parents.

Betty

Betty is a school nurse at a very affluent elementary school. Today she dealt with the following: the allergies of a student who will die if he comes in contact with peanuts in any form (if he puts his forearm on a lunch table that has any peanut butter residue, for example) and the threat of litigation should there be an incident, the daily medications for a student with ADHD, a mother who wants to know word-for-word the conversation the nurse had with her child about the girl's menstrual cycle, and a parent who wants to know her credentials to be a nurse. Where was she educated? What kind of degree does she have? Does she have any pharmaceutical background? Is she authorized to dispense medications? What is the privacy policy of her office about medical issues? How does she protect medication from misuse by other students?

Betty also had to deal with an incident involving a sixth-grade student who had failed to take his medication and had to be carried out of the building to his mother's car. It took four people—one holding each leg and each arm—to carry the young man out of the building.

In Betty's refrigerator are medications, carefully labeled with student names and dosages. For several parents she documents *every day* the time and the amount of the medication that was dispensed to their child.

As though she oversees the lunchroom as well (she doesn't), several of the parents have given her written instructions about what their child is *not* allowed to eat.

Jennifer

Jennifer is an elementary school nurse in a very impoverished neighborhood with many minoritized residents. This morning she provided clean clothes to two students and underwear for five students because they had accidents on the way to school. She never has enough underwear for children.

In her refrigerator she keeps food from the "share table" in the cafeteria. The share table is where students can put food that they have not eaten on a table so that it can be shared. If another child is hungry, they can get extra food from the share table. After lunch is over, if there is still food on the share table, Jennifer will put it in her office refrigerator.

One of the issues in this school is that they have had to start having breakfast in the classrooms. Too many parents were bringing younger children with them for morning breakfast and taking part of the food from the elementary students' plates to feed the younger children. When students come into Jennifer's office hungry, a daily occurrence, she gives them food from the share table—if she has any.

Today she dealt again with a kindergartner who has juvenile diabetes. His blood sugar was off the chart when he came into her office. His mother does not care about his blood sugar and will not give him his shots or monitor his food, so the nurse is teaching the 5-year-old how to do it for himself. Every morning he checks in with her. She gives him a star each day that he takes his shot and eats before he comes to school. He can redeem the stars at the end of the week for a reward.

Today she also had a child with an infected tooth who was in a great deal of pain. When she called the mother, the mother said, "I know. Just have her rinse her mouth with salt water. I cannot afford a dentist."

Jennifer has a fourth-grader who was abused as a 3-year-old and was placed in foster care. The fourth-grader still has her bowel movements on the floor of the bathroom and not in the toilet. The principal asks the nurse if she will please help potty train the student.

She has a sixth-grade boy whose mother is bedridden. He takes care of her every day before he comes to school, all through the night, and every evening. He takes the government check that comes twice a month and walks to the neighborhood convenience store and buys food. He is exhausted and falls asleep in class. The boy begs the nurse not to say anything about his mother because he knows that he will be placed in foster care if the authorities find out.

Jennifer currently has three sick children in her office—one with a temperature over 101, one with a stomach virus, and one with pinkeye—because the parents sent them to school so the parents could go to work. When she calls them, only one parent returns her call. The parent cries and says that she could not miss work—otherwise her child would go hungry. So Jennifer keeps the child.

Two students were sent home today because she found lice in their hair. When she called the parents to come get their children, the parents told her that she was racist and that she was sending them home for a race issue. She explained that it was a legal, public health issue—that the children were contagious and they legally had to go home.

The police were also in today to interview Jennifer about a first-grade boy who was sold by his mother to two men. What contact did Jennifer have with the boy? Had she seen any warning signs?

Finally, Johnny came in today. He has been cutting himself again, and Jennifer has referred him to mental health services. She bandages his arm before school starts. It was bleeding through his shirt. He watched his brother get shot six months ago.

These two stories illustrate the different ways health issues intersect with other issues in both high- and low-poverty schools.

A disability can further complicate the intersectionality of health, race, and poverty. According to the "2016 Disability Statistics Annual Report":

- All disability types (hearing, vision, cognitive, ambulatory, self-care, and independent living) have increases in disability percentages with age; cognitive disabilities show the least change between age groups.

- About 7.6% of individuals under the age of 18 are disabled.

- The poverty rate of adults who are disabled is 21% compared to 13.4% of adults who are not disabled. Overall, the median income for a disabled working adult is about two thirds of that of a non-disabled working adult.[161]

What does that mean for a student whose parent is disabled? First of all, the student will take on adult roles in order to help with the household work. Second, for most students, there is simply less access to resources.

Sexism Against Females

Poverty around the world tends to be feminized, with more women in poverty than men because the burden of raising children usually falls on women. The highest percentage of children in poverty come from female-headed, single-parent households.[162] Poverty and gender often go hand in hand.

Families in Poverty by Family Structure

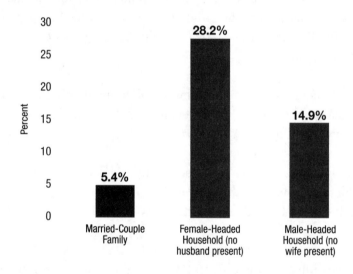

Source: U.S. Census Bureau, *Current Population Survey, 2015 and 2016, Annual Social and Economic Supplements* (Table 4).

Sexism, racism, and classism show up in pay-scale differences. On average, women earn just 80% as much as their male counterparts. For white women it is 79%, whereas for black women it is just 63%.[163] These differences occur all the way up to the few women and members of minoritized groups who are on boards of corporations.

Sexism Against Males

Sexism often shows up in school and has negative effects for males: 85% of educators are female, but 50% of the student population is male. However, the majority of discipline referrals, nonreaders, special education students, and dropouts are male. The obvious answer is that there is a form of systemic sexism at work.

If you are a minoritized male, particularly a black male, the odds against you becoming educated rise. In the U.S. only 17.2% of black males between the ages of 25 and 35 have a college degree. Compare that with the nearly half of white women the same age who have completed their degrees (44.7%), and you begin to see the long reach of a problem that starts in K–12.[164]

Students Suspended from School Compared to Student Population, by Race, Sex, and Disability Status, School Year 2013–14

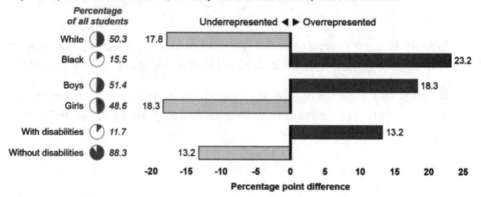

This chart shows whether each group of students was underrepresented or overrepresented among students suspended out of school. For example, boys were overrepresented by about 18 percentage points because they made up about 51% of all students, but nearly 70% of the students suspended out of school.

Source: U.S. Government Accountability Office, "K–12 Education."

This chart illustrates the intersectionality of race, gender, and disability in school discipline.[165]

A Common Thread

In many ways intersectionality is like the warp and weft of the fabric of our lives—many individual threads weave together, intersecting over and over to create the fabric of individuals and their environments. It is often very difficult, if not impossible, to separate the threads. It is not unusual for issues related to immigration, sexism, race, and poverty to be interwoven, especially in the U.S.

For our students, focusing on threads in ways that marginalize and minoritize may create a fabric that eventually destroys the opportunity to learn. Therefore, it is key for teachers to consider all factors when interventions and support systems are developed. The common thread of poverty and living closer to survival mode comes with some common threads across these issues, and those are the threads that we begin our work with in this book.

What Does This Information Mean in the School or Work Setting?

- Equity is not the same as equality. To treat students equitably, we need to take into account all of the factors that intersect to make each student's situation unique.

- Poverty is not a prerequisite for intersectionality. Remember that students from middle class and wealth also have intersecting aspects of their identities.

- Building relationships of mutual respect with students and their parents will help you better understand how intersectionality affects their lives inside and outside of the classroom.

Chapter 11

Poverty and the Brain: How Poverty Impacts Brain Development

In the last several years, studies exploring the relationship between the brain and socioeconomic status (SES) have multiplied, giving us much better data than we have ever had before. While there is still a great deal of debate about how to measure poverty and about how to measure brain performance (neurologically, with MRI scans, etc.), the information is getting better.

It should be noted that there are serious limitations in the research at this point in time. These include limited understandings of the effects of the timing and sequence of poverty on brain development; the lack of long-term studies; changes in methodology, technology, and measurement; and the fact that poverty does not occur in isolation and is so deeply interwoven with other issues.

Having said that, looking at the current research, one of the models that I think is easiest to understand comes from a review of the current research published in the journal *Pediatrics*.[166] The model "draws on a framework based on animal neuroscience research advanced by Sheridan and McLaughlin, which posits that the environments of poverty shape neurodevelopment by depriving the brain of key stimuli and increasing its exposure to negative input."[167]

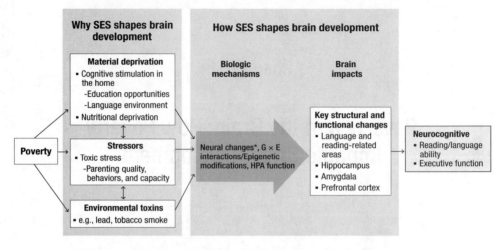

A framework based on animal neuroscience research. G × E, gene–environment interaction. *Neural changes = changes in neural plasticity, pruning, synaptic connections, dendritic branching, myelination.

Source: "State of the Art Review: Poverty and the Developing Brain" by S. Johnson et al.

Note that the neural changes the chart refers to are biologic mechanisms that are being changed by the environment of poverty. HPA function = hypothalamic-pituitary-adrenal glands.

In this article, the researchers looked at the studies published in the previous five years that were related to poverty and brain development. They state:

> As a group, children in poverty are more likely to experience developmental delay, perform worse on cognitive and achievement tests, and experience more behavioral and emotional problems than their more advantaged peers … In addition, child socioeconomic status (SES) is tied to educational attainment, health, and psychological well-being decades later … Poverty may shape the brain at the molecular, neural, cognitive, and behavioral levels.[168]

In other words, the environment changes the biology, which changes the structure and function of the brain, which impacts neurocognitive outcomes.

Why Does Socioeconomic Status Shape Brain Development?

What is it about poverty that impacts the development of the brain?

In this medical model, three aspects of the environment are addressed: (a) material deprivation, (b) stressors, and (c) environmental toxins. In the book *Scarcity*, authors Mullainathan and Shafir examine what happens to the brain when necessities—money, time, food, etc.—are scarce and the brain is forced to make choices between them.[169] The research indicates that facing these choices lowers the IQ of an individual by 13 points simply because the brain is on overload and is unable to process all of the information. Also, often when choices are forced, the time frame is very limited, so the speed at which you have to decide—sometimes for survival—is an additional stressor. If you have plenty of time and money, the stress of decision making tends to be reduced.

Material deprivation and stressors lead to instability over time. There are not enough resources in poverty. When there are fewer resources, it is more difficult to plan. Eventually, it can become a vicious cycle.

Material deprivation is not just about money and time but also about access to language and educational opportunities. As discussed elsewhere in the book, Hart and Risley found that a child in a welfare household hears about half the amount of language a child in a working class home hears (13 million words by age 4 compared with 26 million words), and fewer than one third of the words a child in a professional household hears (45 million words).[170] Language is the tool by which experience is mediated and labeled. It is critical for school performance.

Beyond exposure to language in the home, other formal and informal educational opportunities are often limited in poverty. The following stories illustrate how both rural and urban poverty can cut people off from education.

A Story from a Rural Area

Susan is the oldest of four children in a rural area, and at 7 years old she is very bright. Neither her mother or father have gone to college, but both graduated from high school. Her father farms, and her mother is a stay-at-home mom. Susan and her three siblings are being homeschooled with materials purchased at the local teachers' supply store and through a local homeschooling network. Susan's grandmother subscribes to a book service for Susan. Susan loves to read, but recently her father took her books away from her because she was reading too late at night.

Her brother, a year younger, is mechanically inclined and street smart. He is 6 years old but does not know how to add or subtract yet, and he does not know how many pennies are in a nickel, dime, or quarter.

All four children play with their cousins and go to church every Sunday. There are no trips to the zoo, ball games, or movies, and there is very little travel. The nearest big town is one hour away, and the family will not drive to it because the car is unreliable. They have TV but no cable. They have a tablet but no Internet access. They *do* know how to grow a garden and do chores, and they like to play board games when the chores are done.

A Story from an Urban Area

Dahlia is 7 years old and lives in a city of about 300,000 people in Texas. She lives in the poorest part of the city. She rarely goes farther than five blocks from her home except on school field trips. The Gulf Coast is only about 10 miles from where she lives, but she has never seen it. She has cable TV. Her mother works two jobs, and her grandmother keeps Dahlia and her three siblings after school. They do not have a car. She has been to McDonald's only twice, but she has been to Mexico once.

As both of these stories indicate, educational opportunities—e.g., camp, sports, theater, music, art, travel, etc.—are often almost nonexistent in poverty. Educational opportunities provide language *and* schemas. What is a schema? Schemas are the cognitive structures (conceptual frameworks) that the brain creates to store information. In the brain research on learning, the prefrontal cortex can take in only so much information.

Generally, the more experiences one has, the greater the amount of information that can be absorbed, and the more quickly the information is absorbed. Experience moves the learning from details to larger groups of concepts ("wheel" leads to "car," and that leads to "airplane," etc., which leads to the overarching idea of transportation). The brain sorts in patterns, and so the greater the number of patterns, the greater the learning.

Being exposed to many different patterns isn't the only important factor, however. Something as basic as the food that we eat can impact cognitive development.

Nutritional Deficiencies

Access to adequate, nutritional food (fruits, vegetables, and protein) is limited in poverty because of cost, access, and preparation issues.

Of particular concern is prenatal care, specifically the protein intake by the mother during pregnancy, which is related to the thickness of the myelin sheaths that form around the nerve cells in vitro. The thickness of these myelin sheaths is highly correlated to the speed with which a person can process information—i.e., intelligence.

A part of many people's nutritional deficiencies has to do with food insecurity—there simply is not enough food. The data in the following graphic are by household.[171]

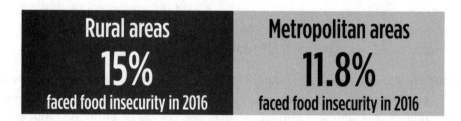

Source: "Rural Hunger in America" by Food Research and Action Center.

Food insecurity is linked to poorer health, less exercise, and lower grades. Mothers who are food insecure are more likely to be in poor/fair health and suffer from depression. Being overweight and obese is often linked to food insecurity.[172]

Johnson et al. write:

> Micronutrients such as vitamin B_{12}, folate, retinoic acid, omega-3 fatty acids, zinc, and iron play a role in regulating gene expression that guides brain development in modulating neuroplasticity, dendritic arborization, synaptogenesis, and myelination ... For example, early childhood iron deficiency is associated with poor academic performance; cognitive, emotional, and attention problems; and less educational attainment in adulthood.[173]

Stressors

Several studies have identified how environmental stressors change people's processing and physical response to all kinds of situations. Allostatic load—basically, stress—increases significantly in poverty. Schamberg writes:

> Allostasis is an attempt by the brain to readjust physiological parameters within neuroendocrine, autonomic nervous, metabolic, cardiovascular, and immune systems in order to meet the changing demands of the environment (Sterling and Eyer, 1988) ... A chronically active allostatic state is known as *allostatic load.*[174]

To be more specific, allostatic load

> refers to the costs of trying to adapt to chronically stressful life events; biologically speaking, this process manifests as cumulative wear and tear on regulatory systems in the body (McEwen & Stellar, 1993). Unpredictability in the environment requires immediate physiological response (allostasis) to promote adaptation.[175]

Schamberg's study was done in rural Upstate New York and took place between 1997 and 2006 with 339 children (52% male, 97% white) in three waves. "The findings ... suggest that poverty, over the course of childhood and early adolescence, increases allostatic load, and this dysregulation, in turn, explains some of the subsequent deficits in working memory four years later."[176]

Stressors can come from multiple sources, including neighborhood effects, early puberty, household violence, mental illness, drug addiction, etc. Low-income neighborhoods have more violence, crime, gangs, early pregnancies, food deserts, homelessness, mobility, and sex offenders, as well as less healthcare access.

The study "Parenting in Poverty: Attention Bias and Anxiety Interact to Predict Parents' Perceptions of Daily Parenting Hassles" adds to the literature on neurocognitive models of parenting. This is the neuroscience of parents in poverty.

A quick summary: The study looks at "primarily low-income Latino/a parents of young children living in urban areas of concentrated disadvantage."[177] Basically, the more the parents were stressed over things such as physical safety, financial hardship, or partner violence, the more they perceived parenting to be a hassle. When parents could not regulate their emotions and anxiety, their interactions rode a wave related to cortisol and their inability to pay attention to their children. Basically, if they were able to give the children attention, they did not see parenting as so big of a hassle as those who paid more attention to their own anxiety or angry feelings. Finegood et al. write:

Specifically, parents who reported higher levels of anxiety (including persistent feelings of nervousness, worry, and restlessness) reported significantly higher amounts of hassles in the parenting role on average. This finding is in keeping with prior research with clinical and nonclinical samples, where difficulty modulating feelings of anxiety has been argued to exert a debilitating effect on adults' cognitions about parenting and their parenting behavior.[178]

Additional stressors include overcrowded homes, violence, neighborhood disorder, and mobility.

Environmental Toxins

Factors in the environment of poverty can have a big impact as well. Among the findings:

Low-income families have greater risk of iron deficiency, which can increase the absorption of lead, which impacts neurofunction. "Lead alters the transmission of glutamate and dopamine, resulting in changes in the neuronal plasticity and synaptic communication with particular effects on the prefrontal cortex, hippocampus and cerebellum."[179]

Smoking and second-hand smoke both negatively impact cognitive outcomes for children. More undereducated adults smoke than educated adults, so there is a higher percentage of adults who smoke in poverty. "The greater the exposure to different substances in utero—as, for example, to two legal drugs, alcohol and cigarettes—the greater the loss of brain volume and cortical grey matter."[180]

Maternal obesity is more prevalent in lower-income communities and among less-educated women. "Obese women frequently have or are developing diabetes, and either situation leads to more problems in pregnancy, including serious birth defects, preterm births, and growth retardation."[181]

Lower-income women have more stress during pregnancy—another factor that results in children with low birth weight. Low birth weight causes cognitive and behavioral difficulties in children.[182]

Pollutants in the environment include mercury in food, lead, polychlorinated biphenyls (PCBs), pesticides, and anything that decreases air quality. Both lead and mercury poisoning can appear in children as ADHD, hyperactivity, and lack of impulse control. Children of parents who were exposed to pesticides may be more likely to develop chronic health issues.

Air quality and the number of children with asthma are related. Asthma is found in greater concentration among children in poverty because of airborne pollution like household mold, mouse and rat droppings, and pollution from industry and traffic. When interstate highways run through cities, they often traverse poor neighborhoods.

How Does Socioeconomic Status Shape Brain Development?

By changing the biology, chemistry, structure, and function of the brain.

Three ways are often cited: neural changes, epigenetics, and glandular function (hypothalamic-pituitary-adrenal axis, or HPA).

Epigenetics

Epigenetics is "the study of changes in organisms caused by modification of gene expression rather than alteration of the genetic code itself."[183] Another explanation is that epigenetics investigates how the environment can "turn genes on and off."

> Here's an analogy that might further help you to understand what epigenetics is. Think of the human lifespan as a very long movie. The cells would be the actors and actresses, essential units that make up the movie. DNA, in turn, would be the script—instructions for all the participants of the movie to perform their roles. Subsequently, the DNA sequence would be the words on the script, and certain blocks of these words that instruct key actions or events to take place would be the genes. The concept of genetics would be like screenwriting. Follow the analogy so far? Great. The concept of *epi*genetics, then, would be like directing. The script can be the same, but the director can choose to eliminate or tweak certain scenes or dialogue, altering the movie for better or worse.[184]

Poverty can lead to epigenetic changes. In other words, poverty can turn genes "on and off." Some of these genes affect neural changes (synaptic plasticity, neuroplasticity, neurogenesis) and glandular functions (like the HPA axis, as discussed earlier).

Prenatal stress can "program" the HPA axis to produce more hyperactivity in this region of the brain. Stress, disruptions to the parent-child relationship, and parenting behaviors all impact the brain as well. Children raised in poverty are more likely to experience harsh and inconsistent discipline, and that can overstimulate the HPA axis. Negative parenting is linked to less gray and white matter in the brain and a smaller hippocampal volume in adulthood.[185]

About the Brain

All functions of the brain are either a chemical or electrical interaction. A chemical interaction occurs on the face of the cell and continues down the tail (axon) of the cell as an electrical impulse. When the electrical impulse enters the dendrites and synapses, causing their structure to permanently change, learning has occurred.

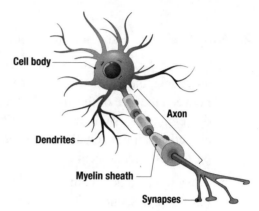

Therefore, learning is physiological. That's why it takes so long to "unlearn" something that has been learned incorrectly.

Poverty impacts these four brain areas:

1. Left occipitotemporal and perisylvian regions of the brain: where language and reading are processed.

2. Left perisylvian/language system: "a complex, distributed system encompassing semantic, syntactic, and phonological aspects of language."[186]

3. Parietal/spatial cognition: "mentally represent and manipulate the spatial relationships among objects."[187]

4. Occipitotemporal/visual cognition: "pattern recognition and visual mental imagery, translating image from visual representations into more abstract representations of object shape and identity, and reciprocally translating visual memory knowledge into mental images."[188]

These areas of the brain may also be affected:

1. **Hippocampus** – learning and memory

   a. Medial temporal/memory system "is responsible for one-trial learning, the ability to retain a representation of a stimulus after one exposure to it (which contrasts with the ability to gradually strengthen a representation through conditioning-like mechanisms), and is dependent on the hippocampus and related structures."[189]

   b. In one study students from poverty were found to have smaller hippocampi, which is associated with more behavioral problems.[190]

   c. Furthermore, nurturance is positively related to the development and size of the hippocampus.[191]

d. In other words, the volume of the hippocampus, where learning memory occurs, is lower if the child was in poverty. The good news is that nurturance—not money—causes this area of the brain to grow. If there is more nurturance in early childhood, this makes a difference in the brain.

2. **Amygdala** – fear and emotional processing

   a. Because the amygdala is where emotions are processed, having a larger amygdala means that more processing occurs there. The relationship between the size of the amygdala and the hippocampus predicts emotional dysregulation, such as greater levels of depression. The higher the amygdala-hippocampal volume ratio, the more processing of emotions, particularly fear, occurs.[192]

   b. The amygdala is structured initially before the age of 3 and is restructured during adolescence. Children with depressed mothers tend to have larger amygdalae than children with no exposure to maternal depression. These children with depressed mothers also have higher levels of cortisol output. Cortisol creates anxiety.[193]

   c. Insecure bonding and attachment is also linked to the development of a larger amygdala. Interestingly, "stressful life events associated with increased activation to fearful faces in the right amygdala; traumatic life events positively associated with left amygdala activity in sad faces."[194]

3. **Prefrontal cortex** – executive functioning; the prefrontal cortex does three things:

   a. Working memory: holds information ready, maintains it over an interval, and manipulates it. (This is not long-term memory.)[195]

   b. Cognitive control: "Resist the most routine or easily available response in favor of a more task-appropriate response."[196]

   c. Reward processing: "regulating our responses in the face of rewarding stimuli ... resisting the immediate pull of an attractive stimulus to maximize more long-term gains."[197]

At the University of California, Berkeley, researchers compared low-income 9- and 10-year-old brains with wealthy children's brains using EEGs.[198] Mark Kishiyama, lead researcher, stated,

> It is similar to a pattern that's seen in patients with strokes that have had lesions in their prefrontal cortex [which deals with executive function] ... It suggests that in these kids, prefrontal function is reduced or disrupted in some way.[199]

However, this is not the end of the story. The article goes on to say, "Such deficiencies are reversible through intensive intervention such as focused lessons and games that encourage children to think out loud or use executive function."[200]

What Does This Information Mean in the School or Work Setting?

- You have to teach students to plan (build executive function) because the prefrontal cortex is not as developed.

- Visual images (mental models) can be used to translate new ideas to the concrete. Visual imaging capability is not affected by poverty. Because the hippocampus is not as developed for learning and memory, visuals help students learn.

- Vocabulary acquisition can be taught by using sketching, a visual activity.

- Procedural processes must be taught (these build executive function in the prefrontal cortex). Details can be managed using visuals and step sheets.

- Well-organized, non-chaotic schools and classrooms reduce allostatic load. Classroom management is a must because it allows working memory to function better.

- Link reward systems to planning by giving rewards to recognize completion of a plan. This helps develop the prefrontal cortex.

- Use visuals to translate from the concrete sensory world to the abstract representational world of paper, ideas, numbers, letters, drawings, etc.

- Question making helps students deal with nonroutine tasks and problem solving (builds executive function).

- There will be more behavioral issues in poverty because of the larger amygdala and smaller hippocampus. Regulation of behavior must be taught.

- The role of nurturance—relationships—in the modulation of allostatic load and gene expression is important in learning.

- You have to manage the irrelevant working memory load. Working memory is like the neck of a bottle in that it limits what can get into the brain—usually about 4–5 pieces of new information at one time. When working memory gets overloaded, it shuts off any new information within 12 seconds. Stress (allostatic load) will further reduce the amount down to one or two pieces of information at a time.

- As you can see in the following graphic, working memory takes in information in two main channels: auditory and visual. When we ask students who are new to the information we are providing to use a third channel, the information dropouts start. For example, if the teacher is lecturing (auditory) and using a slide presentation (visual) and asks the student to take notes (kinesthetic), the student for whom this is new learning will not be able to absorb it all and will start losing information. It is much better to have the students listen to the lecture and see the presentation. After the presentation, give them the notes, and have them work with a partner to highlight the notes.

Human Learning Process

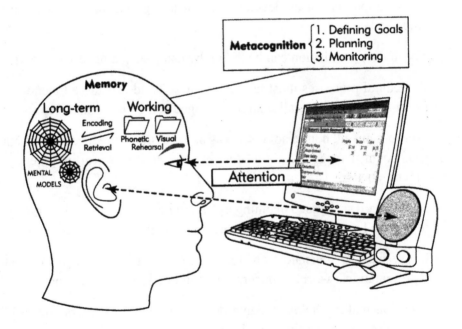

Source: *Building Expertise: Cognitive Methods for Training and Performance* (pp. 50–51), by R. C. Clark, 2008, San Francisco, CA: Pfeiffer. Copyright 2008 by John Wiley & Sons. Reprinted with permission.

Chapter 12

The Parents of Children in Poverty: How to Understand Where They're Coming From

As the demographics in the United States continue to shift, it is important to know who the parents of children in poverty are. Since 41% of children under the age of 18 are either in near poverty or are poor, for every five children, two are having difficulty getting their needs met. The 22% of children in near poverty come from families whose income is less than 200% of the federal poverty threshold. Usually this income is not sufficient to meet basic needs. The other 19% of children are in poverty, which means their families' income is less than 100% of the federal poverty threshold.[201] The free meals these children eat at school are often the only meals they get.

Children by Family Income, 2016

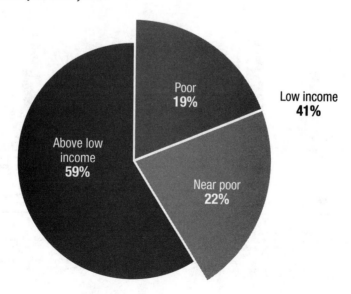

Source: U.S. Census Bureau, "2016 American Community Survey 1-Year Estimates, Poverty Status in the Past 12 Months."

Federal Poverty Thresholds, 2017

Single individual under age 65: $12,752

Single parent with two related children: $19,749

Two parents, two related children: $24,858[202]

Because schools are dependent upon parents as supporters in the education of the child, it is important to know about them both as individuals and also as a group.

What Are the Education Levels of Parents in Poverty by Race?

The table below is from the National Center for Education Statistics (NCES).[203] As you can see, the lower the level of education, the greater the likelihood that the child will be in poverty. This means the interventions that the school designs to work with parents need to be adapted so they can be understood by those who may not have completed high school.

Percentage of Children Under Age 18, in Families Living in Poverty, by Child's Race/ Ethnicity and Parent's Highest Level of Educational Attainment, 2016

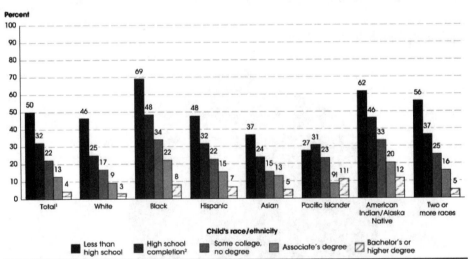

I Interpret data with caution. The coefficient of variation (CV) for this estimate is between 30 and 50 percent.
¹ Total includes races/ethnicities not reported separately.
² Includes parents who completed high school through equivalency programs, such as a GED program.
NOTE: Parents' highest level of educational attainment is the highest level of education attained by any parent residing in the same household as the child. Parents include adoptive and stepparents but exclude parents not residing in the same household as their child. The measure of child poverty includes all children who are related to the householder by birth, marriage, or adoption (except a child who is the spouse of the householder). The householder is the person (or one of the people) who owns or rents (maintains) the housing unit. For additional information about poverty status, see https://www.census.gov/topics/income-poverty/poverty/guidance/poverty-measures.html. Race categories exclude persons of Hispanic ethnicity. Although rounded numbers are displayed, the figures are based on unrounded estimates.

Source: "The Condition of Education 2018" by the National Center for Education Statistics.

You can also see that the highest percentage of children living with parents who did not complete high school were black. By contrast, the lowest percentage of children living with parents who didn't complete high school were Pacific Islanders. Education level and income level are closely related, but being under-educated should not be equated with lack of intelligence. The main difference is that the language and documents that are used by the educated are often in formal register. Many times people in poverty can use only casual register, but that doesn't make them less intelligent than people from other classes who may have had more education.

What Are Family Structures Like in Poverty?

Single-parent households have more poverty than households that have two adults. This is true of mother-only households and father-only households in all races/ethnicities, and it is not a moral issue about what kind of family structure is better than another. It is simply an issue of logistics. When there are two adults in the household, there is more time and money for the children, as you can see in the following table from NCES.[204]

Percentage of Children Under Age 18, in Families Living in Poverty, by Child's Race/Ethnicity and Family Structures, 2016

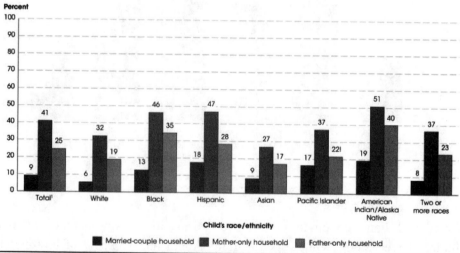

! Interpret data with caution. The coefficient of variation (CV) for this estimate is between 30 and 50 percent.
¹ Total includes races/ethnicities not reported separately.
NOTE: A "mother-only household" has a female householder, with no spouse present (i.e., the householder is unmarried or their spouse is not in the household), while a "father-only household" has a male householder, with no spouse present. Includes all children who live either with their parent(s) or with a householder to whom they are related by birth, marriage, or adoption (except a child who is the spouse of the householder). Children are classified by their parents' marital status or, if no parents are present in the household, by the marital status of the householder who is related to the children. The householder is the person (or one of the people) who owns or rents (maintains) the housing unit. For additional information about poverty status, see https://www.census.gov/topics/income-poverty/poverty/guidance/poverty-measures.html. Race categories exclude persons of Hispanic ethnicity. Although rounded numbers are displayed, the figures are based on unrounded estimates.

Source: "The Condition of Education 2018" by the National Center for Education Statistics.

There is a direct correlation between the ratio of adults to children and student achievement. The higher the ratio of adults to children, the greater the level of achievement of the child.

Are the Parents Working?

Whether or not the parents are employed is a big factor. According to Koball and Jiang from the National Center for Children in Poverty (NCCP), "Children with a full-time, year-round employed parent are less likely to live in a low-income family, compared to children with parents who work part-time/part-year or who are not employed."[205]

Percentage of Children Under Age 18, in Families Living in Poverty, by Child's Race/Ethnicity and Family Structures, 2016

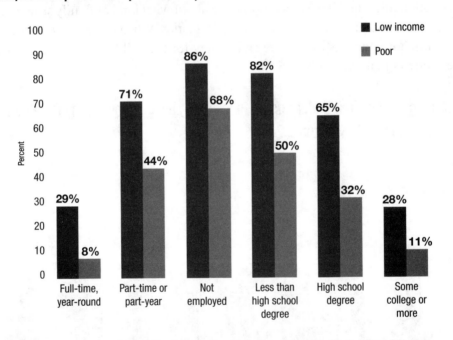

Source: "Basic Facts About Low-Income Children" by H. Koball & Y. Jiang.

Koball and Jiang go on to say, "Nevertheless, many low-income and poor children have parents who work full-time. About half (53.5%) of low-income children and 32% of poor children live with at least one parent employed full-time, year-round."[206]

The more education the adult has, the less likelihood there is that the family will be in poverty.

Where Do People in Poverty Live?

Mostly in the South (see map below). Rural poverty is now equivalent to the urban poverty of the 1980s.[207]

Percentage of Children Under Age 18, in Families Living in Poverty, by State, 2016

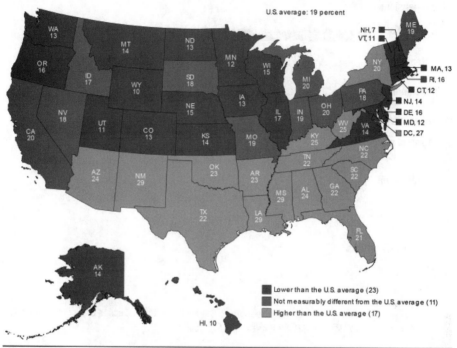

NOTE: The measure of child poverty includes all children who are related to the householder by birth, marriage, or adoption (except a child who is the spouse of the householder). The householder is the person (or one of the people) who owns or rents (maintains) the housing unit. For additional information about poverty status, see https://www.census.gov/topics/income-poverty/poverty/guidance/poverty-measures.html.
SOURCE: U.S. Department of Commerce, Census Bureau, American Community Survey (ACS), 2016. See *Digest of Education Statistics 2017*, table 102.40.

How Do People in Poverty Spend Their Money?

Housing, transportation, and food are the three biggest expenditures for all U.S. Americans—except in the highest-earning 30% of households, which spend more on insurance and pensions than they spend on food.[208]

In poverty, the expenditures for housing, food, and transportation are disproportional to the income. When 41% of income goes to housing, 16% to food, and 14% to transportation, there is not much left over for clothing, medical expenses, or continuing education. If you are working fewer than 40 hours a week, it is even more problematic because you usually have less money and no benefits.

Percent of Annual Household Spending by Income

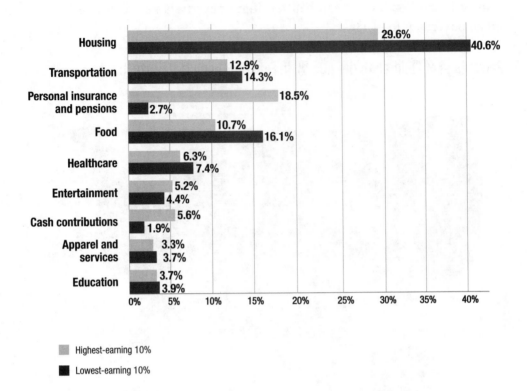

Source: "Consumer Expenditure Survey Table 1110. Deciles of Income Before Taxes" by U.S. Bureau of Labor Statistics.

Mobility

Having a stable environment is so important for child development. But, according to Koball and Jiang, "children living in low-income families are 50% more likely than other children to have moved in the past year and nearly three times as likely to live in families that rent, rather than own, a home."[209]

Residential Instability and Home Ownership by Family Income, 2016

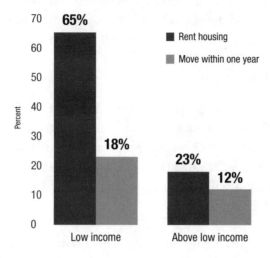

Source: "Basic Facts About Low-Income Children" by H. Koball & Y. Jiang.

What Are the Data on Immigrant Parents?

As the following charts indicate, naturalized citizens have higher levels of educational attainment than noncitizens. The charts are from U.S. Census data as tabulated by the Migration Policy Institute (MPI).[210] The trend in immigration right now is that more college-educated immigrants are coming into the United States.

Educational Attainment by U.S. Citizenship Status
(Foreign-Born Adults, Age 25 and Older)

Naturalized citizens	19,691,977	Noncitizens	18,484,193
Less than high school diploma	20%	Less than high school diploma	38.3%
High school diploma or GED	21.7%	High school diploma or GED	23.2%
Some college or associate's degree	23.1%	Some college or associate's degree	14.1%
Bachelor's degree	20.6%	Bachelor's degree	13.6%
Graduate or professional degree	14.6%	Graduate or professional degree	10.9%

Source: "Data Hub State Immigration Data Profiles: United States" by Migration Policy Institute.

The report "Immigration Data Matters" from MPI supports the idea that more immigrants move into the middle class and working class rather than into deep poverty because of their education level. Only undocumented immigrant families seem to arrive and stay in poverty longer than other groups.[211]

According to Batalova and Alperin:

> The foreign-born share of the U.S. population is at its highest level since 1910, with the approximately 44 million immigrants living in the United States representing 13.5% of the overall population. With U.S. fertility rates at a historic low, the [U.S.] Census Bureau projects that net international migration will be the main driver behind U.S. population growth between 2027 and 2038.[212]

They go on: "About 16% of immigrant families had an annual income below the federal poverty line, compared to 12–14% among the U.S. born."[213]

Sibley and Brabeck write:

> Immigrant groups with the highest proportion of unauthorized parents (Mexican and Dominican immigrants) had the least access to institutional resources such as checking accounts, savings accounts, credit cards, and driver's licenses. Low levels of access to these resources predicted more economic hardship and more parental psychological distress, which in turn were associated with lower scores on child cognitive outcomes.[214]

The Center for American Progress investigates the numbers: "In 2015, the poverty rate for immigrants was 17.3%, compared with 14.3% for the U.S.-born population."[215]

How Do Parents Tend to Parent in Poverty?

In "Targeting Parenting in Early Childhood: A Public Health Approach to Improve Outcomes for Children Living in Poverty," Morris et al. look at families in poverty and how their parenting behaviors impact their children. The study used parent self-reporting and observational assessments. Single-parent families with a father do better than single-parent families with a mother. Maternal depressive symptoms may be a part of the difference.[216]

A study found that married-couple households, regardless of socioeconomic factors, fare better than other models in shielding children from adverse factors such as lack of healthcare or lower cognitive outcomes.

Krueger et al. conclude:

> U.S. children increasingly live in family structures that are associated with poor child well-being. The links between childhood circumstances and socioeconomic and health outcomes in later life mean that children's disadvantages may persist throughout their lives.[217]

The following table is worth revisiting. It is based on information from the book *Unequal Childhoods* by Annette Lareau.[218]

	Concerted cultivation	Accomplishment of natural growth
Key elements	▪ Parent actively fosters and assesses child's talents, opinions, and skills	▪ Parent cares for child and allows child to grow
Organization of daily life	▪ Multiple child leisure activities orchestrated by adults	▪ "Hanging out," particularly with kin, by child
Language use	▪ Reasoning, directives ▪ Child contestation of adult statements ▪ Extended negotiations between parents and child	▪ Directives ▪ Rare questioning or challenging of adults by child ▪ General acceptance by child of directives
Interventions in institutions	▪ Criticisms and interventions on behalf of the child ▪ Training of child to take on this role	▪ Dependence on institutions ▪ Sense of powerlessness and frustration ▪ Conflict between child-rearing practices at home and school
Consequences	▪ Emerging sense of entitlement on the part of the child	▪ Emerging sense of constraint on the part of the child

Source: *Unequal Childhoods* by Annette Lareau.

If the parents come from poverty themselves, they tend to have these patterns. Lareau studied both black and white families at both the poverty and middle-class levels of economics. What the study found is that the differentiating factor in discipline was not race but economic level. Both black and white families in the middle class taught their children to negotiate institutions while both black and white families from poverty taught their children to react strongly to or avoid institutions.

What Are the Patterns When Parents Grew Up in Poverty?

If you grew up in poverty, you'll have a harder time escaping it as an adult than someone who grew up in middle class or wealth. In other words, it's harder to get out of generational poverty than it is to get out of situational poverty. The more years you spend in poverty as a child, the more difficult it will be to get out.[219]

If you were poor as a child	Likelihood of being poor at ages 20 and 25
Never in poverty	5%
In poverty 1–7 years	13%
In poverty 8–14 years	46% at age 20; 40% at age 25

Source: "How Poverty Can Follow Children into Adulthood" by P. Boghani.

Poverty often follows children into adulthood. The chart above also shows that only 6% of the poor adults who experienced the most poverty as children were able to get out of poverty between ages 20 and 25. Compare that with the 40% who couldn't escape. Boghani goes on to state:

1. "The longer you grow up in poverty, the harder it is to graduate … 37% of children who were never poor graduated from college by age 25. Only 3% of children from persistently poor backgrounds were able to do the same."[220]

2. "Growing up poor can carry long-term health implications … children who grow up in poverty are also more likely to develop chronic illnesses such as asthma or obesity—the latter can lead to further health problems, including diabetes and heart disease."[221]

3. "Poverty can also harm a child's brain development and lifelong mental health."[222]

What Does This Information Mean in the School or Work Setting?

- Resources are tools that individuals use to stabilize their lives. Find out about parents' resources. Show parents the list of resources in the book (emotional, physical, etc.), and ask them to help you identify the resources they have a lot of. For example, maybe a family doesn't have financial resources, but they are strong emotionally, and positive role models are available. Find out what resources they have to help their child. Often, the parents have more resources than they know.

- Rather than ask parents for their "educational attainment level," ask them how many years they went to school. That is better for immigrant parents too because schooling patterns and levels are different in other parts of the world.

- Understand that immigrant parents will discipline differently than parents who grew up in the United States. Provide guidelines about what is legal and not legal to do with your children in the U.S.

- Make sure all documents that are sent home from school are in simple, clear language and include graphics and visuals. Stay away from complex, formally written documents.

- Understand that housing costs and transportation create more student mobility between schools, reduce school access, and make it harder for everyone to meet the timetables of school.

- It is worth saying again: When you are dealing with a parent from poverty, do not assume that the educational level is the same as the intelligence level. It is not.

Conclusion

One of the topics as yet untouched is the need to grieve and go through the grieving process as one teaches or works with the poor. The Kübler-Ross stages in the grieving process are anger, denial, bargaining, depression, and acceptance.[223]

As one meets and works with a particular family or individual, there is such frustration and, ultimately, grieving because many situations are so embedded, even intractable, as to seem hopeless. It's like dealing with the mythical Hydra; each time a head is removed, two more appear. Particularly for the adults, so many choices have been made that virtually preclude any resolution that would be acceptable from an educated perspective. Yet the role of the educator or social worker or employer is not to save the individual but rather to offer a support system, role models, and opportunities to learn, which will increase the likelihood of the person's success. Ultimately, the choice always belongs to the individual.[224]

Yet another notion among the middle class, wealthy class, and educated is that if the poor had a choice, they would live differently. Financial resources would certainly help make a difference. Even with financial resources, however, not every individual who received those finances would choose to live differently. There is a freedom of verbal expression, an appreciation of individual personality, a heightened and intense emotional experience, and a sensual, kinesthetic approach to life usually not found among the middle class, the wealthy, the educated. These patterns are so enmeshed and intertwined in the daily life of the poor that to have those cut off would be akin to losing a limb. Even some who have the opportunity choose not to live a different life—in the way that some middle-class people (with the opportunity) prefer not to join the wealthy class and all that comes with it. And, to be sure, for some in poverty, alcoholism, laziness, lack of motivation, addictions, etc., in effect make the choices *for* them.[225]

It is the responsibility of educators and others who work with the poor to teach the differences and skills/rules that will allow each individual to make the choice. As things now stand for many of those in poverty, the choice never exists.[226]

Appendixes

Appendix A

Resources and Interventions

For each case study (see Chapter 1), let's debrief the resources and look at possible interventions.

Case Study #1: Alexa

Resource	Alexa (student)	Sharon (mother)
Financial	1 very limited, but they have food and shelter	1
Emotional	2	2 lots of stress in this environment; no time or help to grieve; happened overnight
Mental/cognitive	4 is very gifted	2 can read/write/compute but little work experience
Spiritual (future story)	3 has hope that with better education comes a better life	3 going to secretarial school
Physical	4 body is healthy	4
Support systems	1 very thin; her mother is supporting her as best she can	0 no support system for the mother
Relationships/ role models	3 strong positive bond between mother and daughter; mother is a role model; good relationships at school	3
Knowledge of hidden rules at school and work	4 both understand these rules	4
Language/ formal register	4 identification of being gifted is almost always linked to formal-register vocabulary	4

This is an example of situational poverty that occurs almost overnight. The hurricane and then the suicide put Alexa and her mother, Sharon, into extreme poverty with few resources.

What are the strengths in this situation? First of all, Alexa is very bright so she needs to develop a clear and detailed future story in order to have a plan. Plans allow one to focus on the long term where there would be hope. Alexa is doing well in school and has tremendous potential. Second, she has the language to debrief the experience with a counselor to begin the grieving process.

What are the needs in this situation? The needs are transportation (part of a support system), grief counseling, and employment for the mother.

What are the interventions that might need to be made?

1. Alexa needs to make certain she knows her counselor and vice versa.

2. Alexa needs to develop a future story.

3. A peer group of other students who have lost a parent could be established once a month at lunch as a way to emotionally begin working through the experience.

4. Perhaps a parent whose child is staying after school could drop off Alexa from the longer session.

Case Study #2: Duane

Resource	Duane (student)	Roney (father)
Financial	1	1 money is tight, and work is unstable
Emotional	2 frustration with school	4 has no emotional issues that interfere with work
Mental/cognitive	2 learning disability	? dropped out of high school but could be very mentally able
Spiritual (future story)	3 has a future story	?
Physical	4 athletically gifted	3 can and does work
Support systems	0 is the support system for his siblings	0 no support system for him
Relationships/ role models	3 lots of support at school; Dad loves him	? loves his children

Resource	Duane (student)	Roney (father)
Knowledge of hidden rules at school and work	2 some; gets in trouble at school	3 knows them enough to have work
Language/ formal register	2	2

Duane and his father, Roney, are an example of a household where there is virtually no support system for either the student or the parent. When a child is forced to act as a parent, in effect, in order for the household to survive, the normal emotional development is suspended while acting as an adult. The child doesn't have a childhood. There is a great amount of resentment and anger around that issue for the child. Further, the child is forced to make decisions for siblings and help them when there has been little or no instruction or preparation. When the child is the support system for the siblings, the child's own homework doesn't get done. Learning disabilities often lead to emotional frustration, which Duane evidences. His salvation is athletics, in which he excels.

The strengths in this situation are Duane's abilities in sports, the support the father is providing (the father has not abandoned the children), and the football coach.

The needs in this situation are learning supports for Duane, transportation after football practice, and childcare while Duane goes to practice.

Interventions could include:

1. Because Duane is LD (learning disabled), homework demands need to be modified so that he can finish the work.

2. Provide nonfiction text that relates to football and sports, as well as academic subjects because he is motivated in those areas. The research on reading indicates that simply the act of reading is a key determinant in reading achievement.

3. Work with community agencies to find after-school childcare for the siblings so that Duane can attend some of the football practices.

4. Arrange for a high school student who needs National Honor Society service credits (who also is involved in sports) to tutor Duane before school or on weekends (when the father is home to watch the children) in order both to build a relationship with Duane and to provide Duane with a role model who does well in school.

Case Study #3: Michael

Resource	Michael	Father
Financial	1 has food and shelter	2 has a job; stressed finances
Emotional	2 although he is classified ED (emotionally disabled), his emotional responses do stabilize as he gets older and away from his mother	3 can hold a job
Mental/cognitive	2 has learning disabilities	?
Spiritual (future story)	3 wants to go into the military	?
Physical	3 small for his age	3 can hold a job
Support systems	4 his stepmother's parents are a strong support system	3 has the support of his mother and his wife's parents
Relationships/ role models	3 has his father, stepmother, and her parents	3
Knowledge of hidden rules at school and work	3 graduates from high school against the odds	2 holds a job
Language/ formal register	2	2

Michael and his father are an example of a household that is disrupted by addiction and drug use. Both are very fortunate to have the maternal grandparents as a support system, with whom to build relationships and experience role models. Furthermore, the stepmother's parents know the hidden rules of work and school and help teach those to Michael. His stepmother's mother is a school administrator, and she knows how to help Michael negotiate special education and access resources within the school system.

The strengths of this situation are his stepmother's parents and the support system they provide, his future story, and his relationship with his father and his stepmother.

Interventions could include:

1. Bring the stepmother's mother (school administrator) in on decisions about Michael's interventions and progress.

2. Do backwards planning with Michael to help him build in all the steps necessary to reach his future story.

3. Provide/structure relationships with other students so that Michael has a peer group to belong to as part of his learning strategies.

Case Study #4: Wadell and Destinie

Resource	Wadell or Destinie	Grandmother
Financial	1 have shelter, some food, tribal assistance	1
Emotional	4 strongest one in the household; no drugs	0
Mental/cognitive	4	?
Spiritual (future story)	4 strong future story	?
Physical	4	0 age
Support systems	2 Destinie and school	1 tribal assistance
Relationships/ role models	2 some tribal leaders and school	?
Knowledge of hidden rules at school and work	4	?
Language/ formal register	4	?

The Wadell case study examines the situation when the student is the support system for the household and functions as the *de facto* adult in the household. It is only because of school, tribal support, and his own personal strength that Wadell survives as well as he does.

Strengths include his motivation because of his relationship with his sister, his strong emotional and mental resources, his future story, his love of music, and his strong interest in the tribal ways that will help Wadell succeed.

The needs here are a strong male role model, transportation, and planning backwards to reach the future story and goals.

Interventions could include:

1. Have Wadell develop a detailed plan for his future story that includes education.

2. Provide a male tribal role model for Wadell.

3. Provide stories for him to read of individuals who have made it through very difficult times.

4. Find an adult who would be willing to provide transportation on some occasions for Wadell.

5. Make certain that Wadell has a strong relationship with the music teacher at school.

Case Study #5: Julius ('Jughead')

Resource	Julius	Grandfather
Financial	1 has food and shelter	1 government assistance
Emotional	3 does not engage in destructive behaviors	0 encourages destructive behaviors—setting the car on fire, etc.
Mental/cognitive	0 illiterate	0
Spiritual (future story)	0 no future story	0
Physical	3	2
Support systems	1	1 extended family all in one place
Relationships/ role models	1 role models problematic	1
Knowledge of hidden rules at school and work	0	0
Language/ formal register	0	0

This case study examines illiteracy, isolation, incestuous/closed thinking, and survival patterns in poverty. Furthermore, it is an example of a situation where there are very few resources. Because the grandfather will do everything he can to isolate Julius from outside influence (unless he gets paid to include him), a key issue for Julius is the ways in which he continues to have access to the "outside" world.

The strengths in this situation are few. Interventions could include:

1. Have Julius develop a future story. Backward-plan exactly what he would need to do to get to that future story.

2. Provide access during school to a computer. One assignment is for him to establish a relationship with another student in another place (his age), and then they exchange information about themselves (needs to be supervised). This will allow Julius to know there is a world beyond the one in which he lives.

3. Provide reading instruction and tutoring. Allow Julius to read to someone much younger—e.g., a first-grade student.

4. Provide an adult mentor/tutor for Julius who also would function as a role model.

Case Study #6: Gabriela

Resource	Gabriela	Grandmother
Financial	3 has a car, cell phone, dresses well	?
Emotional	2 disrespectful	0 requires a great deal of attention
Mental/cognitive	3 can do well	?
Spiritual (future story)	3 has a future story—college	?
Physical	4	?
Support systems	1 is the support system; does have relatives	1 Gabriela
Relationships/ role models	1 parents in prison	?
Knowledge of hidden rules at school and work	2	?
Language/formal register	3	0

Gabriela is again an example of being the primary support system for the household, but she has an external support system in terms of extended family that helps negate the lack of available parents. However, her emotional resources are increasingly frayed because of the lack of supports.

Strengths in this situation include her future story, her mental abilities, her use of formal register, her knowledge of hidden rules, and her extended support system.

Needs in this situation are her emotional resources.

Interventions could include:

1. Provide a counselor who would help Gabriela through the paperwork of getting into community college.

2. Put together a small group of secondary students who are also the "adult" in their home situation. Have the counselor do a lunch with them once a month and examine "what if" scenarios—e.g., *What do you do if you don't have food or money? What do you do when a younger sibling is sick?*

3. Find a female role model for Gabriela.

Case Study #7: Raymond

Resource	Raymond	Mother or father
Financial	3	3
Emotional	0	1
Mental/cognitive	2	2 has a job as a skilled laborer
Spiritual (future story)	? future story was to play football; he gave that up	?
Physical	4	3 holds a job
Support systems	1 mother to live with	?
Relationships/ role models	1 parents love him, but father abandons him	?
Knowledge of hidden rules at school and work	2	2
Language/ formal register	2	2

This case study examines the connection between emotional resources and relationships—and what happens to the emotional resources of a student when the adults don't have emotional resources either.

What interventions might work in this case?

1. Raymond needs a replacement male role model because his father has abandoned him.

2. Raymond needs a very different future story—one that doesn't involve sports and something that he would be good at doing without the memories of his father.

3. Raymond needs to move away from the area—with another relative— where he can literally start again or perhaps consider the military.

4. Raymond needs to get his GED and go to community college with a different future story.

5. It would be helpful if Raymond also could get counseling as a way to deal with the abandonment and anger.

Case Study #8: Ciera

Resource	Ciera	Father
Financial	0 no job; food and shelter are in question	0 in jail
Emotional	3 does not engage in destructive behavior; takes care of younger brothers	0 DUI
Mental/cognitive	4	?
Spiritual (future story)	4 does not want to be like her mother	?
Physical	4	?
Support systems	1 counselor at school	?
Relationships/ role models	1 counselor at school	?
Knowledge of hidden rules at school and work	3	?
Language/ formal register	4	?

Ciera is an example of an individual who has given up all the adult relationships in poverty in order to excel at school and have a different life. Her future story is in the negative (to not be like her mother), but it is a future story. As noted in the Introduction and Chapter 4, the four reasons an individual leaves poverty tend to be: It's too painful to stay, a vision or goal, a special talent or skill, or a key relationship. And Ciera has two of those: It's too painful to stay and a key relationship. Further, this is an example of a situation where the adults have almost no resources. The only resources external to her come from school. In this case, it's a counselor.

Strengths in this situation are Ciera's amazing resiliency, her strong emotional resources, the clarity of her future story, the counselor, and her motivation to have things be different.

The needs are to provide shelter, food, and a support system for Ciera and her brothers.

Interventions could include:

1. Linking Ciera and her brothers with a church or social agency that could help provide resources

2. A female role model for Ciera who could meet and talk with her on a regular basis

Excerpt from *Understanding and Engaging
Under-Resourced College Students*[227]

Chapter 2
What Are the Causes of Poverty?

The Research Continuum

In the United States many of us tend to be confused about the causes of poverty and, therefore, not sure what to do about it.[228] A review of research on poverty indicates that the dialogue has been polarized between those who believe poverty is caused by individual behaviors and those who believe poverty is caused by political/economic structures. Proponents of both of these views often make "either/or" assertions: If poverty is caused by individual behaviors, then political or economic structures are not at fault and vice versa. Taking a "both/and" approach, however, is more productive. "Poverty is caused by both the behavior of the individual and political/economic structures—and everything in between."[229] This book's authors categorize the research into four clusters along a continuum of causes of poverty:

- Behaviors of the individual

- Absence of human and social capital

- Exploitation

- Political/economic structures

Alice O'Connor, in her book *Poverty Knowledge,* states that society typically focuses on race and gender when considering poverty. She suggests that efforts to ameliorate poverty would be better served by examining it through the lens of economic class instead.[230] In the postsecondary arena, this approach emphasizes faculty interaction with students, support services, and student programming to give more attention to building students' resources and creating sustainable communities.

There is valid research that points to strategies and/or solutions to the causes of poverty. As long as there is a range of strategies following the continuum of causes, it is possible to consider how to end poverty. The lists and examples that follow are not exhaustive but rather examples of what might fall into each area of research.

Behaviors of the individual	Community conditions	Exploitation	Political/economic structures
Definition: Research on the choices, behaviors, and circumstances of people in poverty	*Definition:* Research on resources and human and social capital in the city or county	*Definition:* Research on the impact of exploitation on individuals and communities	Definition: Research on political, economic, and social policies and systems at the organizational, city/county, state, national, and international levels
Sample topics: Racism Discrimination by age, gender, disability, race, sexual identity Bad loans Credit-card debt Lack of savings Skill sets Dropping out Lack of education Alcoholism Disabilities Job loss Teen pregnancies Early language experience Child-rearing strategies Bankruptcy due to health problems Street crime White-collar crime Dependency Work ethic Lack of organizational skills Lack of amenities	*Sample topics:* Racism Discrimination by age, gender, disability, race, sexual identity Layoffs Middle-class flight Plant closings Underfunded schools Weak safety net Criminalizing poverty Employer insurance premiums rising in order to drop companies with record of poor health Charity that leads to dependency High rates of illness leading to high absenteeism and low productivity Brain drain City and regional planning Mix of employment/wage opportunities Loss of access to high-quality schools, childcare, and preschool Downward pressure on wages	*Sample topics:* Racism Discrimination by age, gender, disability, race, sexual identity Payday lenders Lease/purchase outlets Subprime mortgages Sweatshops Human trafficking Employment and labor law violations Wage and benefits theft Some landlords Sex trade Internet scams Drug trade Poverty premium (the poor pay more for goods and services) Day labor	*Sample topics:* Racism Discrimination by age, gender, disability, race, sexual identity Financial oligarchy—the military, industrial, congressional complex Return on political investment (ROPI) Corporate lobbyists Bursting "bubbles" Free trade agreements Recessions Lack of wealth-creating mechanisms Stagnant wages Insecure pensions Healthcare costs Lack of insurance De-industrialization Globalization Increased productivity Minimum wage, living wage, self-sufficient wage Declining middle class Decline in unions Taxation patterns Wealth-creating mechanisms

Source: *Getting Ahead in a Just-Gettin'-By World* by P. E. DeVol.

The first cluster of research on poverty holds that **individual initiative**—being on time, staying sober, becoming motivated—would reduce poverty. Indeed, voter research echoes this finding as 40% of voters said that poverty is due to lack of effort on the part of individuals in poverty.[231]

This area of research focuses on the individual as the cause of poverty and draws its conclusions primarily from correlative studies of choices and lifestyles of the poor. The research topics include intergenerational character traits, dependency, single parenthood, work ethic, breakup of families, violence, addiction and mental illness, and language experiences. In the past 60 years, considerable funding and time have been spent on these areas of research, with the focus on changing the thinking and behavior of the poor through such strategies as "work first," literacy education, treatment interventions, a cluster of abstinence issues, and programs that promote marriage. Overall, the intention of these strategies is to improve the choices, education, and internal resources of the poor. This cluster of research, however, does not take into account the influences of outside factors that tend to work against personal assets and choices.

1. The second area of research involves the absence of **human and social capital**—examining how communities provide resources and infrastructure so that individuals can achieve and maintain personal economic stability. In this cluster, topics of research include employment and education issues, declining neighborhoods, and middle-class flight—all of which may lead to "donut cities" where suburbs thrive while the urban core from which people moved collapses, leaving a hole in the center.

Local governments, service providers, and schools are held accountable for poverty through state audits, federal and state reviews of participation rates, and assessment scores. Therefore, the strategies often suggested for improving human and social capital include providing programming to enhance skills and build educational access (such as Head Start), growth in the labor market in order to offer full employment opportunities, antipoverty programs, and improved policing of communities. When individuals discuss how to end poverty from this perspective, the role of business and community development is crucial. Some businesses contribute by thinking not only of their "bottom line" but also about their contribution to their employees and to a sustainable local community.

2. **Exploitation,** the third area of the research continuum, involves abusing and taking advantage of dominated groups and markets for profit. Exploitation takes many forms. For example, people who cannot protest low wages for fear of losing their job work in slavery, sweatshops, and/or in migrant farming. Large corporations that hire employees for only 30 hours a week to avoid paying healthcare and other benefits also are preying on the people who need jobs and security. Exploitation of dominated groups for markets includes the drug trade, "buy here/pay here" car lots where the interest rate is 15.7%, as well as the "rent to own" stores that charge as much as 121% interest. The college student is particularly susceptible to predatory lending at cash-advance and payday lender storefronts in order to make financial ends meet.

Further, exploitation can happen to groups when geographic regions are plundered for their raw materials. Examples include the timber and coal being taken from Appalachian areas in the U.S. or oil being taken from the delta region of Nigeria, because the local people do not benefit from the local resources. Another example is the Native Americans who were driven onto reservations. These groups of people are out of the decision-making and profit-sharing loop. Unfortunately, dominant cultures are frequently reluctant to acknowledge exploitive practices. While half the states in the U.S. have passed antipredatory lending laws, the laws are in danger of being erased due to pressure from the lenders and lobbyists. Strategies to end exploitation found in the research include:

- Educating individuals and groups about exploitation
- Recognizing the role of government in sustaining or eradicating the exploitation
- Finding ways to make the system fair for getting money, products, services, and loans

3. Research topics relevant to how **social, economic, and political structures** contribute to poverty and prosperity examine why poverty exists from the standpoint of who benefits from it. For example:

- Deindustrialization and its toll on small communities across the United States
- The "race to the bottom" in which lower labor costs were meant to bring in new business but result in U.S. jobs moving overseas
- Increased productivity through high-tech equipment, which leads to job loss
- Corporate influence on legislators

Researchers who concentrate on this last category believe that studying poverty is not the same as studying the poor, noting that political/economic structures are a principal cause of poverty. Proponents believe in systemic change that enables people in middle class and poverty to influence the political and economic structures that affect them, just as the wealthy have done for generations if not centuries.

The following summarizes political and economic issues affecting public education in the United States.

> A study from the National Commission on Teaching and America's Future (NCTAF, 2004) shows that high-poverty schools are more likely than low-poverty schools to have many teachers unlicensed in the subjects they teach, limited technology access, inadequate facilities, inoperative bathrooms, vermin infestation, insufficient materials, and multiple teacher vacancies. Other studies show that high-poverty schools implement less rigorous curricula (Barton, 2004), employ fewer experienced teachers (Barton, 2004; Rank, 2004), have higher student-to-teacher ratios (Barton, 2003; Karoly, 2001), offer lower teacher salaries (Karoly, 2001), have larger class sizes (Barton, 2003), and receive less funding (Carey, 2005; Kozol, 1992) than low-poverty schools. The study concludes: the most disadvantaged children attend schools that do not have basic facilities and conditions conducive to providing them with a quality education (NCTAF, 2005, p. 7).[232]

A strategy for changing the political/economic structures includes creating a sustainable economy, with the intent of creating economic stability for all. Further suggestions include implementing measures of accountability beyond the shareholders' profits in business and government, as well as creating "whole-system planning," such as the Social Health Index (SHI) described by Miringoff and Miringoff.[233]

Other Areas of Research into Causes of Poverty: Race and Gender

Race and gender—more specifically, racism and sexism that involve the cultural dominance white males hold over people of color and women in America—are two additional areas of research into the causes of poverty. There are numerous other individual characteristics that intersect with economic class (disabilities, sexual orientation, age, religion), but none has as much impact on individuals, communities, and society as does race. Race/racism is so inextricably linked to economic class that it must be addressed directly as its own category.

As wealth is created over generations, it is estimated that 80% of assets come from transfers from the prior generations, not from income.[234] Past policies and conditions clearly caused huge economic disparities between whites and people of color in the United States. The concepts of income and wealth are as fundamentally different as the concepts of situational poverty and generational poverty. In situational poverty, someone who once had economic stability becomes poor due to a circumstance—death, disease, disability, and so on. These individuals will react to the situation differently and have a greater chance of regaining economic stability than persons coming from two or more generations of poverty. Similarly, income—today's paycheck, lottery ticket, or stock dividend— is different from wealth. Income can change in the short term, but wealth changes over generations and is closely tied to policies that have historically benefited people (especially males) who are white. Wealth is far less dependent on daily income than most people imagine.

America's economic, social, and political policy and structures built and supported a white middle class. Slavery exponentially magnified racial disparities in income and wealth. Generations of African-Americans were subjected to captivity, hard labor, and human rights controlled by slaveholders. The economic advantages slavery afforded to the slave owners is calculated in *The Color of Wealth*. During the mid to late 1800s U.S. government policy supported agriculture by giving lands taken from Mexico and Native Americans to white settlers (e.g., Manifest Destiny, the Gold Rush, and the Homestead Act). Land ownership was largely restricted to whites. U.S. policies continued to develop during the Industrial Revolution, which spawned the working class. Child labor was outlawed, tariffs made U.S. goods more desirable (hence more Americans could be employed), Ford mechanized production (and improved working conditions to a degree), unions developed to help protect workers, and some employers began to provide healthcare and pensions in order to compete for workers in a tight labor market. But segregation and discrimination limited employment opportunities. The white-collar middle class emerged and was supported by the GI Bill, mortgages, Social Security, and Medicare. Between 1930 and 1960, just 1% of all U.S. mortgages were issued to African-Americans, and segregation in colleges meant there were not enough openings for black GIs to go to school on the GI Bill.[235]

In 1994 the median net worth of whites was $94,500, compared with $19,000 for people of color. By 2005 white median net worth increased 48% (to $140,500), compared with nonwhite median net worth, which increased only 31% (to $24,900).

In 2006 the Minnesota Collaborative Anti-Racism Institute (MCARI) developed training materials on systemic racism for inclusion in the *Getting Ahead* workbook curriculum.[236] MCARI presents four features of racism that can validate the experience and intuition of people of color and shift the perspectives of whites so that they become intentionally aware of the daily advantages and disadvantages precipitated by racial identity.[237]

Four Features of Racism

1. **Race matters.** Compared with many countries in the world, the history of the United States is short. Though laws have been passed to change racial, economic, political, and social injustices, including segregation, racial identity still makes a difference, still "invoking mythological moral and intellectual superiority and inferiority."[238]

2. **Racism is more than the historical black-white dichotomy.** This country's early laws and policies required definition of white and nonwhite. In the past, nonwhite primarily meant black. Today, the black/white dichotomy affects every community of color by paradoxically resulting in blindness to the issues of such other communities as Native Americans.

3. **Racism and other oppressions interact.** Race, gender, and economic class are so interrelated that some would argue one can't address one without accounting for the other two. Like economic class, "race shapes how we experience other socially defined identities."[239] Race, gender, and class are relative to one another, such that the experience of one is inescapably connected to the experience of the other. "A white man's experience of gender is dramatically different [from] a black man's. Race is the most powerful factor ... in how one experiences other systemic oppressions."[240]

4. **Identity formation, or racialization,** "is the core feature of racism that reveals its forcefulness," according to MCARI.[241] In the United States we're all assigned, for life, to a racial category that also holds social meaning. Even the national census every decade underscores the importance of identifying oneself by race. Racialization shapes individual, institutional, and cultural identity with cumulative and synergistic effects. Racism is enacted every day upon individuals—and broadly within communities and political and economic structures.

Payne's *A Framework for Understanding Poverty*—referred to henceforth in the text as *Framework*—describes the patterns of behaviors seen in schoolchildren from poverty and their families. Its purpose is to help schoolteachers, drawn largely from the white middle class, understand their students better and teach more effectively. In *Framework* Payne does not present an analysis of the political and economic structures that perpetuate poverty—and does not outline strategies to address them. Nor does she deal in depth in *Framework* with racial, gender, and religious issues. Payne has been straightforward from the start that her focus is on the impact of economic class on issues related to poverty, middle class, and wealth. Nevertheless, by improving teaching and hence the educational system, the *Framework* approach does make important contributions to impacting systemic issues, particularly for students and families in the environment of poverty.[242]

There are those who seem intent on translating Payne's descriptions of perceived patterns, hidden rules, and resources into negative stereotypes and indictments of individuals, as well as reinforcement of classist or racist attitudes. But such critics' focus tends to be on only one area of the research continuum (usually the political and economic structures *or* exploitation and racism), and this fuels polarizing arguments that oversimplify the problems of poverty and demand overarching societal reform from K–12 teachers who are only marginally equipped for the task. The critics offer little help to individuals themselves—or to those practitioners within the system who also seek change. Part of the thinking expressed in the research on exploitation and political/economic structures is that the individual is powerless and has little influence within the system. But many individuals do make it out of poverty, largely due to relationships and education. And most of them make it out *in spite of* the system. Society's systems are only as moral as the people who create and run them, and ignorance is a brutal form of oppression.[243] Payne, therefore, has offered a practical framework for helping teachers understand how to teach, build relationships, foster relational learning, and direct-teach skills for educational success. These strategies create awareness, build cognitive ability, and accelerate language acquisition to make up for the lags caused by growing up in a low-resource environment.

Poverty traps people in the tyranny of the moment,
making it ... difficult to attend to abstract information
or plan for the future—the very things needed to build
[toward the attainment of a college degree].

–Philip DeVol[244]

What Information Does *A Framework for Understanding Poverty* Have That Cannot Be Obtained Easily from Other Sources? Why Do Critics Love to Hate It and Practitioners Love to Use It?

Ruby K. Payne, Ph.D.

What is it that makes *A Framework for Understanding Poverty* so widely embraced and used by practitioners?[245] Some critics attribute the popularity to the bias of the readers. But that hardly makes sense because so many educators are the first generation to be college-educated in their families. Many of their parents came from poverty, so the information resonates with them. Therefore, what actually does the work offer that individuals cannot get from other sources?

Most studies of class issues are statistical or descriptive and use one of four frames of reference to identify what constitutes class. These four frames are:

- Individual choices
- Resources of the community
- Racial/gender exploitation
- Economic/political systems and structures

Most current studies describe poverty as a systemic problem involving racial/gender exploitation. Yes, this is a significant contributor to poverty. Such a *sole* approach, however, does not answer this question: If the system is to blame, why do some people make it out and others never do? Thirty percent of Americans born in the lowest-earning quintile make it out of that quintile.[246] And furthermore, why is it that the first waves of political refugees who have come to the United States in abject poverty usually have recreated, within one generation, the asset base they left behind? They make it out because of human capital. Ignorance is just as oppressive as any systemic barrier. Human capital is developed through education, employment, the intergenerational transfer of knowledge, and bridging social capital. Money makes human capital development easier, but money *alone* does not develop human capital. Further, any system in the world will oppress you if you are uneducated and unemployed.

This analysis of class is a *cognitive approach* based on a 32-year longitudinal study of living next to and in a poverty neighborhood of mostly whites. It examines the *thinking* that comes from the "situated learning" environment of generational poverty.[247] It is the accumulation of years of living with and next to this situated-learning environment. This book does not assign moral value to the thinking or the behaviors but rather says, *These are patterns that you see. These are why individuals use these patterns, and here is what you can do to help those individuals make the transition to the "decontextualized" environment of formal schooling, if they desire to make that transition.*

In the book *Change or Die,* Deutschman says that for people to change, three things must happen. They must relate, reframe, and repeat.[248] And that is precisely what *Framework* does: It identifies what one must do to develop relationships, what must be reframed to go from poverty to the decontextualized world of formal schooling, and the skills and behaviors that must be repeated in order to do that. And whether one likes it or not, both schools and social agencies have as their bottom line: *change.* That is what they are getting paid to do.

Again, not everyone wants to change. The question is this: Do you have a choice not to live in poverty? If you are not educated or employed, then choice has been taken from you.

So what is it about this book that is so important to practitioners? Why do so many practitioners love to use it?

1. **A language to talk about the experience of generational poverty**

   In order to reframe anything, one must have language to do that. You must have language to talk about your current experience and the experience to which you are moving. Class, just like race, is experienced at a very personal level first and impacts thinking.[249] The book explains the patterns in the situated-learning environment of generational poverty and is very careful to say that not everyone will have those patterns. As one person who grew up in extreme poverty said to me, "Growing up in poverty is like growing up in a foreign country. No one explains to you what you do know, what you do not know, or what you could know."

2. **The resource base of themselves or other individuals used to negotiate an environment in order to know which interventions to use**

   Many professionals think poverty and wealth are related to money. They actually are much more related to a set of resources to which one has access. Interventions work because the resources are there to make them work. If that basic concept is not understood, then any intervention will not be successful. For example, if a parent cannot read (mental resource), then there is no success in asking the parent to read to the child.

3. The basic patterns in the mindset differences between/among classes so that one can have bridging social capital

In order to relate to someone different from you, there must be enough understanding of that person's reality to have a conversation. The "hidden rules" allow you to understand that there may be thinking different from yours. Members of a group that has the most people (dominant culture), the most money, or the most power tend to believe that their "hidden rules" are the best. In fact, hidden rules are often equated with intelligence. Knowing different sets of hidden rules allows one to negotiate more environments successfully. "Bridging social capital" is individuals you know who are different from you because they can impact your thinking if there is mutual respect.[250] As we say to audiences, "Bonding social capital helps you *get by,* whereas bridging social capital helps you *get ahead."*

4. The key issues in transition

A huge issue for the secondary students and adults with whom we work is transition. If individuals desire to be better educated, make a change in their living situation, end addiction, have better health, or have a better job, then what is it that those individuals need to know in order to do that? We find that they must assess and develop a resource base, develop bridging relationships, have a language to talk about their own experience and the one they are moving to, and live in a "decontextualized" world of paper/computers. *Framework* provides the understandings and tools to do this.

5. Key issues in the intergenerational transfer of knowledge

Part of human capital is a knowledge base. Knowledge bases are a form of privilege, just as social access and money are. Such knowledge bases also can be passed on intergenerationally. In an Australian study, which followed 8,556 children for 14 years, the researchers found they could predict with reasonable accuracy the verbal reasoning scores of 14-year-olds based on the maternal grandfather's occupation.[251]

Part of the intergenerational transfer of knowledge is also vocabulary. Hart and Risley put tape recorders in homes by economic class and recorded the language that children have access to between the ages of 1 and 4. By age 4, children in welfare households had heard 13 million words compared with 45 million words in a professional household.[252] Vocabulary is key in negotiating situations and environments.

6. **The abstract representational skills and procedural planning skills that one has to have in order to go from the situated learning of poverty to the decontextualized environment of formal schooling**

Lave and Wenger indicate that beginning learning is always about a "situated environment" that has "people, relationships, context, tasks and language."[253] They add that when an individual makes the transition to formal schooling, learning becomes decontextualized. The context is taken away, relationships are not considered in the learning, reasoning is not with stories but with laws and symbols (abstract representational systems). The research indicates that to make the transition between those two environments, one needs relationships and support systems.

Furthermore, in a study released in 2008 using EEG scans with poor and middle-class children, the researchers found that the prefrontal cortex of the brain (executive function) in poor children was undeveloped and resembled the brains of adults who have had strokes. The executive function of the brain handles impulse control, planning, and working memory. The researchers went on to state that it is remediable, but there must be direct intervention.[254] So teaching planning is critical for success in the decontextualized environment of school because it is not taught in the environment of generational poverty.

The book provides the tools to assist with this transition.

7. **The necessity of relationships of mutual respect in learning**

All learning is double-coded—emotionally and cognitively.[255] The nature of the relationship makes a huge difference in how the information is coded emotionally and therefore received. In a study of 910 first-graders, even when the pedagogy of both teachers was excellent, at-risk students would not learn from a teacher if the students perceived the teacher as being "cold and uncaring."[256]

In short, *Framework* provides the tools to give choice to people who do not want to live in poverty. It provides the tools for practitioners themselves to relate, reframe, and repeat.

Why do so many critics love to hate it?

In the last five years, critics have attacked the work, and almost all are connected with higher education in some manner (adjunct faculty, assistant professors, et al.). A large part of it appears to have to do with the nature of the role.

First of all, researchers ask questions and must have a clean methodology in order to publish. Researchers need to publish in order to get tenure and to keep their jobs. You cannot publish if your methodology is not clean, your details are not perfect, all the qualifiers are not included, and your definitions are not exact. Researchers are trained to critique ideas, details, theory, methodology, and findings but not to assess the practicality of the suggestions or situations.

Furthermore, many researchers apparently believe that "researched" information has much more value than information acquired through "practice." In fact, Bohn asks, "How had someone so widely hailed in the public schools as an expert on poverty been ignored by national research institutes, higher education, and all the major, published authorities on the subject of poverty?"[257] In other words, the information does not have value because it has not been acknowledged by higher education.

Practitioners, on the other hand, must have solutions to practical problems. Working with people involves a messy social ecology. To keep your job you must handle and solve problems quickly. If you are a teacher in a classroom with 30 students, then details are not the focus, patterns are; methodology is seldom considered; group well-being ensures safety of individuals; and the focus is on working with each student for high achievement results.

Moreover, there is simply not the time to document all the details or identify the theoretical frames of the situation. Practitioners deal with people and situations and must have a level of understanding about them in order to meet their needs. Change is one of the agendas of practitioners, so efforts focus on that as well.

Why do critics love to hate the work? Quite simply, the work breaks the rules of higher education around the issue of credibility. Here are some of the most common charges leveled against it.

1. *It does not document every detail with the source.*[258]

2. *It does not explain the information with details and qualifiers but rather in patterns or stereotyping.*[259]

3. *It does not reference systems issues or exploitation issues or racial or gender information and their roles in poverty. It does not address the macro-level issues.*[260]

4. *It does not have a clean methodology. It has a mixed methodology.*

5. *It looks at what students cannot do and what needs to be taught—deficit model.*[261]

6. *It can be misused and misunderstood, so therefore it is dangerous.*[262]

7. *The writer self-published. The book is not peer-reviewed. (It could be argued that selling more than 1.8 million copies is a form of peer review.)*

8. *Race and class are not talked about together. Therefore, the work is racist.*[263] *(As an aside, past editions of the book do not discuss gender and class together either, and poverty tends to be feminized around the world.)*

What seems to be an additional outrage in the criticism is the number of books that have been sold; almost every critic mentions it. Rather than asking why so many people would find the information helpful, the critics belittle the readers for not having enough intelligence to know their own biases.[264]

In defense of higher education, however, there is not a good research methodology for social ecologies. Neither quantitative nor qualitative methods address social ecologies very well. Norretranders explains that the research in entropy leads to the understandings of information technology.[265] Perhaps fractal or chaos theory would provide a better theoretical model for researching social ecologies.

Does it work? Does it help make changes? Does it build human capital?

Unequivocally, yes. In some places more so than other places that use the work. Implementation is always messy and uneven. We have collected research against a set of fidelity instruments for more than seven years in K–12 settings; these data have been compiled by Dr. William Swan and have been peer reviewed.[266]

A few key findings were ...

- When using the normal distribution to determine expected frequencies and analyzing the observed versus the expected frequencies: In mathematics, there were twice as many positive findings as would be expected in a normal distribution (statistically significant at the .05 level); in literacy/language arts, there were three times as many positive results as would be expected in a normal distribution (statistically significant at the .001 level).

- These results led Swan to conclude, "The large number of statistically significant findings for the Payne School Model strongly supports the efficacy of the Model in improving student achievement in mathematics and English/reading/literacy/language arts."[267]

- Additionally, an external review of nine research reports on the Payne School Model, led by Dr. C. Thomas Holmes, professor at the University of Georgia, was completed. Holmes, along with four other reviewers, concluded that the design employed in these studies was appropriate, the statistical tests were well-chosen and clearly reported, and the author's conclusions followed directly from the obtained results.[268]

We have hard data about the impact on adults as well. Using *Getting Ahead in a Just-Gettin'-By World* by Philip DeVol and using concepts and tools in *Framework,* we are seeing phenomenal results. YWCA National named "Bridges Out of Poverty/Getting Ahead" as a model program in December 2008. These are the results that the YWCA of Saint Joseph County, Indiana, has been getting.

Increase in participants	Positive change in 3 months	Positive change in 6 months
Income	26%	84%
Education	36%	69%
Employment	32%	63%
Support systems	13%	84%

Conclusion

The book is about developing human capital through relationships and education at the micro level.

I am baffled why the discussion so often must be polarized; in other words, if one idea is right, then another idea must be wrong. Poverty is multifaceted. In fact, the subject is analogous to the fable about the six blind men and the elephant. If we are ever going to successfully address poverty, it will take all the ideas from all quarters, as well as greater understandings than we have at present.

References

Bohn, A. (2006). Rethinking schools online: A framework for understanding Ruby Payne. Retrieved from http://www.rethinkingschools.org/archive/21_02/fram212.shtml

Bomer, R., Dworin, J., May, L., & Semingson, P. (2008). Miseducating teachers about the poor: A critical analysis of Ruby Payne's claims about poverty. *Teachers College Record, 110,* 2497–2531.

DeVol, P. E. (2004). *Getting ahead in a just-gettin'-by world: Building your resources for a better life* (2nd ed.). Highlands, TX: aha! Process.

Deutschman, A. (2007). *Change or die: The three keys to change at work and in life.* New York, NY: HarperCollins.

Goleman, D. (1995). *Emotional intelligence: Why it can matter more than IQ.* New York, NY: Bantam Books.

Gorski, P. (2005). Savage unrealities: Uncovering classism in Ruby Payne's framework [Abridged version]. Retrieved from http://www.edchange.org/publications/Savage_Unrealities_abridged.pdf

Greenspan, S. I., & Benderly, B. L. (1997). *The growth of the mind and the endangered origins of intelligence.* Reading, MA: Addison-Wesley.

Hart, B., & Risley, T. R. (1995). *Meaningful differences in the everyday experience of young American children.* Baltimore, MD: Paul H. Brookes.

Holmes, C. T. (n.d.). Review of program evaluations. Retrieved from https://www.ahaprocess.com/wp-content/uploads/2013/09/External-Review-Dr.-Thomas-Holmes.pdf

Isaacs, J. B., Sawhill, I. V., & Haskins, R. (n.d.). Getting ahead or losing ground: Economic mobility in America. Retrieved from http://www.pewtrusts.org/uploadedFiles/wwwpewtrustsorg/Reports/Economic_Mobility/Economic_Mobility_in_America_Full.pdf

Kishiyama, M. M., Boyce, W. T., Jimenez, A. M., Perry, L. M., & Knight, R. T. (2009). Socioeconomic disparities affect prefrontal function in children. *Journal of Cognitive Neuroscience, 21*(6), 1106–1115.

Lave, J., & Wenger, E. (1991). *Situated learning: Legitimate peripheral participation.* Cambridge, England: Cambridge University Press.

Najman, J. M., Aird, R., Bor, W., O'Callaghan, M., Williams, G., & Shuttlewood, G. (2004). The generational transmission of socioeconomic inequalities in child cognitive development and emotional health. *Social Science and Medicine, 58,* 1147–1158.

Norretranders, T. (1991). *The user illusion: Cutting consciousness down to size.* New York, NY: Penguin.

Payne, R. K. (2005). *A framework for understanding poverty* (4th ed.). Highlands, TX: aha! Process.

Putnam, R. D. (2000). *Bowling alone: The collapse and revival of American community.* New York, NY: Simon & Schuster.

Results and best practices. (2018). aha! Process. Retrieved from https://www.ahaprocess.com/solutions/k-12-schools/results-best-practices

NOTE: Appendix C is adapted nearly verbatim from Chapter 11 in *From Understanding Poverty to Developing Human Capacity* (2012) by R. K. Payne.

Extreme Poverty, Poverty, and Near Poverty Rates for Children Under Age 5, by Living Arrangement: 2016

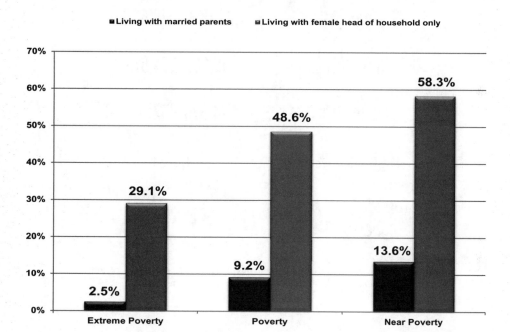

The data for Extreme Poverty, Poverty, and Near Poverty Rates for Children Under Age 5, by Living Arrangement are from table POV03 (50% of poverty, 100% of poverty, and 125% of poverty) People in Families by Family Structure, Iterated by Income-to-Poverty-Ratio, U.S. Census Bureau, *Current Population Survey, 2017 Annual Social and Economic Supplement.*

Extreme poverty: Below 50% of poverty
Poverty: Below 100% of poverty
Near poverty: Below 125% of poverty

For periodic updates on the poverty statistics in Appendix D, please visit www.ahaprocess.com

Household Income in 20% Increments of Total: 2016

Group	Average Household Income Ranges: 2016
Lowest 20%	$0–$24,002
Second 20%	$24,003–$45,600
Third 20%	$45,601–$74,875
Fourth 20%	$74,876–$121,018
Highest 20%	$121,019+
Top 5% (part of highest 20%)	$225,251+

Source: U.S. Census Bureau, *Current Population Survey, 2017 Annual Social and Economic Supplement* (households as of March of the following year).

Breakdown of U.S. Households, by Total Money Income: 2016

Income	# of U.S. Households (in millions)	% of All U.S. Households
<$10k	8,016	6.35
$10k–$14.9k	6,122	4.89
$15k–$24.9k	12,083	9.57
$25k–$34.9k	11,858	9.35
$35k–$49.9k	16,303	12.92
$50k–$74.9k	21,405	16.96
$75k–$99.9k	15,474	12.26
$100k–$149.9k	17,835	14.13
$150k–$199.9k	8,775	6.95
$200k +	8,353	6.62

Source: U.S. Census Bureau, *Current Population Survey, 2017 Annual Social and Economic Supplement* (households as of March of the following year).

Estimated Median Household Income: $57,617

Source: U.S. Census Bureau, *Current Population Survey, 2017 Annual Social and Economic Supplement* (households as of March of the following year).

Number and Percentage of Children in Poverty, by Race: 2016

	Number of children in poverty	Percentage of children in poverty
All Races	13,253,000	18.0%
White	4,050,000	10.8%
African American	3,418,000	30.8%
Hispanic *	4,890,000	26.6%
Asian American	430,000	11.1%
American Indian and Alaska Native **	241,905	33.8%
Native Hawaiian and other Pacific Islander **	79,092	22.9%

* Hispanics may be of any race.
** Data from U.S. Census Bureau, *2017 American Community Survey 1-Year Estimates.*

Source: U.S. Census Bureau, *Current Population Survey, 2017 Annual Social and Economic Supplement.*

U.S. Median Income for Persons Age 25 and Older, by Sex and Educational Attainment: 2016

	Overall	Less Than Ninth Grade	Grades 9–12 (no diploma)	HS Diploma (includes GED)	Associate's Degree	Bachelor's Degree	Master's Degree	Professional Degree	Doctorate
Numbers of persons with earnings (in thousands)									
Male	75,263	2,552	3,954	21,382	7,511	17,577	7,219	1,420	1,902
Female	66,942	1,314	2,467	15,423	8,516	17,188	8,437	1,110	1,368
Median earnings, in 2016 dollars									
Male	$48,213	$26,778	$30,030	$37,409	$48,416	$65,672	$80,539	$106,689	$106,283
Female	$35,017	$17,021	$17,938	$25,691	$32,290	$45,602	$57,816	$81,395	$72,195

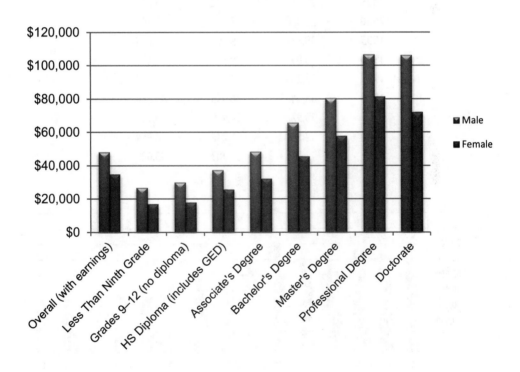

Source: U.S. Census Bureau, *Current Population Survey, 2017 Annual Social and Economic Supplement.*

U.S. Per-Capita Income, Median Household Income, and Median Family Income: 1967 to 2011

Year	Per-Capita Income	Median Household Income	Median Family Income
2016	31,128	57,617	71,062
2015	32,653	53,657	76,697
2014	30,176	53,657	66,632
2013	28,184	52250	64,030
2012	27,319	51,371	62,527
2011	26,708	50,502	69,821
2010	26,059	50,046	60,609
2009	26,409	50,221	61,082
2008	27,589	52,029	63,366
2005	25,035	46,242	55,832
2000	22,970	43,162	52,148
1995	19,871	39,306	46,843
1990	18,894	39,324	46,429
1985	17,280	37,059	43,518
1980	15,844	36,035	42,776
1975	13,972	34,980	39,784
1970	12,543	35,232	38,954
1967	11,067	32,783	35,629

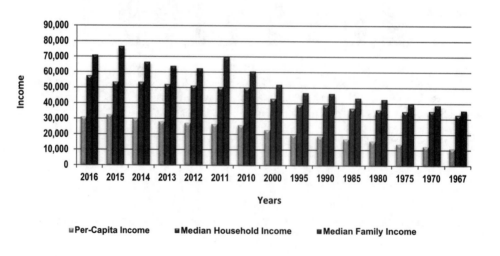

Source: U.S. Census Bureau, *2017 American Community Survey 1-Year Estimates.*

Percentage of U.S. Persons Below Poverty Level, by Race and Ethnicity: 1976 to 2016

Year	All Races	Black	White	Hispanic	Year	All Races	Black	White	Hispanic
2016	12.7	22.0	10.8	19.4	1995	13.8	29.3	11.2	30.3
2015	13.5	24.1	11.6	21.4	1994	14.5	30.6	11.7	30.7
2014	14.8	26.2	12.7	23.6	1993	15.1	33.1	12.2	30.6
2013	14.5	27.2	12.3	23.5	1992	14.8	33.4	11.9	29.6
2012	18.0	28.1	11.0	25.4	1991	14.2	32.7	11.3	28.7
2011	15.0	27.6	12.8	25.3	1990	13.5	31.9	10.7	28.1
2010	15.1	27.4	13.0	26.6	1989	12.8	30.7	10.0	26.2
2009	14.3	25.8	12.3	25.3	1988	13.0	31.3	10.1	26.7
2008	13.2	24.7	11.2	23.2	1987	13.4	32.4	10.4	28.0
2007	12.5	24.5	10.5	21.5	1986	13.6	31.1	11.0	27.3
2006	12.3	24.3	10.3	20.6	1985	14.0	31.3	11.4	29.0
2005	12.6	24.9	10.6	21.8	1984	14.4	33.8	11.5	28.4
2004	12.7	24.7	10.8	21.9	1983	15.2	35.7	12.1	28.0
2003	12.5	24.4	10.5	22.5	1982	15.0	35.6	12.0	29.9
2002	12.1	24.1	10.2	21.8	1981	14.0	34.2	11.1	26.5
2001	11.7	22.7	9.9	21.4	1980	13.0	32.5	10.2	25.7
2000	11.3	22.5	9.5	21.5	1979	11.7	31.0	9.0	21.8
1999	11.9	23.6	9.8	22.7	1978	11.4	30.6	8.7	21.6
1998	12.7	26.1	10.5	25.6	1977	11.6	31.3	8.9	22.4
1997	13.3	26.5	11.0	27.1	1976	11.8	31.1	9.1	24.7
1996	13.7	28.4	11.2	29.4					

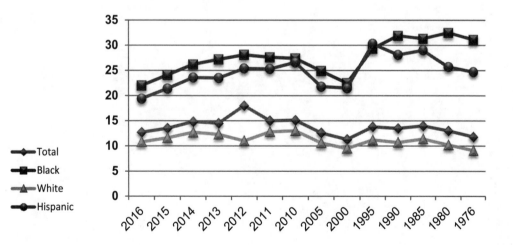

Source: U.S. Census Bureau, *Current Population Survey, 2017 Annual Social and Economic Supplement.*

Where Do We Go from Here? How Do Communities Develop Intellectual Capital and Sustainability?

by Ruby K. Payne, Ph.D.

A key discussion in the United States in the new millennium centers on community. Urban areas have not had a good model for community. Rural areas are losing population and the sense of community they have always had. In fact, the only community that many rural areas have anymore is the local school district. As the student count shrinks and conversations about consolidation begin, many communities vigorously resist that effort because intuitively they understand the need for community.

For the purposes of this article, the definition of community will be the one used by Carl Taylor and Daniel Taylor-Ide in the book *Just and Lasting Change: When Communities Own Their Futures.* They write: "Community, as we use the term, is any group that has something in common and the potential for acting together."[269]

Taylor and Taylor-Ide have been involved with community development for many years around the world.

> *The key to building better lives, is not technical breakthroughs but changing behavior at the community level ... in ways that fit local circumstances ...* Playing an essential role in these processes are the formation and maintenance of a genuine three-way partnership among people in the community, experts from the outside, and government officials.[270]

Community development is becoming more imperative because of the relationship between the intellectual capital in the community and its economic well-being.

What is intellectual capital?

Thomas Stewart, in his book *Intellectual Capital: The New Wealth of Organizations,* defines it as the "intangible assets—the talents of its people, the efficacy of its management systems, the character of its relationships to its customers ..."[271] It is the ability to take existing information and turn it into useful knowledge and tools.

Intellectual capital has become the economic currency of the 21st century. In the 1900s the economic currency was industry-based. In the 1800s it was agriculture-based. One of the issues for many communities is the loss of jobs related to industry and agriculture. Wealth creation is now linked to intellectual capital.

What is the relationship between economic well-being and the development of capital?

Right now in the world and in the United States there is a direct correlation between the level of educational attainment in a community or country and its economic wealth. In the book *As the Future Catches You,* Juan Enriquez gives the following statistic: In 1980 the differential between the richest and poorest country in the world was 5:1 as measured by gross national product (GNP). In 2001 the differential between the richest and the poorest country in the world was 390:1 as measured by GNP.[272] GNP is directly linked to the level of educational attainment. So growth is not incremental; it is exponential.

For the future well-being of communities, it becomes necessary to begin the serious and deliberate development of intellectual capital. This is easier said than done.

How do communities develop intellectual capital? How do you translate between the poor and the policymakers/power brokers?

Systems tend to operate out of default and are amoral. Systems are only as moral as the people who are in them. One of the big issues is how different economic groups translate the issues. For a group to work together, there must be a shared understanding and vocabulary. What is a huge issue to an individual in poverty often doesn't translate as an issue in wealth. The policymakers/power brokers tend to be at the wealth level, while the bureaucrats are at the middle-class level. In the book *Seeing Systems,* Barry Oshry talks about the difficulty the three levels have in communicating with each other.[273]

The following chart identifies how issues are addressed at different economic levels.

Poverty	Middle class	Wealth
Having a job Hourly wages	Appropriate, challenging job Salary and benefits	Maintenance and growth of assets Quality and quantity of workforce
Safety of schools	Quality of schools	K–12 higher education continuum Technical innovation Intermediate colleges and trade schools
A place to rent/live Affordable housing	Property values Quality of schools Quality of neighborhood	Corporate investment potential Infrastructure to support development
Welfare benefits	Taxes	Balance of trade Percentage of taxes Tort liability Corporate contributions Percentage of government indebtedness
Fairness of law enforcement Gangs	Safety Crime rates	Risk management Bond ratings Insurance ratings
Access to emergency rooms	Cost of medical insurance Quality and expertise of medical profession	Cost/predicted costs of medical benefits Workers' compensation
Public transportation	Network of freeways Traffic congestion Time commuting	Systems of transportation (railway, bus, air, etc.) Maintenance of the infrastructure
Having enough food	Access to quality restaurants Variety/quality of food available	Access to high-quality restaurants Amenities for clients Availability of fresh food

Source: *Seeing Systems* by B. Oshry.

As you can see, the same issue is approached and viewed very differently, depending on the economic level of the individual.

What would be the advantage to a community to translate between and among levels for a shared understanding?

With shared understandings, one can develop community, create economic well-being, and develop sustainability.

What is sustainability?

Many people believe that the first major revolution in the world was the agricultural revolution when people were not moving but "stayed put" and had time to develop crafts and skills—and devote time to learning. Many also believe that the second major revolution was the industrial revolution when tools were used to spur development. Finally, the third major revolution may well be the development of sustainability—with intellectual capital as its driving force. In other words, how do we use our resources, yet have enough available for the next generation? How do we live in our environment, yet maintain it for our children?

The following index lists major areas of sustainability.

Sustainable Development Index (SDI)[274]

1. Human rights, freedom, quality	A. Politics and human rights
	B. Equality
2. Demographic development and life expectancy	C. Demographic development
	D. Life expectancy, mortality
3. State of health and healthcare	E. Healthcare
	F. Disease and nutrition
4. Education	G. Education
	H. Technologies and information sharing
5. Economic development and foreign indebtedness	I. Economy
	J. Indebtedness

continued on next page

continued from previous page

6. Resource consumption, eco-efficiency	K. Economy—genuine savings
	L. Economy—resource consumption
7. Environmental quality, environmental pollution	M. Environment—natural resources, land use
	N. Environment—urban and rural problems

Source: "Sustainable Development Assessment" by P. Mederly et al.

It is from the first four elements in the chart that intellectual capital is developed. Those four are foundational to the development of all others.

Why must equity precede sustainability?

One of the most interesting dynamics in communities is the impact of critical mass and equity on change. Thomas Sowell, a historical and international demographer, states that if a community allows any group to be disenfranchised for any reason (religion, race, class, etc.), the whole community becomes economically poorer. What happens is as follows:

| 10% | 20% | 30% | 40% | 50% | 60% | 70% | 80% | 90% | (top 10%) |

Let's use poverty as an example. When 10% of a community is poor, most members of the community will say they have no poverty. When the number climbs to 20%, most will say there is very little poverty. When the number climbs to 30%, the comment will be that there are a few individuals in poverty in the community. But when it hits 35 to 40%, the community becomes alarmed. (Thirty-five to 40% is typically the point of critical mass. Critical mass is when enough people are involved that the issue/behavior gets onto the radar screen, and the community notices.) Comments are made that, all of a sudden, all these poor people came!

At that point, the wealthiest 10% of the community, which has most of the money and resources, will typically pass laws and ordinances to control the 40% in poverty. In the United States the top 20% of households (as measured by income) pays 67.9% of all federal taxes.[275] The bottom 50% of households pays 4% of federal taxes. By the time the poor population reaches 60 to 70% of the total community population, most of the top 10% of households will move out, leaving the community with very few resources. The community is no longer sustainable.

What process can communities use to develop both intellectual capital and sustainability?

To foster community involvement, it's important to use processes that are relatively simple and involve a large number of people, so that critical mass can be achieved. This process must be at least a 20- to 25-year plan, because it takes that long to get critical mass. As futurist and technology forecaster Paul Saffo states, "Most ideas take 20 years to become an overnight success."[276]

It is my recommendation that communities secure endowments. What the endowment does is ensure that for 25 years the ensuing process is followed, data are collected, and three groups are always involved: people in the community, outside experts, and government officials.

The process I recommend takes a minimum of 20 years and follows these steps:

Step 1:

A community group gets together. The members of the group identify what their ideal community would be like 20 years hence. They identify six or seven issues (using the sustainability index as a guide) that would most enhance their community.

Step 2:

The group identifies the key markers for each issue that would indicate progress toward that ideal.

Step 3:

The group identifies the current status of those indicators by gathering "real" community data.

Step 4:

The group works backwards and identifies what the marker would look like 18 years from the goal, 16 years from the goal, etc. Measurements for the markers are established.

Step 5:

The group goes to the larger community (including government officials) and asks all agencies, foundations, charities, churches, businesses, etc., which if any of the markers they are currently working on or would be willing to help address. The larger community agrees to gather data and report that information once a year.

Step 6:

The individuals overseeing the endowment gather the information, put it into a report, and, once a year, gather the larger community for a breakfast and report the data. The leadership persons make recommendations for external expert assistance. The larger community recommits for another year to the larger goals and collection of data.

Step 6 is repeated every year.

It will take 10 to 12 years before much progress at all is seen. Then the progress will become noticeable. Within 20 years the progress will likely be dramatic.

Why use this process?

According to Taylor and Taylor-Ide, in the history of community development, one of four approaches tends to be used: blueprint, explosion, additive, or biological. The biological approach is one of tensegrity. "Tensegrity is the biological form of building," say the authors. "It works by balancing systems in flexible homeostasis rather than by building in a mechanical way that attaches its components rigidly."[277] Taylor and Taylor-Ide also state that tensegrity has these characteristics:

- It allows forms to move and reshape.
- It uses self-assembly in locally specific patterns.
- The whole is different from the member parts.
- It has information feedback.
- It has an efficient distribution and redistribution system.
- It brings accountability; when one part is irresponsible, the whole system is out of balance.[278]

What can you do to get individuals from poverty involved in community issues?

1. Understand the nature of systems. What appeals to the decision makers and power brokers doesn't have the same appeal in poverty and vice versa.
2. Work on real issues—issues that impact day-to-day life.

3. Approach the poor as problem solvers, not victims.
4. Teach the adult voice.
5. Teach question making.
6. Teach "backwards" planning ("begin with the end in mind").
7. Start the process by building relationships of mutual respect, using videos, food, and entertainment; identify the power brokers in the poor community (corner grocers, hairdressers, barbers, ministers, et al.) and bring them into the process.
8. Pay them for their time (e.g., with inexpensive gift cards).
9. Let them bring their children.
10. Identify common tasks so that conversation can occur.
11. Provide constructive outlets for frustration and criticism.
12. Use mental models to help identify, with a minimum of emotion, the areas of needed change.
13. *Gather real data.*

Why would a community consider such an endowed process?

Again quoting Taylor and Taylor-Ide:

> For rich and poor alike, the expansion of trade, changes in the Earth's environment, and the unraveling of social systems make the future uncertain. Even wealthy societies are increasingly unable to care for their growing numbers of poor, alienated youth, forgotten elderly, marginalized mothers, hostile homeless, and exploited minorities ... To achieve a more just and lasting future, we must continually update our definition of development. We can advance more confidently and effectively into that unknown territory by drawing lessons from past successes—and from past failures—and by tailoring solutions for each community to its specific hopes, capabilities, and resources.[279]

In short, community development—based on intellectual capital—is not a choice. Our sustainability, even survival, depends on it.

References

Enriquez, J. (2001). *As the future catches you.* New York, NY: Crown Business.

Oshry, B. (1995). *Seeing systems: Unlocking the mysteries of organizational life.* San Francisco, CA: Berrett-Koehler Publishers.

Saffo, P. (2007, July-August). Six rules for effective forecasting. *Harvard Business Review.* Retrieved from https://hbr.org/2007/07/six-rules-for-effective-forecasting

Sowell, T. (1998, October 5). Race, culture and equality. *Forbes.*

Sowell, T. (1997). *Migrations and cultures: A world view.* New York, NY: HarperCollins.

Stewart, T. A. (1997). *Intellectual capital: The new wealth of organizations.* New York, NY: HarperCollins.

Taylor, C., & Taylor-Ide, D. (2002.) *Just and lasting change: When communities own their futures.* Baltimore, MD: Johns Hopkins University Press.

NOTE: Appendix E is adapted nearly verbatim from Chapter 7 in *From Understanding Poverty to Developing Human Capacity* (2012) by R. K. Payne.

Appendix F

Study Guide
A Framework for Understanding Poverty

Introduction

1. What are four reasons people leave poverty? What *examples* of one or more of these points come to mind for you?

Chapter 1—Resources, 'Reality,' and Interventions: How They Impact 'Situated Learning'

1. What are the nine resources that play a vital role in the success of an individual?
2. Poverty is more about other resources than it is about financial resources. Why? In what ways does the presence and/or absence of other resources impact a person's life? Use examples from your own life or from the lives of those you know.
3. Which resources can an educator influence the most?
4. In which case study in this chapter are the most resources found? The fewest?
5. Which case study affected you most deeply? Why?

Chapter 2—Language and Story: How They Impact Thinking, School, and Work

1. What are the five registers of language? Which one has to be direct-taught in order to be successful in school and the workplace?
2. Which register do most students from poverty not have? What areas of their lives are most influenced by the absence of this register?
3. What did you find the most striking about the Hart/Risley study of early language acquisition by young children in various classes? Why?
4. What usually has to be present in order for the acquisition of language to occur? Why does this present a problem at times?
5. What are the differences between casual and formal story structure?
6. Related to both the Hart/Risley study and "Specificity of Vocabulary," why is a good vocabulary an important contributing factor to success in school and in other settings?

7. What can schools and other organizations do to address casual register, discourse patterns, and story structure?

Chapter 3—Hidden Rules Among Classes: How They Impact Relationships with People Different from You

1. What are hidden rules? And why is understanding them important for individuals in all classes?

2. Did the three mental models "ring true" for you in terms of time priorities? Why or why not? Please respond especially in terms of your own economic class.

3. What were some of your most memorable "aha!" moments as you took the quizzes?

4. What are some of the hidden rules for each class surrounding money, language, possessions, food, and education?

5. What are some of the biggest challenges in getting out of poverty?

6. Why should students be taught the hidden rules of middle class?

7. What was most eye-opening to you about the hidden rules of wealth? Why?

8. What reaction or reactions usually occur when a hidden rule is broken?

9. Why will an understanding of the culture and values of poverty lessen the frustration, even anger, that educators periodically feel when working with students and families from poverty?

Chapter 4—The 'Situated Learning' Reality of Generational Poverty: How It Impacts Navigation of One's Life

1. What are the main differences between generational poverty and situational poverty?

2. Regarding the listing early in the chapter, what do you consider the most difficult aspects of generational poverty for the person caught in that life—and why?

3. What characteristics of generational poverty are present in the "Walter" case study?

4. What makes understanding and dealing with generational poverty so challenging, especially for middle-class people? Why?

5. What makes the family patterns in generational poverty different from the middle class?

6. What emotions were evoked in you from reading Sandy's story? Why?

7. Why is the culture of poverty so often matriarchal ("the mother is invariably at the center")?

8. Why is education the key to getting out of, and staying out of, generational poverty?

Chapter 5—Role Models and Emotional Resources: How They Provide for Stability and Success

1. What are the differences between functional and dysfunctional systems?

2. Why would emotional resources have great importance in school and at work?

3. To move from poverty to middle class or from middle class to wealth, one must trade off _____ for achievement at least for a period of time. Why?

4. How, specifically, do you help provide emotional resources when the student has not had access to appropriate role models?

5. Explain why positive self-talk is a key factor in developing and maintaining strong emotional resources.

6. Why are boundaries important in healthy relationships?

7. What is the greatest free resource available to schools? Why?

Chapter 6—Support Systems and Parents: How They Impact the Ability to Do Homework and to Navigate School and Work

1. What are support systems?

2. In the LaKeitha case study, what types of steps would be beneficial for her—and other students in similar circumstances—to enhance their chances for success?

3. Discuss the nine support systems that schools and other organizations can use to help students. Are there others not listed? If so, what might they be?

4. Why is it important to recognize the role of grief as students and their families cope with the effects of recessions in the United States?

5. What does the insight of Greenspan and Benderly—that all learning is double-coded, both cognitively *and* emotionally—mean to you?

6. To what extent do you agree or disagree with Lareau's comparative analysis of parenting styles in middle-class versus working-class and poor households?

Chapter 7—Creating Relationships: How and Why One Is Motivated to Learn and Change

1. What is the key to achievement for students from poverty? Why?

2. How does a formal institution create relationships?

3. What is the first step in creating relationships with students and adults?

4. Reflect on the concept of deposits and withdrawals with regard to students from poverty. As you relate to individuals in poverty, do you find yourself more on the left side or the right side of the chart? Why do you think you gravitate in the direction you do?

Chapter 8—Discipline: How to Manage Personal Behavior So One Can 'Win' in a Given Environment

1. How does the description of the penance-forgiveness cycle in poverty compare with your understanding of effective discipline?

2. The two anchors of any effective discipline program that moves students to self-governance are structure and choice. Why are these considered anchors?

3. This chapter describes certain behaviors that are related to poverty. Name some of the key interventions for these behaviors. Which interventions do you think are the most effective? Why?

4. What do you consider the most effective part of the "Participation of the Student" exercise? Why?

5. What are the three internal voices that guide an individual, and what are the characteristics and functions of each? Why should students be taught to use the adult voice?

6. What is a metaphor story, and why can it often be effective?

7. What is the most important benefit of reframing? Why?

8. Why do students need to have at least two sets of rules/behaviors from which to choose—one for home and the street and one for school and work settings?

9. Do you agree that discipline should be seen and used as a form of instruction? Why or why not?

Chapter 9—Instruction and Improving Achievement: How to Live in the Abstract Representational World of School and Work

1. What kind of information is generally tested on IQ tests? Why is this important to know?

2. Complete these statements: Teaching is what occurs _____ the head.

    Learning is what occurs _____ the head.

    Why is this important to know?

3. What is mediation, and why is it so essential, especially when working with children from poverty and with children from middle-class households that are struggling to make ends meet?

4. What tends to happen—both short-term and long-term—if an individual cannot plan?

5. Why should instruction in cognitive strategies be part of the curriculum?

6. Why is it important for students and workers to understand abstract representational systems?

7. Which of the eight key instructional issues do you think include the most helpful information for dealing with the students from poverty in your classroom—or the individuals from poverty with whom you relate in non-educational settings?

8. Why should staff development focus on a diagnostic approach rather than a programmatic approach?

Chapter 10—Poverty and Intersectionality: How Poverty Intersects with Race, Health, Immigration

1. What is the definition of intersectionality?

2. How does the story "Black, White, and Green" by Dr. Auzenne-Curl illustrate intersectionality?

3. What are the two distinct phases in the sociology of racism?

4. What are the many "threads" of immigration that create another form of intersectionality?

5. Why is health so interwoven with race and poverty?

6. How does this information on intersectionality apply to your students? How will you use this information to better understand your students?

Chapter 11—Poverty and the Brain: How Poverty Impacts Brain Development

1. Material deprivation, stressors, and nutritional deficiencies all impact brain development. For each of these, identify one specific example and explain how it impacts the development of the brain.

2. What is epigenetics? How does it impact the development of the brain?

3. What are the four areas of the brain that are impacted?

4. Review the list titled "What Does This Information Mean in the School or Work Setting?" What are two things that you will use from that list?

Chapter 12—The Parents of Children in Poverty: How to Understand Where They're Coming From

1. What does the designation of poor and near poor mean as it relates to your students?

2. How does education correlate to children being in poverty?

3. How does family structure correlate to children being in poverty?

4. In what ways is the spending in poverty households different than the spending in your household?

5. How do you interact with parents who are immigrants? What is one thing that you learned about parents who are immigrants?

6. Why is there a tendency, if you were born into poverty, to be in poverty as an adult?

7. How would being taught to react to school (versus being taught to negotiate school) impact your ability to be well schooled?

8. Review the list called "What Does This Mean in the School or Work Setting?" What is one thing you will do from that list?

Appendix A: Resources and Interventions

1. What is your response to the assessments of resources in the case studies? How did these assessments compare with yours?

2. A number of possible interventions are listed for each of the eight case studies. How practical or effective do you think these interventions might be?

Appendix B: What Are the Causes of Poverty? Excerpt from *Understanding and Engaging Under-Resourced College Students*

1. What do you consider the two biggest factors in causing poverty?

2. Why do race and gender need to be part of the discussion when reflecting on the causes of poverty?

3. How can the emphasis on economic *class* be a helpful lens for looking at issues of poverty, along with those of middle class and wealth?

4. How do you understand the phrase "tyranny of the moment," as used by Phil DeVol in the quotation at the end?

Appendix C: What Information Does *A Framework for Understanding Poverty* Have That Cannot Be Obtained Easily from Other Sources? Why Do Critics Love to Hate It and Practitioners Love to Use It?

1. It is pointed out that not everyone wants to change. If you think it strange that some people in poverty choose to stay there (even when they could leave), consider what it might mean for middle-class people to move into wealth—and all that goes with it (see quizzes in Chapter 3). If you're middle class and could join the wealthy class, would you? Why or why not?

2. Think of illustrations in your own life of *bonding* social capital and *bridging* social capital. List a few examples of each.

3. Why is a healthy combination of theory *and* practice needed in addressing issues surrounding poverty? And why do you think a "both/and" approach is favored instead of an "either/or" approach?

4. What to you is the most significant finding in answer to the question "Does it work?"

Appendix D: Poverty Statistics (also available on aha! Process website)

1. What factors exist in the United States that would contribute to poverty being so much higher (4 to 10 times) when a household is headed by a single female compared with a married couple? What do you think the numbers would be for households headed by a single male?

2. Does it surprise you that the 2016 U.S. median income was $57,617? Is that higher or lower than you would have thought? Why?

3. What does it say to you that the U.S. poverty rate (all races) was about the same in 2016 as it was in 1989?

Appendix E: Where Do We Go from Here? How Do Communities Develop Intellectual Capital and Sustainability?

1. Why is a strong foundation of intellectual capital essential to the sustainability of communities in particular and society in general?

2. How might the conversion centuries ago from a nomadic existence to a farming one compare with ways that technology affects us today?

3. What do you think about the six-step process for long-term sustainability outlined here? What do you see as its strengths and weaknesses?

Endnotes

[1] The following section is from my essay "Toward a Cognitive Model for Better Understanding Economic Class," first published in *From Understanding Poverty to Developing Human Capacity.*

[2] M. Gladwell, *Blink;* B. Bloom, *Human Characteristics and School Learning.*

[3] J. B. Isaacs, "Getting Ahead or Losing Ground."

[4] J. S. Brown et al., "Situated Cognition and the Culture of Learning"

[5] U.S. Census Bureau, "Current Population Survey, 2017 Annual Social and Economic Supplement."

[6] Congressional Budget Office, "The Distribution of U.S. Income, 2014."

[7] R. J. Samuelson, "The Culture of Poverty."

[8] J. Marshall, "Children and Poverty"; J. Zins et al., *Building Academic Success on Social and Emotional Learning.*

[9] A. C. Lewis, "Breaking the Cycle of Poverty"; R. Sennett & J. Cobb, *The Hidden Injuries of Class.*

[10] M. Pearce et al., "The Protective Effects of Religiousness and Parent Involvement on the Development of Conduct Problems Among Youth Exposed to Violence."

[11] J. Marshall, "Children and Poverty."

[12] P. Capponi, *Dispatches from the Poverty Line;* N. Zill, "The Changing Realities of Family Life."

[13] R. Sennett & J. Cobb, *The Hidden Injuries of Class;* S. E. Mayer, *What Money Can't Buy;* M. Corcoran & T. Adams, "Race, Sex, and the Intergenerational Transmission of Poverty"; P. Capponi, *Dispatches from the Poverty Line.*

[14] S. E. Mayer, *What Money Can't Buy.*

[15] D. K. Shipler, *The Working Poor;* D. Narayan et al., *Moving out of Poverty.*

[16] C. Harper, "Breaking Poverty Cycles"; P. Glewwe et al., "Early Childhood Nutrition and Academic Achievement"; M. Corcoran, "Rags to Rags"; L.-C. Cheng & D. Page-Adams, "Education, Assets, and Intergenerational Well-Being"; G. Solon, "Intergenerational Mobility in the Labor Market"; C. Harper et al., "Enduring Poverty and the Conditions of Childhood"; J. Brooks-Gunn et al., *Neighborhood Poverty.*

[17] T. Leventhal & J. Brooks-Gunn, "The Neighborhoods They Live in."

[18] B. Sanchez et al., "Makin' It in College"; P. C. Scales et al., "The Role of Developmental Assets in Predicting Academic Achievement"; D. D. Ross et al., "Promoting Academic Engagement Through Insistence"; S. M. Reis et al., "Understanding Resilience in Diverse, Talented Students in an Urban High School"; E. Domagala-Zysk, "The Significance of Adolescents' Relationships with Significant Others and School Failure"; G. J. Duncan & J. Brooks-Gunn, *Consequences of Growing Up Poor.*

[19] A. Lareau, *Unequal Childhoods;* X. Godinot et al., "Resisting Extreme Poverty."

[20] J. Comer, lecture given at Education Service Center, Region IV, Houston, TX.

[21] C. Bicchieri, *The Grammar of Society.*

[22] J. Fernandez-Villaverde et al., "Risk Matters."

[23] B. Hart & T. R. Risley, *Meaningful Differences in the Everyday Experience of Young American Children.*

[24] S. A. Dumais, "Cultural Capital, Gender, and School Success"; G. Farkas, *Human Capital or Cultural Capital;* M. O. Caughy & P. J. O'Campo, "Neighborhood Poverty, Social Capital, and the Cognitive Development of African-American Preschoolers"; D. Narayan et al., *Moving out of Poverty;* D. K. Shipler, *The Working Poor;* M. Woolcock & D. Narayan, "Social Capital: Implications for Development Theory"; A. Krishna, "Escaping Poverty and Becoming Poor."

[25] M. Joos, *The Five Clocks.*

[26] M. R. Montaño-Harmon, presentation to Harris County Department of Education. In her study of Hispanic students who came from Mexico, Montaño-Harmon found that if the family stayed uneducated, the third generation had less formal register in either Spanish or English than the original immigrant had in Spanish. Furthermore, she indicated that the issue for many bilingual students is not that they are bilingual, but that they know only casual register in their native language and casual register in English. I have observed that if the student comes from a household that is religious, though poor and/or uneducated, the student often has formal register because of the exposure to written religious texts—regardless of the specific religion.

[27] S. B. Heath, *Ways with Words;* L. Christenbury, *Making the Journey;* J. R. Rickford, "The Oakland Ebonics Decision"; L. Delpit, *Other People's Children;* W. Wolfram & N. Schilling-Estes, *American English;* W. Labov, "Can Reading Failure Be Reversed?"; J. Baugh, *Beyond Ebonics.*

[28] J. M. Najman et al., "The Generational Transmission of Socioeconomic Inequalities in Child Cognitive Development and Emotional Health."

[29] B. Hart & T. R. Risley, *Meaningful Differences in the Everyday Experience of Young American Children; The Social World of Children;* "American Parenting of Language-Learning Children."

[30] B. Hart & T. R. Risley, "The Early Catastrophe."

[31] D. Walker et al., "Prediction of School Outcomes Based on Early Language Production and Socioeconomic Factors"; R. E. Durham et al., "Kindergarten Oral Language Skill."

[32] A. G. Halberstadt, "Race, Socioeconomic Status, and Nonverbal Behavior"; L. C. Quay & R. L. Blaney, "Verbal Communication, Nonverbal Communication, and Private Speech in Lower and Middle Socioeconomic Status Preschool Children."

[33] R. B. Kaplan, "Cultural Thought Patterns in Inter-Cultural Education"; R. B. Kaplan & R. B. Baldauf, *Language Planning.*

[34] J. P. Gee, "What Is Literacy?"

[35] J. Ogbu, "The Consequences of the American Caste System"; L. M. Koch et al., "Attitudes Toward Black English and Code Switching."

[36] R. S. Wheeler & R. Swords, "Codeswitching"; K. Gilyard, *Voices of the Self;* J. McWhorter, *The Word on the Street;* C. T. Adger et al., *Making the Connection;* T. Perry & L. Delpit, *The Real Ebonics Debate;* G. Smitherman, "'What Go Round Come Round'"; W. Wolfram et al., *Dialects in Schools and Communities.*

[37] M. R. Montaño-Harmon, presentation to Harris County Department of Education. Montaño-Harmon recommended that you teach students to write in casual register and then translate it to formal. She gave this example: Ninth-graders were to write to a friend about something that the friend could do for their health. One of the girls wrote to a friend that the friend "pissed her off" because the friend was smoking and pregnant. In the class the students finally decided that there was no good translation in formal register for "pissed off."

[38] R. Feuerstein et al., *Instrumental Enrichment.*

[39] D. Cummings, "A Different Approach to Teaching Language"; M. Ezarik, "A Time and a Place"; J. Baugh, *Out of the Mouths of Slaves;* J. R. Rickford, "Using the Vernacular to Teach the Standard"; J. M. Schierloh, "Teaching Standard English Usage"; H. U. Taylor, *Standard English, Black English, and Bidialectalism;* R. S. Wheeler, "From Home Speech to School Speech."

[40] G. W. Evans et al., "Parental Language and Verbal Responsiveness to Children in Crowded Homes."

[41] M. A. Callanan, "How Parents Label Objects for Young Children"; C. B. Mervis, "Early Lexical Development."

[42] An exception is C. Harper et al., "Enduring Poverty and the Conditions of Childhood."

[43] S. N. Durlaf, "A Framework for the Study of Individual Behavior and Social Interactions," "The Memberships Theory of Poverty"; G. Akerlof, "Social Distance and Social Decisions"; R. Benabou, "Workings of a City," "Equity and Efficiency in Human Capital Investment," "Heterogeneity, Stratification and Growth"; C. Bicchieri, *The Grammar of Society;* K. A. S. Wickrama & S. Noh, "The Long Arm of Community"; P. Sharkey, "The Intergenerational Transmission of Context."

[44] C. Harper et al., "Enduring Poverty and the Conditions of Childhood"; T. Leventhal & J. Brooks-Gunn, "The Neighborhoods They Live in"; W. J. Wilson, *The Truly Disadvantaged.*

[45] W. J. Wilson, *The Truly Disadvantaged;* R. Stanton-Salazar & S. Dornbusch, "Social Capital and the Reproduction of Inequality"; M. P. Fernandez-Kelly, "Towanda's Triumph"; B. Fine, *Social Capital Versus Social Theory;* M. Gonzalez de la Rocha, *Private Adjustments;* D. Narayan et al., *Crying out for Change;* A. Lareau, "Social Class Differences in Family-School Relationships."

[46] D. K. Shipler, *The Working Poor;* G. J. Duncan & J. Brooks-Gunn, *Consequences of Growing Up Poor;* W. J. Wilson, *The Truly Disadvantaged.*

[47] C. W. Mills, *The Power Elite.*

[48] S. J. Haider & K. McGarry, "Recent Trends in Resource Sharing Among the Poor"; K. Edin & L. Lein, *Making Ends Meet;* D. K. Shipler, *The Working Poor.*

[49] P. L. Carter, "Straddling Boundaries."

[50] R. R. McCrae & P. T. Costa, Jr., "Toward a New Generation of Personality Theories," "A Five-Factor Theory of Personality"; R. R. McCrae et al., "Age Differences in Personality Across the Adult Life Span," "Nature over Nurture."

[51] M. Harrington, "The Invisible Land."

[52] P. A. Jargowsky, *Poverty and Place;* W. J. Wilson, *The Truly Disadvantaged* and *When Work Disappears;* D. Narayan et al., *Crying out for Change;* A. Levine & J. Nidiffer, *Beating the Odds;* T. Mortenson, "A Conversation About Diversity"; L. M. Pachter et al., "Do Parenting and the Home Environment, Maternal Depression, Neighborhood, and Chronic Poverty Affect Child Behavioral Problems Differently in Different Racial-Ethnic Groups?"; J. Carroll, "Speaker Says New 'Culture of Poverty' Sweeping U.S."

[53] G. Hofstede, *Culture's Consequences.*

[54] J. Carroll, "Speaker Says New 'Culture of Poverty' Sweeping U.S."

[55] R. M. Rizzo & L. J. Parks, "The Culture of Generational Poverty"; J. M. Fitchen, *Poverty in Rural America;* E. F. Dubow & M. F. Ippolito, "Effects of Poverty and Quality of the Home Environment on Changes in the Academic and Behavioral Adjustment of Elementary School-Age Children"; J. Iceland, *Poverty in America;* D. P. Moynihan, *Family and Nation;* P. L. Chase-Lansdale & J. Brooks-Gunn, *Escape from Poverty;* P. L. Chase-Lansdale, J. Brooks-Gunn et al., "Young African-American Multigenerational Families in Poverty"; K. A. Cagney et al., "Neighborhood-Level Cohesion and Disorder"; S. M. Monroe, "Modern Approaches to Conceptualizing and Measuring Human Life Stress"; D. K. Shipler, *The Working Poor.*

[56] G. W. Evans & K. English, "The Environment of Poverty"; G. W. Evans, "The Environment of Childhood Poverty."

[57] R. Sennett & J. Cobb, *The Hidden Injuries of Class;* J. MacLeod, *Ain't No Makin' It.*

[58] H. Stier & M. Tienda, "Are Men Marginal to the Family?"

[59] W. Ong, *Orality and Literacy.*

[60] L. J. Rodriguez, *Always Running.*

[61] P. Capponi, *Dispatches from the Poverty Line;* T. Nonn, "Hitting Bottom"; L. Ojeda et al., "Socioeconomic Status and Cultural Predictors of Male Role Attitudes Among Mexican American Men"; R. E. Nisbett & D. Cohen, *Culture of Honor.*

[62] D. Cohen et al., "'When You Call Me That, Smile!'"

[63] D. K. Shipler, *The Working Poor.*

[64] R. L. Flores, "The Effect of Poverty on Young Children's Ability to Organize Everyday Events."

[65] D. H. Fischer, *Albion's Seed;* J. E. Pearce, *Days of Darkness;* K. F. Otterbein, "Five Feuds."

[66] J. Kozol, *Amazing Grace.*

[67] P. E. DeVol, *Getting Ahead in a Just-Gettin'-By World.*

[68] D. Sather, "Al Silva: Escaping Poverty & Achieving Excellence"

[69] S. McLanahan, "Family Structure and the Reproduction of Poverty," "Family Structure and Dependency"; S. McLanahan & K. Booth, "Mother-Only Families"; I. Garfinkel & S. McLanahan, *Single Mothers and Their Children;* F. F. Furstenburg, Jr. et al., "Paternal Participation and Children's Well-Being After Marital Dissolution"; S. McLanahan & G. Sandefur, *Growing Up with a Single Parent;* D. J. Eggebeen & D. T. Lichter, "Race, Family Structure, and Changing Poverty Among American Children"; P. Boss & G. Greenberg, "Family Boundary Ambiguity"; P. Florsheim, "The Economic and Psychological Dynamics of Single Motherhood and Nonresident Paternal Involvement"; E. W. Gordon, "The Myths and Realities of African-American Fatherhood."

[70] S. E. Mayer, *What Money Can't Buy;* J. Brooks-Gunn et al., "Poor Families, Poor Outcomes"; L. J. Rodriguez, *Always Running.*

[71] L. J. Rodriguez, *Always Running;* N. Zill, "The Changing Realities of Family Life."

[72] N. Zill, "The Changing Realities of Family Life."

[73] L. J. Rodriguez, *Always Running.*

[74] R. Sennett & J. Cobb, *The Hidden Injuries of Class;* S. E. Mayer, *What Money Can't Buy.*

[75] Oscar Lewis, "The Culture of Poverty."

[76] D. Goleman, *Social Intelligence: The Hidden Impact of Relationships.*

[77] Oscar Lewis, "The Culture of Poverty."

[78] C. B. Broderick, *Understanding Family Process;* M. J. Cox & B. Paley, "Families as Systems"; R. D. Parke, "Development in the Family."

[79] S. F. Hughes et al., "The Family Life Cycle and Clinical Intervention"; K. Power et al., "A Controlled Comparison of Eye Movement Desensitization and Reprocessing Versus Exposure Plus Cognitive Restructuring Versus Waiting List in the Treatment of Post-Traumatic Stress Disorder."

[80] C. B. Broderick, *Understanding Family Process;* K. Hoff & A. Sen, "The Kin System as a Poverty Trap?"; M. J. Cox & B. Paley, "Families as Systems."

[81] F. Walsh, "A Family Resilience Framework," *Normal Family Processes,* "The Concept of Family Resilience."

[82] Case study written by Michael Dumont.

[83] S. Covey, *The 7 Habits of Highly Effective People;* J. Bradshaw, *Bradshaw on: The Family;* L. Vygotsky, *Mind and Society.*

[84] J. Bradshaw, *Bradshaw on: The Family;* S. Wegscheider-Cruse, *Co-Dependency;* R. Subby, *Lost in the Shuffle;* J. P. Morgan, Jr., "What Is Codependency?"; A. R. Anderson & C. S. Henry, "Family System Characteristics and Parental Behaviors as Predictors of Adolescent Substance Use"; V. S. Dahinten et al., "Adolescent Children of Adolescent Mothers"; M. Beattie, *Beyond Codependency.*

[85] S. McLanahan, "Family Structure and the Reproduction of Poverty."

[86] J. E. LeDoux, "Emotional Memory Systems in the Brain," "Emotion," *The Emotional Brain,* "Emotion, Memory and the Brain"; A. Bechara et al., "Emotion, Decision Making and the Orbitofrontal Cortex"; M. Power et al., *Cognition and Emotion.*

[87] A. Arrien, *The Four-Fold Way,* p. 273.

[88] B. Hart & T. R. Risley, *Meaningful Differences in the Everyday Experience of Young American Children;* M. Linver et al., "Measuring Infants' Home Environment"; A. Lareau, *Unequal Childhoods;* R. H. Bradley & R. F. Corwyn, "Socioeconomic Status and Child Development"; M. K. Eamon, "The Effects of Poverty on Children's Socioemotional Development."

[89] M. Gladwell, *Outliers,* "How David Beats Goliath."

[90] G. Field, "The Psychological Deficits and Treatment Needs of Chronic Criminality"; C. Williams & A. Garland, "A Cognitive-Behavioural Therapy Assessment Model for Use in Everyday Clinical Practices."

91 S. E. Mayer, *What Money Can't Buy;* S. Folkman & R. S. Lazarus, "An Analysis of Coping in a Middle-Aged Community Sample"; S. Folkman et al., "Dynamics of a Stressful Encounter"; Carver et al., "Assessing Coping Strategies"; C. J. Holahan & R. H. Moos, "Risk, Resistance, and Psychological Distress."

92 G. J. Duncan & J. Brooks-Gunn, *Consequences of Growing Up Poor;* M. B. Shure & G. Spivack, "Interpersonal Problem-Solving in Young Children"; B. Benard, "Fostering Resiliency in Kids"; M. Rutter, "Resilient Children"; J. K. Felsman, "Risk and Resiliency in Childhood."

93 J. R. Smith et al., "Consequences of Living in Poverty for Young Children's Cognitive and Verbal Ability and Early School Achievement"; D. K. Shipler, *The Working Poor;* G. J. Duncan & J. Brooks-Gunn, *Consequences of Growing Up Poor;* T. Leventhal & J. Brooks-Gunn, "The Neighborhoods They Live in."

94 D. K. Shipler, *The Working Poor;* G. J. Duncan & J. Brooks-Gunn, *Consequences of Growing Up Poor;* T. Leventhal & J. Brooks-Gunn, "The Neighborhoods They Live in."

95 D. K. Shipler, *The Working Poor;* G. J. Duncan & J. Brooks-Gunn, *Consequences of Growing Up Poor;* T. Leventhal & J. Brooks-Gunn, "The Neighborhoods They Live in"; G. Farkas, *Human Capital or Cultural Capital?;* S. A. Dumais, "Cultural Capital, Gender, and School Success."

96 J. R. Smith et al., "Consequences of Living in Poverty for Young Children's Cognitive and Verbal Ability and Early School Achievement"; A. Morin, "Self-Talk and Self-Awareness."

97 G. J. Duncan & J. Brooks-Gunn, *Consequences of Growing Up Poor;* A. Morin, "Characteristics of an Effective Internal Dialogue in the Acquisition of Self-Information."

98 First published in *Instructional Leader* as R. K. Payne, "Moving from Middle Class to Situational Poverty—from Stability to Instability: What You Can Do to Help Your Students and Parents During the Present Economic Downturn."

99 E. Kübler-Ross, *On Death and Dying.*

100 H. Conway, *Collaboration for Kids.*

101 J. Irwin et al., "Social Assets and Mental Distress Among the Homeless."

102 S. Covey, *The 7 Habits of Highly Effective People;* R. Ferguson, *Toward Excellence with Equity;* S. J. Wolin & S. Wolin, *The Resilient Self;* S. I. Greenspan & B. L. Benderly, *The Growth of the Mind and the Endangered Origins of Intelligence.*

103 A. Lareau, *Unequal Childhoods.*

104 J. P. Shapiro et al., "Invincible Kids."

105 L. J. Rodriguez, *Always Running;* P. Capponi, *Dispatches from the Poverty Line* and *The War at Home;* M. Gladwell, *Outliers;* P. Tough, *Whatever It Takes;* Waxman et al., "Resiliency Among Students at Risk of Academic Failure."

106 S. Covey, *The 7 Habits of Highly Effective People;* R. Ferguson, *Toward Excellence with Equity;* S. J. Wolin & S. Wolin, *The Resilient Self;* S. I. Greenspan & B. L. Benderly, *The Growth of the Mind and the Endangered Origins of Intelligence.*

107 M. Wheatley, *Leadership and the New Science,* pp. 8–13.

108 *Ibid.,* pp. 34–35.

109 P. Capponi, *Dispatches from the Poverty Line.*

110 L. J. Rodriguez, *Always Running;* P. Capponi, *Dispatches from the Poverty Line;* D. K. Shipler, *The Working Poor;* M. Gladwell, *Outliers.*

111 S. Covey, *The 7 Habits of Highly Effective People.*

112 L. J. Rodriguez, *Always Running;* P. Capponi, *Dispatches from the Poverty Line;* D. K. Shipler, *The Working Poor;* M. Gladwell, *Outliers.*

113 L. J. Rodriguez, *Always Running;* P. Capponi, *Dispatches from the Poverty Line.*

114 R. J. Sampson & J. H. Laub, "Urban Poverty and the Family Context of Delinquency"; M. E. Lamb, *Parenting and Child Development in 'Nontraditional' Families;* L. M. Berger & J. Brooks-Gunn, "Socioeconomic Status, Parenting Knowledge and Behaviors, and Perceived Maltreatment of Young Low-Birth-Weight Children"; L. M. Berger, "Socioeconomic Factors and Substandard Parenting"; A. N. LeBlank, *Random Family.*

[115] A. A. Ferguson, *Bad Boys.*

[116] S. E. Mayer, *What Money Can't Buy;* L. J. Rodriguez, *Always Running;* G. J. Duncan & J. Brooks-Gunn, *Consequences of Growing Up Poor;* R. Arum, *Judging School Discipline.*

[117] A. A. Ferguson, *Bad Boys.*

[118] S. E. Mayer, *What Money Can't Buy;* S. McLanahan, "Parent Absence or Poverty"; J. Mathews, *Work Hard. Be Nice;* P. Tough, *Whatever It Takes;* R. H. DuRant et al., "Factors Associated with the Use of Violence Among Urban Black Adolescents."

[119] S. E. Mayer, *What Money Can't Buy;* D. K. Shipler, *The Working Poor;* P. Tough, *Whatever It Takes;* J. Lehrer, "Don't! The Secret of Self-Control"; Barbarin et al., "Children Enrolled in Public Pre-K"; J. Brooks-Gunn et al., "Do Neighborhoods Influence Child and Adolescent Development?"; Caughy et al., "The Effect of Residential Neighborhood on Child Behavior Problems in First Grade."

[120] L. M. McNeil, *Contradictions of Control.*

[121] Cf. R. A. Bailey, *Conscious Discipline;* S. S. Khalsa, *Teaching Discipline and Self-Respect;* H. Walker et al., *Antisocial Behavior in School.*

[122] F. Perls, *Gestalt Therapy;* E. Berne, *Transactional Analysis in Psychotherapy* and *Games People Play;* S. S. Khalsa, *Teaching Discipline and Self-Respect.*

[123] E. Berne, *Transactional Analysis in Psychotherapy* and *Games People Play.*

[124] R. N. Caine & G. Caine, *Making Connections.*

[125] H. L. Hodgkinson, "What Should We Call People?"; A. C. Lewis, "Breaking the Cycle of Poverty"; J. Brooks-Gunn et al., "Poor Families, Poor Outcomes"; J. R. Smith et al., "Consequences of Living in Poverty for Young Children's Cognitive and Verbal Ability and Early School Achievement"; L. Pagani et al., "The Influence of Poverty on Children's Classroom Placement and Behavior Problems"; G. J. Duncan & J. Brooks-Gunn, *Consequences of Growing Up Poor.*

[126] R. Balfanz & V. Byrnes, "Closing the Mathematics Achievement Gap in High-Poverty Middle Schools"; E. C. Crowe et al., "Examining the Core"; Obradovic et al., "Academic Achievement of Homeless and Highly Mobile Children in an Urban School District"; M. J. Farah et al., "Poverty, Privilege, and Brain Development," "Childhood Poverty"; H. Zhang & D. J. Cowen, "Mapping Academic Achievement and Public School Choice Under the No Child Left Behind Legislation"; D. Berliner, "Our Impoverished View of Educational Reform"; U.S. Department of Education, "NAEP Data Explorer"; S. R. Sirin, "Socioeconomic Status and Academic Achievement"; S. Cavanaugh, "Poverty's Effect on U.S. Scores Greater Than for Other Nations."

[127] V. P. John & E. Leacock, "Transforming the Structure of Failure."

[128] R. J. Hernstein & C. Murray, *The Bell Curve.*

[129] Cf. S. J. Gould, *The Mismeasure of Man;* S. P. Verney, "Culture-Fair Cognitive Ability Assessment."

[130] H. L. Minton, "Charting Life History"; J. N. Shurkin, *Terman's Kids;* S. J. Ceci, *On Intelligence;* J. Brooks-Gunn et al., "Ethnic Differences in Children's Intelligence Test Scores."

[131] J. M. Najman et al., "The Generational Transmission of Socioeconomic Inequalities in Child Cognitive Development and Emotional Health."

[132] M. Gladwell, *Outliers.*

[133] L. Pagani et al., "The Influence of Poverty on Children's Classroom Placement and Behavior Problems"; G. J. Duncan & J. Brooks-Gunn, *Consequences of Growing Up Poor.*

[134] R. Feuerstein et al., *Instrumental Enrichment.*

[135] J. P. Lantolf, "Sociocultural Theory and Second Language Acquisition"; R. Donato, "Collective Scaffolding in Second-Language Learning"; A. Aljaafreh & J. P. Lantolf, "Negative Feedback as Regulation and Second-Language Learning in the Zone of Proximal Development"; L. Vygotsky, *Mind and Society;* H. Nassaji & M. Swain, "A Vygotskian Perspective Towards Corrective Feedback in L2"; R. Donato & B. Adair-Hauck, "Discourse Perspectives on Formal Instruction"; R. Rommetveit, "Language Acquisition as Increasing Linguistic Structuring of Experience and Symbolic Behavior Control"; G. W. Evans et al., "The Social Consequences of Self-Control"; G. W. Evans & J. Rosenbaum, "Self-Regulation and the Income-Achievement Gap."

[136] R. Feuerstein et al., *Instrumental Enrichment.*

[137] M. M. Kishiyama et al., "Socioeconomic Disparities Affect Prefrontal Function in Children"; D. R. Lynam et al., "The Interaction Between Impulsivity and Neighborhood Context on Offending"; Morey et al., "The Role of Trauma-Related Distractors on Neural Systems for Working Memory and Emotion Processing in Posttraumatic Stress Disorder."

[138] R. J. Sawyer et al., "Direct Teaching, Strategy Instruction, and Strategy Instruction with Explicit Self-Regulation"; D. H. Schunk & B. J. Zimmerman, *Self-Regulation of Learning and Performance.*

[139] R. Feuerstein et al., *Instrumental Enrichment;* H. Sharron & M. Coulter, *Changing Children's Minds.*

[140] R. Feuerstein et al., *Instrumental Enrichment.*

[141] For a more in-depth look at these strategies, see R. K. Payne, *Research-Based Strategies* and *Under-Resourced Learners.*

[142] A. S. Palincsar & A. L. Brown, "The Reciprocal Teaching of Comprehension-Fostering and Comprehension-Monitoring Activities."

[143] R. K. Payne, *Under-Resourced Learners.*

[144] L. Shulman, "A Union of Insufficiencies."

[145] Cf. D. Conley & K. Albright (Eds.), *After the Bell;* R. Edmonds, "Characteristics of Effective Schools"; D. Levine, "Update on Effective Schools"; D. MacKenzie, "Research for School Improvement."

[146] R. K. Payne, *Under-Resourced Learners,* Chapter 6.

[147] A. H. Wingfield, "About Those 79 Cents."

[148] Children's Defense Fund, "Child Poverty in America 2016."

[149] First published in R. K. Payne, *Emotional Poverty.*

[150] C. Auzenne-Curl, personal correspondence.

[151] M. Clair & J. S. Denis, "Sociology of Racism."

[152] M. Diament, "Audit Warns of Potential SSI Fraud."

[153] Social Security Administration, "Understanding Supplemental Security Income SSI Benefits—2018 Edition."

[154] M. R. Montaño-Harmon, "Presentation Given to Harris County Department of Education, Houston, TX."

[155] Centers for Disease Control and Prevention, "Health, United States, 2015."

[156] *Ibid.*

[157] *Ibid.*

[158] O. Khazan, "Being Black in America Can Be Hazardous to Your Health."

[159] U.S. Department of Health and Human Services, "Facts and Statistics."

[160] *Ibid.*

[161] L. Kraus, "2016 Disability Statistics Annual Report."

[162] U.S. Census Bureau, "Table 4. Families in Poverty by Type of Family."

[163] C. Connley, "Reminder."

[164] R. V. Reeves & K. Guyot, "Black Women Are Earning More College Degrees, But That Alone Won't Close Race Gaps."

[165] U.S. Government Accountability Office, "K–12 Education."

[166] S. Johnson et al., "State of the Art Review."

[167] *Ibid.*

[168] *Ibid.*

[169] S. Mullainathan & E. Shafir, *Scarcity.*

[170] B. Hart & T. R. Risley, *Meaningful Differences in the Everyday Experience of Young American Children.*

[171] Food Research and Action Center, "Rural Hunger in America."

[172] *Ibid.*

[173] S. Johnson et al., "State of the Art Review."

[174] M. Schamberg, "The Cost of Living in Poverty," p. 8.

[175] *Ibid.,* p. 9.

[176] *Ibid.,* p. 20.

[177] E. Finegood et al., "Parenting in Poverty."

[178] *Ibid.*

[179] S. Johnson et al., "State of the Art Review."

[180] D. Berliner, "Poverty and Potential."

[181] *Ibid.*

[182] *Ibid.*

[183] Oxford Dictionaries, "Epigenetics."

[184] What Is Epigenetics, "A Super Brief and Basic Explanation of Epigenetics for Total Beginners."

[185] S. Johnson et al., "State of the Art Review"

[186] M. J. Farah et al., "Poverty, Privilege, and Brain Development," p. 6.

[187] *Ibid.*

[188] *Ibid.*

[189] *Ibid.*

[190] S. Johnson, "State of the Art Review."

[191] *Ibid.*

[192] *Ibid.*

[193] *Ibid.*

[194] *Ibid.*

[195] M. J. Farah et al., "Poverty, Privilege, and Brain Development," p. 7.

[196] *Ibid.,* p. 8.

[197] *Ibid.*

[198] M. M. Kishiyama, "Socioeconomic Disparities Affect Prefrontal Function in Children."

[199] G. Toppo, "Study."

[200] *Ibid.*

[201] U.S. Census Bureau, "2016 American Community Survey 1-Year Estimates, Poverty Status in the Past 12 Months."

[202] U.S. Census Bureau, "Poverty Thresholds."

[203] U.S. Department of Education, National Center for Education Statistics, "The Condition of Education 2018."

[204] *Ibid.*

[205] H. Koball & Y. Jiang, "Basic Facts About Low-Income Children."

[206] *Ibid.*

[207] U.S. Department of Education, National Center for Education Statistics, "The Condition of Education 2018."

[208] U.S. Bureau of Labor Statistics, "Consumer Expenditures Survey Table 1110. Deciles of Income Before Taxes."

[209] H. Koball & Y. Jiang, "Basic Facts About Low-Income Children."

[210] Migration Policy Institute, "Data Hub State Immigration Data Profiles."

[211] J. Batalova et al., "Immigration Data Matters."

[212] J. Batalova & E. Alperin, "Immigrants in the U.S. States with the Fastest-Growing Foreign-Born Populations."

[213] *Ibid.*

[214] E. Sibley & K. Brabeck, "Latino Immigrant Students' School Experiences in the United States."

[215] The Center for American Progess & M. D. Nicholson, "The Facts on Immigration Today: 2017 Edition."

[216] A. S. Morris et al., "Targeting Parenting in Early Childhood."

[217] P. M. Krueger et al., "Family Structure and Multiple Domains of Child Well-Being in the United States."

[218] A. Lareau, *Unequal Childhoods.*

[219] P. Boghani, "How Poverty Can Follow Children into Adulthood."

[220] *Ibid.*

[221] *Ibid.*

[222] *Ibid.*

[223] E. Kübler-Ross, *On Death and Dying.*

[224] R. J. Samuelson, "The Culture of Poverty"; R. Sennett & J. Cobb, *The Hidden Injuries of Class;* L. Pagani et al., "The Influence of Poverty on Children's Classroom Placement and Behavior Problems"; N. Zill, "The Changing Realities of Family Life."

[225] *Ibid.*

[226] N. Zill, "The Changing Realities of Family Life."

[227] K. Becker et al., *Understanding and Engaging Under-Resourced College Students.*

[228] D. K. Shipler, *The Working Poor.*

[229] R. K. Payne et al., *Bridges Out of Poverty,* p. 266.

[230] A. O'Connor, *Poverty Knowledge.*

[231] M. Bostrom, "Together for Success."

[232] P. Gorski, "Savage Unrealities," p. 2.

[233] M. Miringoff & M.-L. Miringoff, *The Social Health of the Nation.*

[234] B. K. Bucks et al., "Changes in U.S. Family Finances from 2004 to 2007."

[235] M. Lui et al., *The Color of Wealth.*

[236] P. E. DeVol, *Getting Ahead in a Just-Gettin'-By World.*

[237] C. Valenzuela & J. Addington, *Four Features of Racism.*

[238] *Ibid.*

[239] *Ibid.*

[240] *Ibid.*

[241] *Ibid.*

[242] R. K. Payne, *A Framework for Understanding Poverty* (4th ed.).

[243] R. K. Payne & P. E. DeVol, "Toward a Deeper Understanding of Issues Surrounding Poverty."

[244] P. E. DeVol, *Facilitator Notes for Getting Ahead in a Just Gettin'-By World,* p. 1.

[245] R. K. Payne, *A Framework for Understanding Poverty* (4th ed.).

[246] J. B. Isaacs et al., "Getting Ahead or Losing Ground."

[247] J. Lave & E. Wenger, *Situated Learning.*

[248] A. Deutschman, *Change or Die.*

[249] J. Lave & E. Wenger, *Situated Learning.*

[250] R. D. Putnam, *Bowling Alone.*

[251] J. M. Najman et al., "The Generational Transmission of Socioeconomic Inequalities in Child Cognitive Development and Emotional Health."

[252] B. Hart & T. R. Risley, *Meaningful Differences in the Everyday Experience of Young American Children.*

[253] J. Lave & E. Wenger, *Situated Learning.*

[254] M. M. Kishiyama et al., "Socioeconomic Disparities Affect Prefrontal Function in Children," p. 1.

[255] S. I. Greenspan & B. L. Benderly, *The Growth of the Mind and the Endangered Origins of Intelligence.*

[256] D. Goleman, *Emotional Intelligence.*

[257] A. P. Bohn, "A Framework for Understanding Ruby Payne," para. 4.

[258] R. Bomer et al., "Miseducating Teachers About the Poor."

[259] A. P. Bohn, "A Framework for Understanding Ruby Payne"; R. Bomer et al., "Miseducating Teachers About the Poor"; P. Gorski, "Savage Unrealities."

[260] *Ibid.*

[261] R. Bomer et al., "Miseducating Teachers About the Poor"; P. Gorski, "Savage Unrealities."

[262] A. P. Bohn, "A Framework for Understanding Ruby Payne."

[263] P. Gorski, "Savage Unrealities."

[264] A. P. Bohn, "A Framework for Understanding Ruby Payne"; R. Bomer et al., "Miseducating Teachers About the Poor"; P. Gorski, "Savage Unrealities."

[265] T. Norretranders, *The User Illusion.*

[266] W. Swan, "The Payne School Model's Impact on Student Achievement," p. 2.

[267] *Ibid.,* p. 2.

[268] C. T. Holmes, "Review of Program Evaluations."

[269] C. Taylor & D. Taylor-Ide, *Just and Lasting Change,* p. 19.

[270] *Ibid.,* pp. 17–18.

[271] T. A. Stewart, *Intellectual Capital.*

[272] J. Enriquez, *As the Future Catches You.*

[273] B. Oshry, *Seeing Systems.*

[274] P. Mederly et al., "Sustainable Development Assessment." This is the Sustainable Development Index (SDI) developed in 2000–01 by the Central European Node of the Millennium Project through the American Council for the United Nations University. In 1987 the World Commission on Environment and Development defined sustainability as a concept. In 1992 a total of 178 states agreed at the United Nations Conference of Environment and Development to include this concept in official development measures. Consensus appears to be emerging that sustainable development may well be "the third global revolution," following the agricultural and industrial revolutions (Mederly et al., pp. 5, 8).

[275] Congressional Budget Office, "The Distribution of U.S. Income, 2014."

[276] P. Saffo, "Six Rules for Effective Forecasting."

[277] C. Taylor & D. Taylor-Ide, *Just and Lasting Change,* p. 58.

[278] *Ibid.*

[279] *Ibid.,* p. 30.

Bibliography

Adger, C. T., Christian, D., & Taylor, O. (Eds.). (1999). *Making the connection: Language and academic achievement among African-American students.* Washington, DC: Center for Applied Linguistics.

Akerlof, G. (1997). Social distance and social decisions. *Econometrica, 65,* 1005–1028.

Aljaafreh, A., & Lantolf, J. P. (1994). Negative feedback as regulation and second-language learning in the zone of proximal development. *The Modern Language Journal, 78*(4), 465–483.

American Association for Higher Education. (1992). *A new framework prepared by the commission on Chapter 1: Making schools work for children in poverty.* Washington, DC: Author.

Anderson, A. R., & Henry, C. S. (1994). Family system characteristics and parental behaviors as predictors of adolescent substance use. *Adolescence, 29*(114), 405–420.

Anderson, J., Hollinger, D., & Conaty, J. (1993). Re-examining the relationship between school poverty and student achievement. *ERS Spectrum, 11*(2), 21–31.

Arrien, A. (1997). *The four-fold way: Walking the paths of the warrior, teacher, healer and visionary.* New York, NY: HarperCollins.

Arum, R. (2003). *Judging school discipline.* Cambridge, MA: Harvard University Press.

Bailey, R. A. (2000). *Conscious discipline: 7 basic skills for brain smart classroom management.* Oviedo, FL: Loving Guidance.

Balfanz, R., & Byrnes, V. (2006). Closing the mathematics achievement gap in high-poverty middle schools: Enablers and constraints. *Journal of Education for Students Placed at Risk, 11*(2), 143–159.

Bandler, R., & Grinder, J. (1979). *Frogs into princes.* Moab, UT: Real People Press.

Barbarin, O., Bryant, D., McCandies, T., Burchinal, M., Early, D., Clifford, R., ... Howes, C. (2006). Children enrolled in public pre-K: The relation of family life, neighborhood quality, and socioeconomic resources to early competence. *American Journal of Orthopsychiatry, 76*(2), 265–276.

Barnitz, J. G. (1994). Discourse diversity: Principles for authentic talk and literacy instruction. *Journal of Reading, 37,* 586–591.

Bartholomae, D. (1985). Inventing the university. In M. Rose (Ed.), *When a writer can't write* (pp. 134–166). New York, NY: Guilford Press.

Batalova, J., & Alperin, E. (2018, July 10). Immigrants in the U.S. states with the fastest-growing foreign-born populations. Retrieved from https://www.migrationpolicy.org/article/immigrants-us-states-fastest-growing-foreign-born-populations

Batalova, J., Shymonyak, A., & Mittelstadt, M. (2018, March). Immigration data matters. Retrieved from https://www.migrationpolicy.org/research/immigration-data-matters

Baugh, J. (1999). *Out of the mouths of slaves: African-American language and educational malpractice.* Austin, TX: University of Texas Press.

Baugh, J. (2000). *Beyond Ebonics: Linguistic pride and racial prejudice.* New York, NY: Oxford University Press.

Beattie, M. (1989). *Beyond codependency.* Center City, MN: Hazelden.

Bechara, A., Damasio, H., & Damasio, A. R. (2000). Emotion, decision making and the orbitofrontal cortex. *Cerebral Cortex, 10*(3), 295–307.

Becker, K. A., Krodel, K. M., & Tucker, B. H. (2009). *Understanding and engaging under-resourced college students: A fresh look at the influence of economic class on teaching and learning in higher education.* Highlands, TX: aha! Process.

Bell, A. (1984). Language style as audience design. *Language in Society, 13,* 145–204.

Benabou, R. (1993). Workings of a city: Location, education and production. *Quarterly Journal of Economics, 108*(3), 619–652.

Benabou, R. (1996). Equity and efficiency in human capital investment: The local connection. *Review of Economic Studies, 62,* 237–264.

Benabou, R. (1996). Heterogeneity, stratification and growth: Macroeconomic effects of community structure. *American Economic Review, 86,* 584–609.

Benard, B. (1991). Fostering resiliency in kids: Protective factors in the family, school, and community. Retrieved from https://eric.ed.gov/?id=ED335781

Berger, K. S. (2011). *The developing person through the life span* (8th ed.). New York, NY: Worth.

Berger, L. M. (2007). Socioeconomic factors and substandard parenting. *Social Service Review, 81*(3), 485–522.

Berger, L. M., & Brooks-Gunn, J. (2005). Socioeconomic status, parenting knowledge and behaviors, and perceived maltreatment of young low-birth-weight children. *Social Service Review, 79*(2), 237–267.

Berliner, D. (1988). Implications of studies of expertise in pedagogy for teacher education and evaluation. In J. Pfleiderer (Ed.), *New directions for teacher assessment: Proceedings of the 1988 ETS invitational conference* (pp. 39–68). Princeton, NJ: Educational Testing Service.

Berliner, D. (2006). Our impoverished view of educational reform. *Teachers College Record, 108*(6), 949–995.

Berliner, D. C. (2009, March 9). Poverty and potential: Out-of-school factors and school success. National Educational Policy Center. Retrieved from https://nepc.colorado.edu/publication/poverty-and-potential

Berne, E. (1961). *Transactional analysis in psychotherapy: A systematic individual and social psychiatry.* New York, NY: Ballantine Books.

Berne, E. (1964). *Games people play: The psychology of human relationships.* New York, NY: Grove Press.

Berne, E. (1996). *Games people play: The psychology of human relationships* (2nd ed.). New York, NY: Ballantine Books.

Bianchi, S. M. (1990). America's children: Mixed prospects. *Population Bulletin, 45*(1), 1–42.

Biber, D., & Finegan, E. (Eds.). (1994). *Sociolinguistic perspectives on register.* New York, NY: Oxford University Press.

Bicchieri, C. (2006). *The grammar of society.* Cambridge, England: Cambridge University Press.

Bloom, B. (1976). *Human characteristics and school learning.* New York, NY: McGraw-Hill.

Boals, B. M., and others. (1990). Children in poverty: Providing and promoting a quality education. Retrieved from https://files.eric.ed.gov/fulltext/ED351126.pdf

Boghani, P. (2017, November 22). How poverty can follow children into adulthood. *Frontline.* Retrieved from https://www.pbs.org/wgbh/frontline/article/how-poverty-can-follow-children-into-adulthood

Bohn, A. P. (2006). A framework for understanding Ruby Payne. Retrieved from http://www.rethinkingschools.org/archive/21_02/fram212.shtml

Bomer, R., Dworin, J., May, L., & Semingson, P. (2008). Miseducating teachers about the poor: A critical analysis of Ruby Payne's claims about poverty. *Teachers College Record, 110,* 2497–2531.

Boss, P., & Greenberg, G. (2004). Family boundary ambiguity: A new variable in family stress theory. *Family Process, 23*(4), 535–546.

Bostrom, M. (2004). Together for success: Communicating low-wage work as economy, not poverty. Retrieved from http://www.topospartnership.com/wp-content/uploads/2013/03/TogetherforSuccess.pdf

Bradley, R. H., & Corwyn, R. F. (2002). Socioeconomic status and child development. *Annual Review of Psychology, 53,* 371–399.

Bradshaw, J. (1988). *Bradshaw on: The family.* Deerfield Beach, FL: Health Communications.

Broderick, C. B. (1993). *Understanding family process: Basics of family systems theory.* Newbury Park, CA: Sage.

Brooks-Gunn, J., Duncan, G. J., & Aber, J. L. (Eds.). (1997). *Neighborhood poverty: Context and consequences for children.* New York, NY: Russell Sage.

Brooks-Gunn, J., Duncan, G. J., Klebanov, P. K., & Sealand, N. (1993). Do neighborhoods influence child and adolescent development? *American Journal of Sociology, 99*(2), 353–395.

Brooks-Gunn, J., Duncan, G. J., & Maritato, N. (1997). Poor families, poor outcomes: The well-being of children and youth. In G. J. Duncan & J. Brooks-Gunn (Eds.), *Consequences of growing up poor* (pp. 1–17). New York, NY: Russell Sage.

Brooks-Gunn, J., Klebanov, P. K., & Duncan, G. J. (1996). Ethnic differences in children's intelligence test scores: Role of economic deprivation, home environment, and maternal characteristics. *Child Development, 67*(2), 396–408.

Brouwer, S. (1998). *Sharing the pie: A citizen's guide to wealth and power in America.* New York, NY: Henry Holt.

Brown, J. S., Collins, A., & Duguid, P. (1989). Situated cognition and the culture of learning. *Educational Researcher, 18*(1), 32–42.

Bucks, B. K., Kennickell, A. B., Mach, T. L., & Moore, K. B. (2009). Changes in U.S. family finances from 2004 to 2007: Evidence from the survey of consumer finances. Retrieved from http://www.federalreserve.gov/pubs/bulletin/2009/pdf/scf09.pdf

Cagney, K. A., Glass, T. A., Skarupski, K. A., Barnes, L. L., Schwartz, B. S., & Mendes de Leon, C. F. (2009). Neighborhood-level cohesion and disorder: Measurement and validation in two older adult urban populations. *The Journals of Gerontology Series B: Psychological Sciences and Social Sciences, 64B*(3), 415–424.

Caine, R. N., & Caine, G. (1994). *Making connections: Teaching and the human brain.* Menlo Park, CA: Addison-Wesley.

Callanan, M. A. (1985). How parents label objects for young children: The role of input in the acquisition of category hierarchies. *Child Development, 56,* 508–523.

Campbell, J. K. (1966). Honour and the devil. In J. G. Peristiany (Ed.), *Honour and shame: The values of Mediterranean society* (pp. 141–170). Chicago, IL: University of Chicago Press.

Capponi, P. (1997). *Dispatches from the poverty line.* Toronto, Ontario, Canada: Penguin Books Canada.

Capponi, P. (2000). *The war at home: An intimate portrait of Canada's poor.* Toronto, Ontario, Canada: Penguin Books Canada.

Carroll, J. (2006, October 6). Speaker says new 'culture of poverty' sweeping U.S. Retrieved from https://www.northtexascatholic.org/NTC_10.6.06.pdf

Carter, P. L. (2006). Straddling boundaries: Identity, culture and school. *Sociology of Education, 79*(4), 304–328.

Carver, C. S., Scheier, M. F., & Weintraub, J. K. (1989). Assessing coping strategies: A theoretically based approach. *Journal of Personality and Social Psychology, 56,* 267–283.

Caughy, M. O., Nettles, S. M., & O'Campo, P. J. (2008). The effect of residential neighborhood on child behavior problems in first grade. *American Journal of Community Psychology, 42,* 39–50.

Caughy, M. O., & O'Campo, P. J. (2006). Neighborhood poverty, social capital, and the cognitive development of African-American preschoolers. *American Journal of Community Psychology, 37,* 141–154.

Cavanaugh, S. (2007). Poverty's effect on U.S. scores greater than for other nations. *Education Week, 27*(15), 1, 13.

Ceci, S. J. (1996). *On intelligence: A bioecological treatise on intellectual development.* Cambridge, MA: Harvard University Press.

The Center for American Progess, & Nicholson, M. D. (2017, April 20). The facts on immigration today: 2017 edition. Retrieved from https://www.americanprogress.org/issues/immigration/reports/2017/04/20/430736/facts-immigration-today-2017-edition

Centers for Disease Control and Prevention. (2016). Health, United States, 2015. Retrieved from https://www.cdc.gov/nchs/data/hus/hus15.pdf

Chase-Lansdale, P. L., & Brooks-Gunn, J. (Eds.). (1995). *Escape from poverty: What makes a difference for children?* New York, NY: Cambridge University Press.

Chase-Lansdale, P. L., Brooks-Gunn, J., & Zamsky, E. S. (1994). Young African-American multigenerational families in poverty: Quality of mothering and grandmothering. *Child Development, 65,* 373–393.

Cheng, L.-C., & Page-Adams, D. (1996). Education, assets, and intergenerational well-being: The case of female headed families. Working paper no. 96-4. St. Louis. MO: Center for Social Development. Retrieved from https://openscholarship.wustl.edu/cgi/viewcontent.cgi?article=1194&context=csd_research

Children's Defense Fund. (2017, September 18). Child poverty in America 2016: National analysis. Retrieved from https://www.childrensdefense.org/wp-content/uploads/2018/06/child-poverty-in-america-2016.pdf

Christakis, D. A., Gilkerson, J., Richards, J. A., Zimmerman, F. J., Garrison, M. M., Xu, D., … Yapanel, U. (2009). Audible television and decreased adult words, infant vocalizations, and conversational turns. *Archives of Pediatric Adolescent Medicine, 163*(6), 554–558.

Christenbury, L. (2000). *Making the journey: Being and becoming a teacher of English language arts* (2nd ed.). Portsmouth, NH: Boynton/Cook Heinemann.

Clair, M., & Denis, J. S. (2015). Sociology of racism. *International Encyclopedia of the Social & Behavioral Sciences,* 2nd edition, Volume 19. doi:10.1016/B978-0-08-097086-8.32122-5

Clark, R. C. (2008). *Building expertise: Cognitive methods for training and performance improvement* (3rd ed.). San Francisco, CA: Pfeiffer.

Cohen, D., Vandellow, J., Puente, S., & Rantilla, A. (1999). 'When you call me that, smile!' How norms for politeness, interaction styles, and aggression work together in Southern culture. *Social Psychology Quarterly, 62*(3), 257–275.

Collins, B. C. (1997). *Emotional unavailability: Recognizing it, understanding it, and avoiding its trap.* Lincolnwood, IL: NTC/Contemporary Publishing.

Comer, J. (1995). Lecture given at Education Service Center, Region IV. Houston, TX.

Comer, J. (2001, April 23). Schools that develop children. *The American Prospect, 12*(7). Retrieved from http://prospect.org/article/schools-develop-children

Congressional Budget Office. (2018, March 19). The distribution of U.S. income, 2014. Retrieved from https://www.cbo.gov/publication/53597

Conley, D., & Albright, K. (Eds.). (2004). *After the bell: Family background, public policy and educational success.* New York, NY: Routledge.

Connell, R. W. (1994). Poverty and education. *Harvard Educational Review, 64*(2), 125–150.

Connley, C. (2018, April 10). Reminder: Today isn't Equal Pay Day for black, Latina, or Native American women. Retrieved from https://www.cnbc.com/2018/04/10/today-isnt-equal-pay-day-for-black-latina-or-native-american-women.html

Conway, H. (2006). *Collaboration for kids.* Highlands, TX: aha! Process.

Cook, J. T., & Brown, L. J. (1993). *Two Americas: Racial differences in child poverty in the U.S.: A linear trend analysis to the year 2010.* Research-in-progress working paper. Medford, MA: Tufts University.

Cook, T. D., Church, M. B., Ajanaku, S., Shadish, W. R., Kim, J., & Cohen, R. (1997). The development of occupational aspirations and expectations among inner-city boys. *Child Development, 67*(6), 3368–3385.

Coontz, S. (1995). The American family and the nostalgia trap. *Phi Delta Kappan, 76*(7), 1–20.

Corcoran, M. (1995). Rags to rags: Poverty and mobility in the United States. *Annual Review of Sociology, 21,* 237–267.

Corcoran, M., & Adams, T. (1997). Race, sex, and the intergenerational transmission of poverty. In G. J. Duncan & J. Brooks-Gunn (Eds.), *Consequences of growing up poor* (pp. 461–517). New York, NY: Russell Sage.

Covey, S. (1989). *The 7 habits of highly effective people.* New York, NY: Free Press.

Cox, M. J., & Paley, B. (1997). Families as systems. *Annual Review of Psychology, 48,* 243–267.

Crowe, E. C., Connor, C., & Petscher, Y. (2009). Examining the core: Relations among reading curricula, poverty, and first through third grade reading achievement. *Journal of School Psychology, 47*(3), 187–214.

Cummings, D. (1997, January 9). A different approach to teaching language. *The Atlanta Constitution,* p. B1.

Cunningham, P. M., & Allington, R. L. (2003). *Classrooms that work* (3rd ed.). Boston, MA: Pearson Education.

Dahinten, V. S., Shapka, J. D., & Willms, J. D. (2007). Adolescent children of adolescent mothers: The impact of family functioning on trajectories of development. *Journal of Youth and Adolescence, 36*(2), 195–212.

Danziger, S., Heflin, C., Corcoran, M., Oltmans, E., & Wang, H.-C. (2002). Does it pay to move from welfare to work? *Journal of Policy Analysis and Management, 21,* 671–692.

Delpit, L. (1995). *Other people's children: Cultural conflict in the classroom.* New York, NY: New Press.

Dennison, P. E., & Dennison, G. E. (1994). *Brain gym.* Ventura, CA: Edu-Kinesthetics.

Deutschman, A. (2007). *Change or die: The three keys to change at work and in life.* New York, NY: HarperCollins.

DeVol, P. E. (2013). *Facilitator notes for Getting Ahead in a Just-Gettin'-By World: Building your resources for a better life* (3rd ed.). Highlands, TX: aha! Process.

DeVol, P. E. (2015). *Getting ahead in a just-gettin'-by world: Building your resources for a better life* (3rd. rev. ed.). Highlands, TX: aha! Process.

Diament, M. (2016, March 8). Audit warns of potential SSI fraud. Retrieved from https://www.disabilityscoop.com/2016/03/08/audit-warns-potential-ssi-fraud/22011

Domagala-Zysk, E. (2006). The significance of adolescents' relationships with significant others and school failure. *School Psychology International, 27*(2), 232–247.

Donato, R. (1994). Collective scaffolding in second-language learning. In J. P. Lantolf & G. Appel (Eds.), *Vygotskian approaches to second-language research* (4th ed., pp. 33–56). Norwood, NJ: Ablex.

Donato, R., & Adair-Hauck, B. (1992). Discourse perspectives on formal instruction. *Language Awareness, 1,* 73–90.

Donato, R., & McCormick, D. (1994). A sociocultural perspective on language learning abilities: The role of mediation. *The Modern Language Journal, 78*(4), 453–464.

Dubow, E. F., & Ippolito, M. F. (1994). Effects of poverty and quality of the home environment on changes in the academic and behavioral adjustment of elementary school-age children. *Journal of Clinical Child Psychology, 23,* 401–412.

Duckworth, A. L., Peterson, C., Matthews, M. D., & Kelly, D. R. (2007). Grit: Perseverance and passion for long-term goals. *Journal of Personality and Social Psychology, 92*(6), 1087–1101.

Dumais, S. A. (2002). Cultural capital, gender, and school success: The role of habitus. *Sociology of Education, 75*(1), 44–68.

Duncan, G. J., & Brooks-Gunn, J. (Eds.). (1997). *Consequences of growing up poor.* New York, NY: Russell Sage.

DuRant, R. H., Cadenhead, C., Pendergrast, R. A., Slavens, G., & Linder, C. W. (1994). Factors associated with the use of violence among urban black adolescents. *American Journal of Public Health, 84*(4), 612–617.

Durham, R. E., Farkas, G., Hammer, C., Tomblin, J. B., & Catts, H. W. (2007). Kindergarten oral language skill: A key variable in the intergenerational transmission of socioeconomic status. *Research in Social Stratification and Mobility, 25*(4), 294–305.

Durlaf, S. N. (2000). A framework for the study of individual behavior and social interactions. Retrieved from http://www.irp.wisc.edu/publications/dps/pdfs/dp122001.pdf

Durlaf, S. N. (2000). The memberships theory of poverty: The role of group affiliations in determining socioeconomic outcomes. Paper presented at Understanding Poverty in America: Progress and Problems. Madison, WI. Retrieved from http://www.irp.wisc.edu/publications/dps/pdfs/dp122101.pdf

Eamon, M. K. (2001). The effects of poverty on children's socioemotional development: An ecological systems analysis. *Social Work, 46*(3), 256–266.

Edelman, P. B., & Ladner, J. (Eds.). (1991). *Adolescence and poverty: Challenge for the 1990s.* Washington, DC: Center for National Policy.

Edin, K., & Lein, L. (1997). *Making ends meet.* New York, NY: Russell Sage.

Edmonds, R. (1986). Characteristics of effective schools. In U. Neisser (Ed.), *The school achievement of minority children: New perspectives* (pp. 93–104). Hillsdale, NJ: Lawrence Erlbaum.

Educational attainments of students living in poverty: Report of the department of education to the governor and the general assembly of Virginia. Senate document number 13. (1993). Richmond, VA: Virginia State Department of Education.

Eggebeen, D. J., & Lichter, D. T. (1991). Race, family structure, and changing poverty among American children. *American Sociological Review, 56*(6), 801–817.

Einbinder, S. D. (1993). *Five million children: 1993 update.* New York, NY: National Center for Children in Poverty.

Eitzen, D. S. (1992). Problem students: The sociocultural roots. *Phi Delta Kappan, 73*(8), 584–590.

Ellis, J., & Ure, J. (1969). Language varieties: Register. In A. R. Meetham (Ed.), *Encyclopedia of linguistics, information and control* (pp. 251–259). London, England: Pergamon Press.

Enriquez, J. (2001). *As the future catches you.* New York, NY: Crown Business.

Ervin-Tripp, S. M., & Dil, A. S. (1973). *Language acquisition and communicative choice.* Palo Alto, CA: Stanford University Press.

Evans, G. W. (2004). The environment of childhood poverty. *American Psychologist, 59*(2), 77–92.

Evans, G. W., & English, K. (2002). The environment of poverty: Multiple stressor exposure, psychophysiological stress, and socioemotional adjustment. *Child Development, 73*(4), 1238–1248.

Evans, G. W., Maxwell, L. E., & Hart, B. (1999). Parental language and verbal responsiveness to children in crowded homes. *Developmental Psychology, 35*(4), 1020–1023.

Evans, G. W., & Rosenbaum, J. (2008). Self-regulation and the income-achievement gap. *Early Childhood Research Quarterly, 23*(4), 504–514.

Evans, T. D., Cullen, F. T., Burton, V. S., Dunaway, R. G., & Benson, M. L. (1997). The social consequences of self-control: Testing the general theory of crime. *Criminology, 35*(3), 475–504.

Ezarik, M. (2002, May 1). A time and a place. Retrieved from https://www. districtadministration.com/article/time-and-place

Faircloth, B. S., & Hamm, J. V. (2005). Sense of belonging among high school students representing four ethnic groups. *Journal of Youth and Adolescence, 34*(4), 293–309.

Farah, M. J., Noble, K. G., & Hurt, H. (2008). Poverty, privilege, and brain development: Empirical findings and ethical implications. In J. Illes (Ed.), *Neuroethics in the 21st century.* New York, NY: Oxford University Press.

Farah, M. J., Shera, D. M., Savage, J. H., Betancourt, L., Giannetta, J. M., Brodsky, N. L., … Hurt, H. (2006). Childhood poverty: Specific associations with neurocognitive development. *Brain Research, 110*(1), 166–174.

Farkas, G. (1996). *Human capital or cultural capital? Ethnicity and poverty groups in an urban school district.* Hawthorne, NY: Aldine de Gruyter.

Farson, R. (1997). *Management of the absurd: Paradoxes in leadership.* New York, NY: Touchstone.

Felsman, J. K. (1989). Risk and resiliency in childhood: The lives of street children. In T. Dugan & R. Coles (Eds.), *The child in our times* (pp. 56–80). New York, NY: Brunner/ Mazel.

Ferguson, A. A. (2000). *Bad boys: Public schools in the making of black masculinity.* Ann Arbor, MI: University of Michigan Press.

Ferguson, R. (2008). *Toward excellence with equity: An emerging vision for closing the achievement gap.* Cambridge, MA: Harvard Education Press.

Fernald, G. M. (1988). *Remedial techniques in basic school subjects.* Austin, TX: Pro-Ed.

Fernandez-Kelly, M. P. (1994). Towanda's triumph: Social and cultural capital in the transition to adulthood in the urban ghetto. *International Journal of Urban and Regional Research, 18,* 88–111.

Fernández-Villaverde, J., Guerrón-Quintana, P. A., Rubio-Ramírez, J., & Uribe, M. (2009). Risk matters: The real effects of volatility shocks. NBER working papers 14875, National Bureau of Economic Research. Retrieved from https://ideas.repec.org/p/nbr/nberwo/14875.html

Feuerstein, R., Rand, Y., Hoffman, M. B., & Miller, R. (1980). *Instrumental enrichment: An intervention program for cognitive modifiability.* Glenview, IL: Scott, Foresman.

Field, G. (1986). The psychological deficits and treatment needs of chronic criminality. *Federal Probation, 50*(4), 60–66.

Fine, B. (2001). *Social capital versus social theory: Political economy and social science at the turn of the millennium.* London, England: Routledge.

Finegood, E. D., Raver, C. C., DeJoseph, M. L., & Blair, C. (2017). Parenting in poverty: Attention bias and anxiety interact to predict parents' perceptions of daily parenting hassles. *Journal of Family Psychology, 31*(1), 51–60. doi:10.1037/fam0000291

Fischer, D. H. (1989). *Albion's seed: Four British folkways in America.* Oxford, England: Oxford University Press.

Fitchen, J. M. (1995). *Poverty in rural America: A case study.* Prospect Heights, IL: Waveland Press.

Flores, R. L. (2004). The effect of poverty on young children's ability to organize everyday events. *Journal of Children and Poverty, 10*(2), 99–118.

Florsheim, P. (1998). The economic and psychological dynamics of single motherhood and nonresident paternal involvement. *The CEIC Review, 7*(1).

Folkman, S., & Lazarus, R. S. (1980). An analysis of coping in a middle-aged community sample. *Journal of Health and Social Behavior, 21,* 219–239.

Folkman, S., Lazarus, R. S., Dunkel-Schetter, C., DeLongis, A., & Gruen, R. J. (1986). Dynamics of a stressful encounter: Cognitive appraisal, coping, and encounter outcomes. *Journal of Personality and Social Psychology, 50,* 992–1003.

Food Research and Action Center. (2018). Rural hunger in America: Get the facts. Retrieved from http://frac.org/wp-content/uploads/rural-hunger-in-america-get-the-facts.pdf

Forward, S., with Frazier, D. (1998). *Emotional blackmail.* New York, NY: HarperCollins.

Fox, S. (1997). The controversy over Ebonics. *Phi Delta Kappan, 79*(3), 237–240.

Freedman, J., & Combs, G. (1996). *Narrative therapy: The social construction of preferred realities.* New York, NY: W. W. Norton.

Freire, P. (1999). *Pedagogy of the oppressed.* New York, NY: Continuum.

Furstenburg, F. F., Jr., Morgan, P. S., & Allison, P. D. (1987). Paternal participation and children's well-being after marital dissolution. *American Sociological Review, 52*(5), 695–701.

Fussel, P. (1983). *Class: A guide through the American status system.* New York, NY: Ballantine Books.

Galeano, E. (1998). *Upside down: A primer for the looking-glass world.* New York, NY: Metropolitan Books.

Gans, H. J. (1995). *The war against the poor.* New York, NY: Basic Books.

Gardner, H. (1991). *The unschooled mind: How children think and how schools should teach.* New York, NY: Basic Books.

Garfinkel, I., & McLanahan, S. (1986). *Single mothers and their children: A new American dilemma.* Washington, DC: Urban Institute Press.

Garmezy, N. (1991). Resiliency and vulnerability to adverse developmental outcomes associated with poverty. *American Behavioral Scientist, 34*(4), 416–430.

Gee, J. P. (1987). What is literacy? *Teaching and Learning, 2*(1), 3–11.

Ghadessy, M. (Ed.). (1988). *Registers of written English: Situational factors and linguistic features.* London, England: Frances Pinter.

Ghadessy, M. (Ed.). (1993). *Register analysis: Theory and practice.* London, England: Frances Pinter.

Gilyard, K. (1991). *Voices of the self: A study of language competence.* Detroit, MI: Wayne State Press.

Gladwell, M. (2007). *Blink.* New York, NY: Back Bay Books.

Gladwell, M. (2008). *Outliers: The story of success.* New York, NY: Little, Brown.

Gladwell, M. (2009, May 11). How David beats Goliath: When underdogs break the rules. *The New Yorker, 85*(13), 40–49.

Glewwe, P., Jacoby, H., & King, E. (1999). Early childhood nutrition and academic achievement: A longitudinal analysis. doi:10.1016/S0047-2727(00)00118-3

Godinot, X., Heyberger, C., Heyberger, P., Ugarte, M., & Ugarte, R. (2007). Resisting extreme poverty: Learning from families in Burkina Faso and Peru. In D. Narayan, D. Narayan-Parker, & P. L. Petesch (Eds.), *Moving out of poverty* (pp. 273–306). Washington, DC: World Bank.

Goleman, D. (1995). *Emotional intelligence: Why it can matter more than IQ.* New York, NY: Bantam Books.

Goleman, D. (2006). *Social intelligence: The hidden impact of relationships.* New York, NY: Random House.

Gonzalez de la Rocha, M. (2000). *Private adjustments: Household responses to the erosion of work.* New York, NY: UNDP-SEPED.

Gordon, E. W. (1998). The myths and realities of African-American fatherhood. *The CEIC Review, 7*(1).

Gorski, P. (2005). Savage unrealities: Uncovering classism in Ruby Payne's framework [Abridged version]. Retrieved from http://www.edchange.org/publications/Savage_Unrealities_abridged.pdf

Gould, S. J. (1981). *The mismeasure of man.* New York, NY: Norton.

Grant, M. (1985). The kinesthetic approach to teaching: Building a foundation for learning. *Journal of Learning Disabilities, 18*(8), 455–462.

Greenspan, S. I., & Benderly, B. L. (1997). *The growth of the mind and the endangered origins of intelligence.* Reading, MA: Addison-Wesley.

Haberman, M. (1995). *Star teachers of children in poverty.* Madison, WI: Phi Delta Kappa.

Haider, S. J., & McGarry, K. (2005, September 23). Recent trends in resource sharing among the poor. NBER working paper 11612. Cambridge, MA: National Bureau of Economic Research. Retrieved from http://www.nber.org/papers/w11612

Halberstadt, A. G. (1985). Race, socioeconomic status, and nonverbal behavior. In A. W. Siegman & S. Feldstein (Eds.), *Multichannel integrations of nonverbal behavior* (pp. 227–266). Hillsdale, NJ: Lawrence Erlbaum.

Hannaford, C. (1995). *Smart moves: Why learning is not all in your head.* Arlington, VA: Great Ocean.

Hannaford, C. (1996). Smart moves: Understanding children. *Learning, 25*(3), 66–68.

Harper, C. (2005). Breaking poverty cycles: The importance of action in early childhood. CHIP policy briefing 8. Retrieved from https://assets.publishing.service.gov.uk/media/57a08c6a40f0b649740011e0/briefing_8.pdf

Harper, C., Marcus, R., & Moore, K. (2003). Enduring poverty and the conditions of childhood: Lifecourse and intergenerational poverty transmissions. *World Development, 31*(3), 535–554.

Harrington, M. (1962). *The other America.* New York, NY: Simon & Schuster.

Harrington, M. (1971). The invisible land. In E. Penchef (Ed.), *Four horsemen: Pollution, poverty, famine, violence* (pp. 142–154). San Francisco, CA: Canfield Press.

Harris, L. C. (1988). Facts about Texas children. Excerpted from *Children, choice, and change.* Austin, TX: Hogg Foundation for Mental Health, Texas University.

Harrison, L. E., & Huntington, S. P. (Eds.). (2000). *Culture matters: How values shape human progress.* New York, NY: Basic Books.

Hart, B., & Risley, T. R. (1992). American parenting of language-learning children: Persisting differences in family-child interactions observed in natural home environments. *Developmental Psychology, 28*(6), 1096–1105.

Hart, B., & Risley, T. R. (1995). *Meaningful differences in the everyday experience of young American children.* Baltimore, MD: Paul H. Brookes.

Hart, B., & Risley, T. R. (1999). *The social world of children: Learning to talk.* Baltimore, MD: Paul H. Brookes.

Hart, B., & Risley, T. R. (2003). The early catastrophe: The 30 million word gap. *American Educator, 27*(1), 4–9.

Heath, S. B. (1983). *Ways with words: Language, life, and work in communities and classrooms.* Cambridge, England: Cambridge University Press.

Henderson, N. (1996). *Resiliency in schools: Making it happen for students and educators.* Thousand Oaks, CA: Corwin Press.

Hernstein, R. J., & Murray, C. (1994). *The bell curve: Intelligence and class structure in American life.* New York, NY: Free Press.

Hodgkinson, H. L. (1995). What should we call people? Race, class, and the census for 2000. *Phi Delta Kappan, 77,* 173–179.

Hoff, K., & Sen, A. (2005). The kin system as a poverty trap? WPS3575. Washington, DC: World Bank. Retrieved from http://elibrary.worldbank.org/content/workingpaper/10.1596/1813-9450-3575

Hofstede, G. (2002). *Culture's consequences: International differences in work- related values* (2nd ed.). Newbury Park, CA: Sage.

Holahan, C. J., & Moos, R. H. (1987). Risk, resistance, and psychological distress: A longitudinal analysis with adults and children. *Journal of Abnormal Psychology, 96,* 3–13.

Hollingsworth, J. R., & Ybarra, S. E. (2008). *Explicit direct instruction: The power of the well-crafted, well-taught lesson.* Thousand Oaks, CA: Corwin Press.

Holmes, C. T. (n.d.). Review of program evaluations. Retrieved from https://www. ahaprocess.com/wp-content/uploads/2013/09/External-Review-Dr.-Thomas-Holmes.pdf

Hughes, S. F., Berger, M., & Wright, L. (1978). The family life cycle and clinical intervention. *Journal of Marital and Family Therapy, 4*(4), 33–40.

Hyerle, D. (1996). *Visual tools for constructing knowledge.* Alexandria, VA: Association for Supervision and Curriculum Development.

Iceland, J. (2003). *Poverty in America.* Los Angeles, CA: University of California Press.

Idol, L., & Jones, B. F. (Eds.). (1991). *Educational values and cognitive instruction: Implications for reform.* Hillsdale, NJ: Lawrence Erlbaum.

Irwin, J., Lagory, M., Ritchey, F., & Fitzpatrick, K. (2008). Social assets and mental distress among the homeless: Exploring the roles of social support and other forms of social capital on depression. *Social Science and Medicine, 67,* 1935–1943.

Isaacs, J. B., Sawhill, I. V., & Haskins, R. (2008, February). Getting ahead or losing ground: Economic mobility in America. Retrieved from http://www.pewtrusts.org/~/media/ legacy/uploadedfiles/pcs_assets/2008/pewempgettingaheadfull2pdf.pdf

Jargowsky, P. A. (1997). *Poverty and place: Ghettos, barrios and the American city.* New York, NY: Russell Sage.

Jaworski, J. (1996). *Synchronicity: The inner path of leadership.* San Francisco, CA: Berrett-Koehler.

John, V. P., & Leacock, E. (1979). Transforming the structure of failure. In D. A. Wilkerson (Ed.), *Educating all our children: An imperative for democracy* (pp. 76–91). Westport, CT: Mediax.

Johnson, S. B., Riis, J. L., & Noble, K. G. (2016). State of the art review: Poverty and the developing brain. *Pediatrics, 137*(4). doi:10.1542/peds.2015-3075

Jones, B. F., Pierce, J., & Hunter, B. (1988). Teaching students to construct graphic representations. *Educational Leadership, 46*(4), 20–25.

Jonides, J., Lewis, R. L., Nee, D. E., Lustig, C. A., Berman, M. G., & Moore, K. S. (2008). The mind and brain of short-term memory. *Annual Review of Psychology, 59,* 193–224.

Joos, M. (1967). *The five clocks.* San Diego, CA: Harcourt, Brace, & World.

Joos, M. (1967). The styles of the five clocks. In R. D. Abraham & R. C. Troike (Eds.), *Language and cultural diversity in American education* (pp. 145–149). Englewood Cliffs, NJ: Prentice Hall.

Kahlenberg, R. D. (2001). Learning from James Coleman. *Public Interest, 144,* 54–72. Retrieved from https://www.nationalaffairs.com/public_interest/detail/learning-from-james-coleman

Kaplan, R. B. (1966). Cultural thought patterns in inter-cultural education. *Language Learning, 16*(1), 1–20.

Kaplan, R. B. (1972). *The anatomy of rhetoric: Prolegomena to a functional theory of rhetoric.* Concord, MA: Heinle & Heinle.

Kaplan, R. B. (Ed.). (1980). *On the scope of applied linguistics.* Rowley, MA: Newbury House Publishers.

Kaplan, R. B. (1984). Cultural thought patterns in intercultural education. In S. McKay (Ed.), *Composing in a second language* (pp. 43–62). Rowley, MA: Newbury House Publishers.

Kaplan, R. B., & Baldauf, R. B., Jr. (1997). *Language planning: From practice to theory.* Bristol, England: Multilingual Matters.

Karpman, S. (1968). Fairy tales and script drama analysis. *Transactional Analysis Bulletin, 7*(26), 39–43.

Khalsa, S. S. (2007). *Teaching discipline and self-respect.* Thousand Oaks, CA: Corwin Press.

Khanna, V. (n.d.). Impossible scenarios: Lives at the intersection of poverty and late capitalism [Digital slideshow]. Presentation at the University of North Carolina at Greensboro. Retrieved from http://www.slideshare.net/Vishal_Khanna/impossible-scenarios-lives-at-the-intersection-of-poverty-and-late-capitalism

Khazan, O. (2018, July/August). Being black in America can be hazardous to your health. Retrieved from https://www.theatlantic.com/magazine/archive/2018/07/being-black-in-america-can-be-hazardous-to-your-health/561740

Kinsella, K. (2005, October). Preparing for effective vocabulary instruction. Aiming High Resource. Retrieved from http://www.scoe.org/docs/ah/AH_kinsella1.pdf

Kinsella, K. (2005, November). Teaching academic vocabulary. Aiming High Resource. Retrieved from http://www.scoe.org/docs/ah/AH_kinsella2.pdf

Kishiyama, M. M., Boyce, W. T., Jimenez, A. M., Perry, L. M., & Knight, R. T. (2009). Socioeconomic disparities affect prefrontal function in children. *Journal of Cognitive Neuroscience, 21*(6), 1106–1115.

Knapp, M. S., Adelman, N., Needels, M., Zucker, A., McCollum, H., Turnbull, B. J., … Shields, P. M. (1992). *Academic challenge for the children of poverty* [Three volumes]. Washington, DC: U.S. Department of Education.

Knapp, M. S., & Shields, P. M. (1990). Reconceiving academic instruction for the children of poverty. *Phi Delta Kappan, 71,* 752–758.

Knapp, M. S., & Shields, P. M. (Eds.). (1991). *Better schooling for the children of poverty: Alternatives to conventional wisdom.* Berkeley, CA: McCutchan.

Koball, H., & Jiang, Y. (2018, January). Basic facts about low-income children. National Center for Children in Poverty. Retrieved from http://www.nccp.org/publications/pub_1194.html

Koch, L. M., Gross, A. M., & Kolts, R. (2001). Attitudes toward Black English and code switching. *Journal of Black Psychology, 27*(1), 29–42.

Kozol, J. (1991). *Savage inequalities.* New York, NY: HarperPerennial.

Kozol, J. (1995). *Amazing grace.* New York, NY: Crown.

Kraus, L. (2017). 2016 disability statistics annual report. Durham, NH: University of New Hampshire. Retrieved from https://disabilitycompendium.org/sites/default/files/user-uploads/2016_AnnualReport.pdf

Kretzmann, J., & McKnight, J. (1993). *Building communities from the inside out: A path toward finding and mobilizing a community's assets.* Chicago, IL: ACTA.

Krishna, A. (2003). Escaping poverty and becoming poor: Who gains, who loses, and why? *World Development, 32*(1), 121–136.

Krueger, P. M., Jutte, D. P., Franzini, L., Elo, I., & Hayward, M. D. (2015). Family structure and multiple domains of child well-being in the United States: A cross-sectional study. *Population Health Metrics, 13*(6). doi:10.1186/s12963-015-0038-0

Kübler-Ross, E. (1969). *On death and dying.* New York, NY: Simon & Schuster.

Laborde, G. Z. (1983). *Influencing with integrity: Management skills for communication and negotiation.* Palo Alto, CA: Syntony.

Labov, W. (1972). *Sociolinguistic patterns.* Philadelphia, PA: University of Pennsylvania Press.

Labov, W. (1995). Can reading failure be reversed? A linguistic approach to the question. In V. Gadsden and D. Wagner (Eds.), *Literacy among African-American youth* (pp. 39–68). Cresskill, NJ: Hampton Press.

Labov, W., & Waletzky, J. (1967). Narrative analysis: Oral versions of personal experience. In J. Helm (Ed.), *Essays on the verbal and visual arts* (pp. 12–44). Seattle, WA: University of Washington Press.

Lamb, M. E. (1999). *Parenting and child development in 'nontraditional' families.* Mahwah, NJ: Lawrence Erlbaum.

Lane, K. L., & Beebe-Frankenberger, M. (2004). *School-based interventions: The tools you need to succeed.* Boston, MA: Pearson Education.

Language barriers are more complex than we might think. (1992, November). *CSBA News, 4*(9). Sacramento, CA: California School Boards Association.

Lantolf, J. P. (2005). Sociocultural theory and second language acquisition. In R. B. Kaplan, W. Grabe, M. Swain, & G. R. Tucker (Eds.), *The Oxford handbook of applied linguistics* (pp. 104–114). New York, NY: Oxford University Press.

Lareau, A. (1987). Social class differences in family-school relationships: The importance of cultural capital. *Sociology of Education, 60,* 73–85.

Lareau, A. (2003). *Unequal childhoods: Class, race and family life.* Berkeley, CA: University of California Press.

Larson, J. (1993, November). Maria Montaño-Harmon: A call for heightened awareness. *Texas Lone Star.*

Lave, J., & Wenger, E. (1991). *Situated learning: Legitimate peripheral participation.* New York, NY: Cambridge University Press.

LeBlank, A. N. (2003). *Random family: Love, drugs, trouble, and coming of age in the Bronx.* New York, NY: Scribner.

LeDoux, J. E. (1993). Emotional memory systems in the brain. *Behavioral Brain Research, 58,* 69–79.

LeDoux, J. E. (1995). Emotion: Clues from the brain. *Annual Review of Psychology, 46,* 209–235.

LeDoux, J. E. (1998). *The emotional brain: The mysterious underpinnings of emotional life.* New York, NY: Simon & Schuster.

LeDoux, J. E. (2002). Emotion, memory and the brain. *Scientific American, 12,* 62–71.

Lehrer, J. (2009, May 18). Don't! The secret of self-control. *The New Yorker,* pp. 26–32.

Leventhal, T., & Brooks-Gunn, J. (2000). The neighborhoods they live in: The effects of neighborhood residence on child and adolescent outcomes. *Psychological Bulletin, 126*(2), 309–337.

Levine, A., & Nidiffer, J. (1996). *Beating the odds: How the poor get to college.* San Francisco, CA: Jossey-Bass.

Levine, D. (1990). Update on effective schools: Findings and implications for research and practice. *Journal of Negro Education, 59,* 577–584.

Lewis, A. C. (1996). Breaking the cycle of poverty. *Phi Delta Kappan, 78*(3), 186.

Lewis, O. (1971). The culture of poverty. In E. Penchef (Ed.), *Four horsemen: Pollution, poverty, famine, violence* (pp. 135–141). San Francisco, CA: Canfield Press.

Lewit, E. M. (1993). Child indicators: Children in poverty. *The Future of Children, 3*(1), 176–182.

Lewit, E. M. (1993). Why is poverty increasing among children? *The Future of Children, 3*(2), 198–207.

Linver, M., Martin, A., & Brooks-Gunn, J. (2004). Measuring infants' home environment: The IT-HOME for infants between birth and 12 months in four national data sets. *Parenting, 4*(2), 115–137.

Loewen, J. W. (2007). *Lies my teacher told me: Everything your U.S. history textbook got wrong* (rev. ed). New York, NY: Touchstone.

Lui, M., Robles, B., Leondar-Wright, B., Brewer, R., & Adamson, R. (2006). *The color of wealth: The story behind the U.S. racial wealth divide.* New York, NY: New Press.

Lynam, D. R., Caspi, A., Moffit, T. E., Wikstrom, P., Loeber, R., & Novak, S. (2000). The interaction between impulsivity and neighborhood context on offending: The effects of impulsivity are stronger in poorer neighborhoods. *Journal of Abnormal Psychology, 109*(4), 563–574.

MacKenzie, D. (1983). Research for school improvement: An appraisal of some recent trends. *Educational Researcher, 12,* 5–17.

MacLeod, J. (1995). *Ain't no makin' it: Aspirations and attainment in a low-income neighborhood.* Boulder, CO: Westview Press.

Marshall, J. (2003). Children and poverty: Some questions answered. CHIP briefing 1. Retrieved from https://assets.publishing.service.gov.uk/media/57a08d1de5274a27b200163f/CHIP_QA.pdf

Marzano, R. J. (1998). *A theory-based meta-analysis of research on instruction.* Aurora, CO: Mid-Continent Regional Educational Laboratory.

Marzano, R. J. (2003). *What works in schools.* Alexandria, VA: Association for Supervision and Curriculum Development.

Marzano, R. J. (2004). *Building background knowledge for academic achievement.* Alexandria, VA: Association for Supervision and Curriculum Development.

Marzano, R. J., & Arredondo, D. (1986). *Tactics for thinking.* Aurora, CO: Mid-Continent Regional Educational Laboratory.

Mathews, J. (2009). *Work hard. Be nice: How two inspired teachers created the most promising schools in America.* Chapel Hill, NC: Algonquin Books.

Mattaini, M. A. (1993). *More than a thousand words: Graphics for clinical practice.* Washington, DC: NASW Press.

Mayer, R. E., & Sims, V. K. (1994). For whom is a picture worth a thousand words? Extensions of a dual-coding theory of multimedia learning. *Journal of Educational Psychology, 86*(3), 389–401.

Mayer, S. E. (1997). *What money can't buy.* Cambridge, MA: Harvard University Press.

McCrae, R. R., & Costa, P. T., Jr. (1990). *Personality in adulthood.* New York, NY: Guilford Press.

McCrae, R. R., & Costa, P. T., Jr. (1996). Toward a new generation of personality theories: Theoretical contexts for the five-factor model. In J. S. Wiggins (Ed.), *The five-factor model of personality: Theoretical perspectives* (pp. 51–87). New York, NY: Guilford Press.

McCrae, R. R., & Costa, P. T., Jr. (1999). A five-factor theory of personality. In L. A. Pervin & O. P. John (Eds.), *Handbook of personality: Theory and research* (2nd ed., pp. 139–153). New York, NY: Guilford Press.

McCrae, R. R., Costa, P. T., Jr., de Lima, M. P., Simoes, A., Ostendorf, F., Angleitner, A., ... Piedmont, R. L. (1999). Age differences in personality across the adult life span: Parallels in five cultures. *Developmental Psychology, 35,* 466–477.

McCrae, R. R., Costa, P. T., Jr., Ostendorf, F., Angleitner, A., Hrebickova, M., Avia, M. D., ... Smith, P. B. (2000). Nature over nurture: Temperament, personality, and life span development. *Journal of Personality and Social Psychology, 78,* 173–186.

McEwan, E. R. (2004). *Seven strategies of highly effective readers.* Thousand Oaks, CA: Corwin Press.

McKnight, J. (1995). *The careless society: Community and its counterfeits.* New York, NY: Basic Books.

McLanahan, S. (1985). Family structure and the reproduction of poverty. *The American Journal of Sociology, 90*(4), 873–901.

McLanahan, S. (1988). Family structure and dependency: Early transitions to female household headship. *Demography, 25*(1), 1–16.

McLanahan, S. (1997). Parent absence or poverty: Which matters more? In G. J. Duncan & J. Brooks-Gunn (Eds.), *Consequences of growing up poor* (pp. 35–48). New York, NY: Russell Sage.

McLanahan, S., & Booth, K. (1989). Mother-only families: Problems, prospects, and politics. *Journal of Marriage and the Family, 51*(3), 557–580.

McLanahan, S., & Sandefur, G. (1994). *Growing up with a single parent: What hurts, what helps.* Cambridge, MA: Harvard University Press.

McNeil, L. M. (1988). *Contradictions of control: School structure and school knowledge.* New York, NY: Routledge.

McWhorter, J. (1998). *The word on the street: Debunking the myth of pure Standard English.* New York, NY: Plenum Press.

Mederly, P., Novacek, P., & Topercer, J. (2003). Sustainable development assessment: Quality and sustainability of life indicators at global, national, and regional level. *Foresight, 5*(5), 42–49.

Mervis, C. B. (1984). Early lexical development: The contributions of mother and child. In C. Sophian (Ed.), *Origins of cognitive skills* (pp. 339–370). Hillsdale, NJ: Lawrence Erlbaum.

Migration Policy Institute. (2018). Data hub state immigration data profiles: United States. Retrieved from https://www.migrationpolicy.org/data/state-profiles/state/language/US

Miller, W. R., & Rollnick, S. (2002). *Motivational interviewing: Preparing people for change* (2nd ed.). New York, NY: Guilford Press.

Mills, C. W. (1956). *The power elite.* New York, NY: Oxford University Press.

Minton, H. L. (1988). Charting life history: Lewis M. Terman's study of the gifted. In J. G. Morawski (Ed.), *The rise of experimentation in American psychology* (pp. 138–162). New Haven, CT: Yale University Press.

Miranda, L. C. (1991). *Latino child poverty in the United States.* Washington, DC: Children's Defense Fund.

Miringoff, M., & Miringoff, M.-L. (1999). *The social health of the nation: How America is really doing.* New York, NY: Oxford University Press.

Mistry, R. S., White, E. S., Benner, A. D., & Huynh, V. W. (2009). A longitudinal study of the simultaneous influence of mothers' and teachers' educational expectations on low-income youth's academic achievement. *Journal of Youth and Adolescence, 38*(6), 826–838.

Monroe, S. M. (2008). Modern approaches to conceptualizing and measuring human life stress. *Annual Review of Clinical Psychology, 4,* 33–52.

Montaño-Harmon, M. R. (1991). Discourse features of written Mexican Spanish: Current research in contrastive rhetoric and its implications. *Hispania, 74*(2), 417–425.

Montaño-Harmon, M. R. (1994). Presentation given to Harris County Department of Education, Houston, TX.

Morey, R. A., Dolcos, F., Petty, C. M., Cooper, D. A., Hayes, J. P., LaBar, K. S., & McCarthy, G. (2009). The role of trauma-related distractors on neural systems for working memory and emotion processing in posttraumatic stress disorder. *Journal of Psychiatric Research, 43*(8), 809–817.

Morgan, J. P., Jr. (1991). What is codependency? *Journal of Clinical Psychology, 47*(5), 720–729.

Morin, A. (1993). Self-talk and self-awareness: On the nature of the relation. *The Journal of Mind and Behavior, 14*(3), 223–234.

Morin, A. (1996). Characteristics of an effective internal dialogue in the acquisition of self-information. *Imagination, Cognition, and Personality, 15*(1), 45–58.

Morris, A. S., Robinson, L. R., Hays-Grudo, J., Claussen, A. H., Hartwig, S. A., & Treat, A. E. (2017). Targeting parenting in early childhood: A public health approach to improve outcomes for children living in poverty. *Child Development, 88*(2), 388–397. doi:10.1111/cdev.12743

Mortenson, T. (1998). A conversation about diversity. *Academe, 84*(4), 42–43.

Mota-Altman, N. (2006, Summer). Academic language: Everyone's 'second' language. *California English.* Retrieved from http://www.nwp.org/cs/public/print/resource/2329

Moynihan, D. P. (1986). *Family and nation.* Orlando, FL: Harcourt Brace Jovanovich.

Moynihan, D. P. (1989). Welfare reform: Serving America's children. *Teachers College Record, 90*(3), 337–341.

Mullainathan, S., & Shafir, E. (2014). *Scarcity: The new science of having less and how it defines our lives.* New York, NY: Picador.

Najman, J. M., Aird, R., Bor, W., O'Callaghan, M., Williams, G., & Shuttlewood, G. (2004). The generational transmission of socioeconomic inequalities in child cognitive development and emotional health. *Social Science and Medicine, 58,* 1147–1158.

Narayan, D., Chambers, R., Shah, M. K., & Petesch, P. (2000). *Crying out for change.* Washington, DC: World Bank.

Narayan, D., Narayan-Parker, D., & Petesch, P. L. (Eds.). (2007). *Moving out of poverty.* Washington, DC: World Bank.

Nassaji, H., & Swain, M. (2000). A Vygotskian perspective towards corrective feedback in L2: The effect of random vs. negotiated help on the learning of English articles. *Language Awareness, 9*(1), 34–51.

Natale, J. A. (1992). Growing up the hard way. *American School Board Journal, 179*(10), 20–27.

National Center for Children in Poverty. (1996). *Wake up America: Columbia University study shatters stereotypes of young child poverty.* New York, NY: Columbia University.

National Center for Children in Poverty. (n.d.). Immigrant children in the United States are growing in number and facing substantial economic hardship. Retrieved from http://www.nccp.org/media/releases/release_1.html

Natriello, G., McGill, E. L., & Pallas, A. M. (1990). *Schooling disadvantaged children: Racing against catastrophe.* New York, NY: Teachers College Press.

Nisbett, R. E., & Cohen, D. (1996). *Culture of honor: The psychology of violence in the South.* Boulder, CO: Westview Press.

Nonn, T. (2007). Hitting bottom: Homelessness, poverty and masculinity. In B. Arrighi (Ed.), *Understanding inequality: The intersection of race/ethnicity, class, and gender* (2nd ed., pp. 281–288). Lanham, MD: Rowman & Littlefield.

Norretranders, T. (1991). *The user illusion: Cutting consciousness down to size.* New York, NY: Penguin.

Obradovic, J., Long, J. D., Cutuli, J. J., Chan, C. K., Hinz, E., Heistad, D., & Masten, A. S. (2009). Academic achievement of homeless and highly mobile children in an urban school district: Longitudinal evidence on risk, growth, and resilience. *Development and Psychopathology, 21,* 493–518.

O'Connor, A. (2001). *Poverty knowledge: Social science, social policy, and the poor in twentieth-century U.S. history.* Princeton, NJ: Princeton University Press.

Ogbu, J. (1986). The consequences of the American caste system. In U. Neisser (Ed.), *The school achievement of minority children: New perspectives* (pp. 19–56). Hillsdale, NJ: Lawrence Erlbaum.

Ojeda, L., Rosales, R., & Good, G. (2008). Socioeconomic status and cultural predictors of male role attitudes among Mexican American men: Son más machos? *Psychology of Men and Masculinity, 9,* 133–138.

O'Neill, J. (1991, September). A generation adrift? *Educational Leadership,* 4–10. Retrieved from http://www.ascd.org/ASCD/pdf/journals/ed_lead/el_199109_oneil.pdf

Ong, W. (1982). *Orality and literacy: The technologizing of the world.* London, England: Methuen.

Oshry, B. (1995). *Seeing systems: Unlocking the mysteries of organizational life.* San Francisco, CA: Berrett-Koehler.

Otterbein, K. F. (2000). Five feuds: An analysis of homicides in eastern Kentucky in the late nineteenth century. *American Anthropologist, 102*(2), 231–243.

Oxford Dictionaries. (2018). Epigenetics. Retrieved from https://en.oxforddictionaries.com/definition/epigenetics

Pachter, L. M., Auinger, P., Palmer, R., & Weitzman, M. (2006). Do parenting and the home environment, maternal depression, neighborhood, and chronic poverty affect child behavioral problems differently in different racial-ethnic groups? *Pediatrics, 117,* 1329–1338.

Pagani, L., Boulerice, B., & Tremblay, R. E. (1997). The influence of poverty on children's classroom placement and behavior problems. In G. J. Duncan & J. Brooks-Gunn (Eds.), *Consequences of growing up poor* (pp. 311–339). New York, NY: Russell Sage.

Palincsar, A. S., & Brown, A. L. (1984). The reciprocal teaching of comprehension-fostering and comprehension-monitoring activities. *Cognition and Instruction, 1*(2), 117–175.

Parke, R. D. (2004). Development in the family. *Annual Review of Psychology, 55,* 365–399.

Payne, R. K. (2005). *A framework for understanding poverty* (4th ed.). Highlands, TX: aha! Process.

Payne, R. K. (2008). *Under-resourced learners: 8 strategies to boost student achievement.* Highlands, TX: aha! Process.

Payne, R. K. (2009). Moving from middle class to situational poverty—from stability to instability: What you can do to help your students and parents during the present economic downturn. *Instructional Leader, 22*(3), 1–4.

Payne, R. K. (2010). *Research-based strategies: Narrowing the achievement gap for under-resourced students* (2nd ed.). Highlands, TX: aha! Process.

Payne, R. K. (2012). *From understanding poverty to developing human capacity.* Highlands, TX: aha! Process.

Payne, R. K. (2013). *A framework for understanding poverty* (5th ed.). Highlands, TX: aha! Process.

Payne, R. K. (2017). *Research-based strategies: Narrowing the achievement gap for under-resourced students* (3rd ed.). Highlands, TX: aha! Process.

Payne, R. K. (2017). *Under-resourced learners: 8 strategies to boost student achievement* (rev. ed). Highlands, TX: aha! Process.

Payne, R. K. (2018). *Emotional poverty in all demographics: How to address anger, anxiety, and violence in the classroom.* Highlands, TX: aha! Process.

Payne, R. K., & DeVol, P. E. (2005). Toward a deeper understanding of issues surrounding poverty: A response to critiques of A Framework for Understanding Poverty. Retrieved from https://www.ahaprocess.com/wp-content/uploads/2013/08/Framework-for-Understanding-Poverty-Deeper-Understanding.pdf

Payne, R. K., DeVol, P. E., & Dreussi-Smith, T. (2009). *Bridges out of poverty: Strategies for professionals and communities* (rev. ed.). Highlands, TX: aha! Process.

Pearce, J. E. (1994). *Days of darkness: The feuds of eastern Kentucky.* Lexington, KY: University Press of Kentucky.

Pearce, M. J., Jones, S. M., Schwab-Stone, M. E., & Ruchkin, V. (2003). The protective effects of religiousness and parent involvement on the development of conduct problems among youth exposed to violence. *Child Development, 74*(6), 1682–1696.

Penchef, E. (Ed.). (1971). *Four horsemen: Pollution, poverty, famine, violence.* San Francisco, CA: Canfield Press.

Perls, F. (1983). *Gestalt therapy.* Hammond, IN: Owls Books.

Perry, T., & Delpit, L. (Eds.). (1998). *The real Ebonics debate: Power, language and the education of African-American children.* Boston, MA: Beacon Press.

PK. (2018, September 10). Who are the one percent in the United States by income and net worth? Don't Quit Your Day Job. Retrieved from https://dqydj.com/who-are-the-one-percent-united-states/

Phillips, K. (2002). *Wealth and democracy: A political history of the American rich.* New York, NY: Broadway Books.

Poor attention in kindergarten predicts lower high school test scores. (2009, May 28). ScienceDaily. Retrieved from http://www.sciencedaily.com/releases/2009/05/090526093928.htm

The poorest among us. (1996). *U.S. News & World Report, 121*(25), 18.

Power, K., McGoldrick, T., Brown, K., Buchanan, R., Sharp, D., Swanson, V., & Karatzias, A. (2002). A controlled comparison of eye movement desensitization and reprocessing versus exposure plus cognitive restructuring versus waiting list in the treatment of post-traumatic stress disorder. *Clinical Psychology and Psychotherapy, 9,* 299–318.

Power, M., Power, M. J., & Dalgleish, T. (2007). *Cognition and emotion: From order to disorder* (2nd ed.). London, England: Psychology Press.

Pransky, J. (1998). *Modello: A story of hope for the inner-city and beyond.* Cabot, VT: NEHRI.

Pressley, M. (1995). *Cognition, teaching, and assessment.* New York, NY: HarperCollins.

Putnam, R. D. (2000). *Bowling alone: The collapse and revival of American community.* New York, NY: Simon & Schuster.

Quay, L. C., & Blaney, R. L. (1992). Verbal communication, nonverbal communication, and private speech in lower and middle socioeconomic status preschool children. *Journal of Genetic Psychology, 153*(2), 129–138.

Reeves, R. V., & Guyot, K. (2017, December 4). Black women are earning more college degrees, but that alone won't close race gaps. Retrieved from https://www.brookings.edu/blog/social-mobility-memos/2017/12/04/black-women-are-earning-more-college-degrees-but-that-alone-wont-close-race-gaps

Reis, S. M., Colbert, R. D., & Hebert, T. P. (2005). Understanding resilience in diverse, talented students in an urban high school. *Roeper Review, 27*(2), 110–120.

Renchler, R. (1993). Poverty and learning. ERIC Digest. Retrieved from https://scholarsbank.uoregon.edu/xmlui/bitstream/handle/1794/3304/digest083.pdf?sequence=1

Results and best practices. (2018). aha! Process. Retrieved from https://www.ahaprocess.com/solutions/k-12-schools/results-best-practices

Rickford, J. R. (1996, December 26). The Oakland Ebonics decision: Commendable attack on the problem. *San Jose Mercury News.* Retrieved from http://www.stanford.edu/~rickford/ebonics/SJMN-OpEd.html

Rickford, J. R. (1997, January 22). Letter to Senator Specter, chairman, U.S. Senate Subcommittee on Labor, Health and Human Services and Education. Retrieved from http://www.stanford.edu/~rickford/ebonics/SpecterLetter.html

Rickford, J. R. (1998, March 25). Using the vernacular to teach the standard. Paper presented at the 1998 California State University Long Beach (CSULB) Conference on Ebonics. Retrieved from http://www.stanford.edu/~rickford/papers/VernacularToTeachStandard.html

Rizzo, R. M., & Parks, L. J. (2007). The culture of generational poverty: Providing meaningful help to the impoverished. Retrieved from http://www.ceus-nursing.com/ceus-courses/material_detail.php?id=120

Robinson, D. H., Corliss, S. B., Bush, A. M., Bera, S. J., & Tomberlin, T. (2003). Optimal presentation of graphic organizers and text: A case for large bites? *Education Communication and Technology, 51*(4), 25–41.

Robinson, D. H., & Kiewra, K. A. (1995). Visual argument: Graphic organizers are superior to outlines in improving learning from text. *Journal of Educational Psychology, 87*(3), 455–467.

Rodriguez, L. J. (1993). *Always running.* New York, NY: Simon & Schuster.

Romaine, S. (1980). Stylistic variation and evaluative reactions to speech. *Language and Speech, 23,* 213–232.

Romaine, S. (2002). Language and social class. In N. J. Smelser & P. B. Baltes (Eds.), *International encyclopedia of the social and behavioral sciences* (pp. 8308–8312). Oxford, England: Pergamon.

Rommetveit, R. (1985). Language acquisition as increasing linguistic structuring of experience and symbolic behavior control. In J. V. Wertsch (Ed.), *Culture, communication, and cognition: Vygotskian perspectives* (pp. 183–204). New York, NY: Cambridge University Press.

Ross, D. D., Bondy, E., Gallingane, C., & Hambacher, E. (2008). Promoting academic engagement through insistence: Being a warm demander. *Childhood Education, 84*(3), 142–145.

Rural children: Increasing poverty rates pose educational challenges. Briefing report GAO/HEHS-94-75BR. (1994). Washington, DC: General Accounting Office. Retrieved from http://www.gpo.gov/fdsys/pkg/GAOREPORTS-HEHS-94-75BR/html/GAOREPORTS-HEHS-94-75BR.htm

Rutter, M. (1984). Resilient children. *Psychology Today, 3,* 57–65.

Saffo, P. (2007, July-August). Six rules for effective forecasting. *Harvard Business Review.* Retrieved from https://hbr.org/2007/07/six-rules-for-effective-forecasting

Sampson, R. J., & Laub, J. H. (1994). Urban poverty and the family context of delinquency: A new look at structure and process in a classic study. *Child Development, 65*(2), 523–540.

Sampson, R. J., Sharkey, P., & Raudenbush, S. W. (2008). Durable effects of concentrated disadvantage on verbal ability among African-American children. *Proceedings of the National Academy of Sciences, 105*(3), 845–852.

Samuelson, R. J. (1997). The culture of poverty. *Newsweek, 129*(18), 49.

Sanchez, B., Reyes, O., & Singh, J. (2006). Makin' it in college: The value of significant individuals in the lives of Mexican American adolescents. *Journal of Hispanic Higher Education, 5*(1), 48–67.

Sapolsky, R. M. (1998). *Why zebras don't get ulcers: An updated guide to stress, stress-related diseases, and coping.* New York, NY: W. H. Freeman & Company.

Sather, D. (2014, April 16). Al Silva: Escaping poverty & achieving excellence. Retrieved from https://www.businessbankoftexas.com/business-resource-center/al-silva-escaping-poverty-achieving-excellence.htm

Sawyer, R. J., Graham, S., & Harris, K. R. (1992). Direct teaching, strategy instruction, and strategy instruction with explicit self-regulation: Effects on the composition skills and self-efficacy of students with learning disabilities. *Journal of Educational Psychology, 84*(3), 340–352.

Scales, P. C., Benson, P. L., Roehlkepartain, E. C., Sesma, A., Jr., & van Dulmen, M. (2006). The role of developmental assets in predicting academic achievement: A longitudinal study. *Journal of Adolescence, 29*(5), 691–708.

Scarcella, R. (2003). *Academic English: A conceptual framework.* Santa Barbara, CA: University of California Linguistic Minority Research Institute.

Schamberg, M. (2008). The cost of living in poverty: Long-term effects of allostatic load on working memory. Retrieved from https://ecommons.cornell.edu/bitstream/handle/1813/10814/Schamberg%20?sequence=1

Schierloh, J. M. (1991). Teaching standard English usage: A dialect-based approach. *Adult Learning, 2*(5), 20–22.

Schmoker, M. (2001). *Results: The key to continuous school improvement* (2nd ed.). Alexandria, VA: Association for Supervision and Curriculum Development.

School age demographics: Recent trends pose new educational challenges. Briefing report to congressional requesters. (1993). Washington, DC: General Accounting Office.

Schunk, D. H., & Zimmerman, B. J. (1994). *Self-regulation of learning and performance.* Mahwah, NJ: Lawrence Erlbaum.

Self-regulation game predicts kindergarten achievement. (2009, June 9). ScienceDaily. Retrieved from http://www.sciencedaily.com/releases/2009/06/090608162547.htm

Senge, P. M. (1994). *The fifth discipline: The art & practice of the learning organization.* New York, NY: Currency Doubleday.

Sennett, R., & Cobb, J. (1972). *The hidden injuries of class.* New York, NY: Alfred A. Knopf.

Shapiro, J. P., Friedman, D., Meyer, M., & Loftus, M. (1996). Invincible kids. *U.S. News & World Report, 121*(19), 62–70.

Sharkey, P. (2008). The intergenerational transmission of context. *American Journal of Sociology, 113*(4), 931–969.

Sharron, H., & Coulter, M. (2004). *Changing children's minds: Feuerstein's revolution in the teaching of intelligence.* Highlands, TX: aha! Process.

Shipler, D. K. (2004). *The working poor: Invisible in America.* New York, NY: Random House.

Shulman, L. S. (1988, November). A union of insufficiencies: Strategies for teacher assessment in a period of educational reform. *Educational Leadership,* 36–41. Retrieved from http://www.ascd.org/ASCD/pdf/journals/ed_lead/el_198811_shulman.pdf

Shure, M. B., & Spivack, G. (1982). Interpersonal problem-solving in young children: A cognitive approach to prevention. *American Journal of Community Psychology, 10*(3), 341–356.

Shurkin, J. N. (1992). *Terman's kids.* New York, NY: Little, Brown.

Sibley, E., & Brabeck, K. (2017). Latino immigrant students' school experiences in the United States: The importance of family-school-community collaborations. *School Community Journal, 27*(1), 137–157. Retrieved from https://eric.ed.gov/?id=EJ1146470

Sirin, S. R. (2005). Socioeconomic status and academic achievement: A meta-analytic review of research. *Review of Educational Research, 75*(3), 417–453.

Smith, J. R., Brooks-Gunn, J., & Klebanov, P. K. (1997). Consequences of living in poverty for young children's cognitive and verbal ability and early school achievement. In G. J. Duncan & J. Brooks-Gunn (Eds.), *Consequences of growing up poor* (pp. 132–189). New York, NY: Russell Sage.

Smith, M. K. (2009). Jean Lave, Etienne Wenger and communities of practice. *The Encyclopedia of Informal Education.* Retrieved from http://www.infed.org/biblio/communities_of_practice.htm

Smitherman, G. (1981). 'What go round come round': King in perspective. In G. Smitherman (Ed.), *Talkin that talk: Language, culture and education in African America* (pp. 132–149). New York, NY: Routledge.

Social Security Administration. (2018). Understanding Supplemental Security Income SSI benefits—2018 edition. Retrieved from https://www.ssa.gov/ssi/text-benefits-ussi.htm

Solon, G. (1999). Intergenerational mobility in the labor market. In O. Ashenfelter & D. Card (Eds.), *Handbook of labor economics* (3rd ed., pp. 1761–1800). Amsterdam, Netherlands: North Holland.

Sowell, T. (1997). *Migrations and cultures: A world view.* New York, NY: HarperCollins.

Sowell, T. (1998, October 5). Race, culture and equality. *Forbes.* Retrieved from http://www.forbes.com/forbes/1998/1005/6207144a.html

Stanton-Salazar, R., & Dornbusch, S. (1995). Social capital and the reproduction of inequality: Information networks among Mexican-origin high school students. *Sociology of Education, 68,* 116–135.

Stern, M. J. (1987). The welfare of families. *Educational Leadership, 44*(6), 82–87.

Stewart, T. A. (1997). *Intellectual capital: The new wealth of organizations.* New York, NY: HarperCollins.

Stier, H., & Tienda, M. (2007). Are men marginal to the family? Insights from Chicago's inner city. In B. Arrighi (Ed.), *Understanding inequality: The intersection of race/ethnicity, class, and gender* (2nd ed., pp. 107–118). Lanham, MD: Rowman & Littlefield.

Stringfield, S. (1994). *Urban and suburban/rural: Special strategies for educating disadvantaged children.* Baltimore, MD: Johns Hopkins University.

Subby, R. (1987). *Lost in the shuffle: The co-dependent reality.* Deerfield Beach, FL: HCI.

Swan, W. (n.d.). The Payne school model's impact on student achievement—a national study. Retrieved from https://www.ahaprocess.com/wp-content/uploads/2014/01/Payne-School-Model-Impact-National-Study.pdf

Sweeney, W. J., Ring, M. M., Malanga, P., & Lambert, M. C. (2003). Using curriculum-based assessment and repeated practice instructional procedures combined with daily goal setting to improve elementary students' oral reading fluency: A preservice teacher training approach. *Journal of Precision Teaching and Celeration, 19*(1), 2–19.

Takeuchi, D. T., Williams, D. R., & Adair, R. K. (1991). Economic stress in the family and children's emotional and behavioral problems. *Journal of Marriage and the Family, 53*(4), 1031–1041.

Tannen, D. (1982). Oral and literate strategies in spoken and written narratives. *Language, 58,* 1–21.

Tannen, D. (1982). *Spoken and written language: Exploring orality and literacy.* Norwood, NJ: Ablex.

Tannen, D. (1984). *Conversational style: Analyzing talk among friends.* Norwood, NJ: Ablex.

Taylor, C., & Taylor-Ide, D. (2002). *Just and lasting change: When communities own their futures.* Baltimore, MD: Johns Hopkins University Press.

Taylor, H. U. (1991). *Standard English, Black English, and bidialectalism: A controversy.* New York, NY: Peter Lang.

Texas school improvement initiative: Peer evaluator training manual. (1995). Austin, TX: Texas Education Agency.

Thornburg, K. R., Hoffman, S., & Remeika, C. (1991). Youth at risk: Society at risk. *Elementary School Journal, 91*(3), 199–208.

Tileston, D. W. (2004). *What every teacher should know about effective teaching strategies.* Thousand Oaks, CA: Corwin Press.

Toppo, G. (2009, January 16). Study: Poverty dramatically affects children's brains. Retrieved from https://www.huffingtonpost.com/2008/12/16/study-poverty-dramaticall_n_151482.html

Tough, P. (2008). *Whatever it takes: Geoffrey Canada's quest to change Harlem and America.* New York, NY: Houghton Mifflin.

Townsend, M. A., & Clarihew, A. (1989). Facilitating children's comprehension through the use of advance organizers. *Journal of Reading Behavior, 21*(1), 15–35.

Tying education to future goals may boost grades more than helping with homework. (2009, May 21). ScienceDaily. Retrieved from http://www.sciencedaily.com/releases/2009/05/090519134711.htm

U.S. Bureau of Labor Statistics. (2017, August). Consumer Expenditure Survey, 2016. Table 1110. Retrieved from https://www.bls.gov/cex/2016/combined/decile.pdf

U.S. Census Bureau. (2012). Table 3: People in poverty by selected characteristics: 2010 and 2011. Retrieved from https://www.census.gov/prod/2012pubs/p60-243.pdf

U.S. Census Bureau. (2017). 2016 American Community Survey 1-year estimates, employment status. Washington, DC: United States Census Bureau. Retrieved from https://factfinder.census.gov/bkmk/table/1.0/en/ACS/16_1YR/S2301/0400000US27

U.S. Census Bureau. (2017). 2016 American Community Survey 1-year estimates, poverty status in the past 12 months. Washington, DC: United States Census Bureau. Retrieved from https://factfinder.census.gov/faces/tableservices/jsf/pages/productview.xhtml?pid=ACS_15_1YR_S1702&prodType=table

U.S. Census Bureau. (2017). Table 4. Families in poverty by type of family: 2015 and 2016. Retrieved from https://www2.census.gov/programs-surveys/demo/tables/p60/259/pov_table4.xls

U.S. Census Bureau. (2018). Current population survey, 2017 annual social and economic supplement. Retrieved from https://www.census.gov/programs-surveys/cps/data-detail.html

U.S. Census Bureau. (2018). Poverty thresholds. Retrieved from https://www.census.gov/data/tables/time-series/demo/income-poverty/historical-poverty-thresholds.html

U.S. Department of Education. (n.d.). NAEP data explorer. Retrieved from https://www.nationsreportcard.gov/ndecore/landing

U.S. Department of Education, National Center for Education Statistics. (2018). The condition of education 2018. Retrieved from https://nces.ed.gov/pubs2018/2018144.pdf

U.S. Department of Health and Human Services. (2017). Facts and statistics. Retrieved from https://www.hhs.gov/fitness/resource-center/facts-and-statistics/index.html

U.S. Government Accountability Office. (2018, April 4). K–12 education: Discipline disparities for black students, boys, and students with disabilities. Retrieved from https://www.gao.gov/products/GAO-18-258

Valenzuela, C., & Addington, J. (2006). *Four features of racism.* (Available from Minnesota Collaborative Anti-Racism Initiative, 1671 Summit Ave., St. Paul, MN 55105.)

Verney, S. P. (2005). Culture-fair cognitive ability assessment. *Assessment, 12*(3), 303–319.

Vobejda, B. (1994, August 30). Diversity of 'typical' family grows even wider. *Houston Chronicle,* p. A1.

Vygotsky, L. (1978). *Mind and society: The development of higher mental processes.* Cambridge, MA: Harvard University Press.

Walker, D., Greenwood, C., Hart, B., & Carta, J. (1994). Prediction of school outcomes based on early language production and socioeconomic factors. *Child Development, 65*(2), 606–621.

Walker, H., Colvin, G., & Ramsey, E. (1995). *Antisocial behavior in school: Strategies and best practices.* Pacific Grove, CA: Brooks/Cole.

Walsh, F. (2002). A family resilience framework: Innovative practice applications. *Family Relations, 51*(2), 130–137.

Walsh, F. (2002). *Normal family processes: Growing diversity and complexity* (3rd ed.). New York, NY: Guilford Press.

Walsh, F. (2004). The concept of family resilience: Crisis and challenge. *Family Process, 35*(3), 261–281.

Washburne, C. (1958). Conflicts between educational theory and structure. *Educational Theory, 8*(2), 87–94.

Waxman, H. C., Gray, J. P., & Padron, Y. N. (2002). Resiliency among students at risk of academic failure. In S. Stringfield & D. Land (Eds.), *Educating at-risk students* (pp. 29–48). Chicago, IL: University of Chicago Press.

Wegscheider-Cruse, S. (1984). *Co-dependency.* Deerfield Beach, FL: HCI.

Wegscheider-Cruse, S. (1990). *Understanding co-dependency.* Deerfield Beach, FL: HCI.

What Is Epigenetics. (2013, July 30). A super brief and basic explanation of epigenetics for total beginners. Retrieved from https://www.whatisepigenetics.com/what-is-epigenetics

Wheatley, M. (1992). *Leadership and the new science.* San Francisco, CA: Berrett-Koehler.

Wheeler, R. S. (2001). From home speech to school speech: Vantages on reducing the achievement gap in inner city schools. *The Virginia English Bulletin, 51,* 4–16.

Wheeler, R. S., & Swords, R. (2009). Codeswitching: Tools of language and culture transform the dialectically diverse classroom. *Developing Writers Workshop 5.* Retrieved from http://www.learner.org/workshops/hswriting/workshops/workshop5/codeswitching.html

White, K., Hohn, R., & Tollefson, N. (1997). Encouraging elementary students to set realistic goals. *Journal of Research in Childhood Education, 12*(1), 48–57.

Wickrama, K. A. S., & Noh, S. (2009). The long arm of community: The influence of childhood community contexts across the early life course. *Journal of Youth and Adolescence, 39*(8), 894–910.

Williams, C., & Garland, A. (2002). A cognitive-behavioural therapy assessment model for use in everyday clinical practices. *Advances in Psychiatric Treatment, 8,* 172–179.

Wilson, W. J. (1987). *The truly disadvantaged: The inner city, the underclass, and public policy.* Chicago, IL: University of Chicago Press.

Wilson, W. J. (1996). *When work disappears: The world of the new urban poor.* New York, NY: Knopf.

Wingfield, A. H. (2016, October 17). About those 79 cents. Retrieved from https://www.theatlantic.com/business/archive/2016/10/79-cents/504386

Wolfram, W., Adger, C. T., & Christian, D. (1999). *Dialects in schools and communities.* Mahwah, NJ: Lawrence Erlbaum.

Wolfram, W., & Schilling-Estes, N. (1998). *American English.* Oxford, England: Basil Blackwell.

Wolin, S. J., & Wolin, S. (1993). *The resilient self: How survivors of troubled families rise above adversity.* New York, NY: Random House.

Wood, J. W. (2005). *The SAALE model for reaching the hard to teach.* Richmond, VA: Virginia Commonwealth University.

Woodard, S. L. (1992). Academic excellence in the urban environment: Overcoming the odds. *NAASP Bulletin, 76*(546), 57–61.

Woolcock, M., & Narayan, D. (2000). Social capital: Implications for development theory. *World Bank Research Observer, 15*(2), 225–251.

Zhang, H., & Cowen, D. J. (2009). Mapping academic achievement and public school choice under the No Child Left Behind legislation. *Southeastern Geographer, 49*(1), 24–40.

Zill, N. (1993). The changing realities of family life. *Aspen Institute Quarterly, 5*(1), 27–51.

Zins, J., Weissberg, R., Wang, M., & Walberg, H. J. (Eds.). (2004). *Building academic success on social and emotional learning: What does the research say?* New York, NY: Teachers College Press.

Index

[Page numbers in *italics* refer to tables or illustrations.]

About the Author

Ruby K. Payne, Ph.D., is CEO and founder of aha! Process and is an author, speaker, publisher, and career educator. She is a leading expert on the mindsets of economic class and on crossing socioeconomic lines in education and work. Payne is recognized internationally for her foundational and award-winning book (2014 Golden Lamp REVERE Award), *A Framework for Understanding Poverty,* now in its sixth edition, which has sold more than 1.8 million copies. Payne has helped students and adults of all economic backgrounds achieve academic, professional, and personal success.

Payne's expertise stems from more than 30 years of experience in public schools. She has traveled extensively and has presented her work throughout North America and in Europe, Australia, China, and India. She has spoken to more than 2 million educators and trained more than 7,000 trainers to do her work. Her speaking engagements have included EARCOS (East Asia Regional Council of Schools) in Malaysia, National Association of School Boards, Central States Bankers Conference, Federal Reserve Board of Governors, Beijing Institute of Education, and Harvard Summer Institute for Principals, as well as thousands of individual school districts and campuses.

Payne has written or coauthored more than a dozen books. Recent publications are *Emotional Poverty in All Demographics: How to Reduce Anger, Anxiety, and Violence in the Classroom; Emotional Poverty, Volume 2: Safer Students and Less-Stressed Teachers; Before You Quit Teaching,* a free, downloadable multimedia book; the revised edition of *Research-Based Strategies: Narrowing the Achievement Gap for Under-Resourced Students,* coauthored with Bethanie H. Tucker, Ed.D., which won the Independent Publisher Bronze Educational Resource Award; *How Much of Yourself Do You Own? A Process for Building*

Your Emotional Resources, coauthored with Emilia O'Neill-Baker, Ph.D.; and the third revised edition of *Removing the Mask: How to Identify and Develop Giftedness in Students from Poverty,* coauthored with Paul D. Slocumb, Ed.D. and Ellen Williams, Ed.D. The previous edition of *Removing the Mask* won a gold medal from the Independent Publisher Book Awards.

Another major publication is *Bridges Out of Poverty,* coauthored with Philip E. DeVol and Terie Dreussi-Smith, which offers strategies for building sustainable communities. Payne's mission of raising student achievement and overcoming poverty has become a cornerstone for school improvement efforts undertaken by educational districts and Bridges communities across the United States.

Other publications include: *Bridges to Health and Healthcare: New Solutions for Improving Access and Services,* coauthored with Terie Dreussi-Smith, Lucy Shaw, and Jan Young, Ph.D.; *Under-Resourced Learners: 8 Strategies to Boost Student Achievement; Hidden Rules of Class at Work,* coauthored with Don Krabill; *School Improvement: 9 Systemic Processes to Raise Achievement,* coauthored with Donna Magee, Ed.D.; *Crossing the Tracks for Love: What to Do When You and Your Partner Grew Up in Different Worlds; Living on a Tightrope: A Survival Handbook for Principals,* coauthored with William Sommers, Ph.D.; *What Every Church Member Should Know About Poverty,* coauthored with Bill Ehlig; and *Achievement for All: Keys to Educating Middle Grades Students in Poverty,* published by the Association for Middle Level Education (AMLE). *Boys in Poverty: A Framework for Understanding Dropout,* coauthored with *Removing the Mask* collaborator Paul Slocumb, was published by Solution Tree Press and received the Distinguished Achievement Award from the Association of Educational Publishers in the professional development category.

Payne received her bachelor's degree from Goshen College, her Master's Degree in English Literature from Western Michigan University, and her Ph.D. in Educational Leadership and Policy from Loyola University Chicago.

Connect with us at ahaprocess.com

- Visit ahaprocess.com for free resources: articles, video clips, and success stories from practitioners—and read our aha! Moments blog!

- Sign up for our latest LIVE online workshop offerings at ahaprocess.com/events:

  - Emotional Poverty Workshops and Trainer Certification
  - Bridges Across Every Divide Workshop
  - Getting Ahead in a Just-Gettin'-By World Facilitator Training

  - Bridges Out of Poverty Workshop and Trainer Certification
  - Tactical Communication Workshop for First Responders
  - Research-Based Strategies
  - Removing the Mask: Identifying Gifted Students from Poverty

- **Register for on-demand workshops at ahaprocess.com/on-demand**

- **If you like *A Framework for Understanding Poverty: A Cognitive Approach, 6th Edition,* check out these publications:**

  - *Emotional Poverty, Volume 2: Safer Students and Less-Stressed Teachers* (Payne)
  - *Emotional Poverty in All Demographics* (Payne)

  - *How Much of Yourself Do You Own? A Process for Building Your Emotional Resources* (Payne & O'Neill-Baker)
  - *Research-Based Strategies: Narrowing the Achievement Gap for Under-Resourced Students* (Payne & Tucker)

  - *Bridges Across Every Divide: Policy and Practices to Reduce Poverty and Build Communities* (DeVol & Krebs)
  - *Workplace Stability: Creating Conditions That Lead to Retention, Productivity, and Engagement in Entry-Level Workers* (Weirich)

  - *Tactical Communication (First Responder Edition): Mastering Effective Interactions with Citizens from Diverse Economic Backgrounds* (Pfarr)

- **Connect with us on Facebook, Twitter, and Instagram—and watch our YouTube channel**

For a complete listing of products, please visit ahaprocess.com

Join us on Facebook

facebook.com/rubypayne
facebook.com/bridgesoutofpoverty
facebook.com/workplacestability
facebook.com/ahaprocess
facebook.com/collegeachievementalliance

Twitter

@rubykpayne
@ahaprocess
#addresspoverty
#BridgesOutofPoverty

Subscribe to our YouTube channel

youtube.com/ahaprocess

Read our blog

ahaprocess.com/blog

Instagram

@ rubykpayne